S67
P9-AFL-429

Black Labor in Richmond, 1865–1890

Black Labor in Richmond, 1865–1890

Peter J. Rachleff

University of Illinois Press
Urbana and Chicago

Illini Books edition, 1989
© 1984 by Temple University
Reprinted by arrangement with Temple University Press
Manufactured in the United States of America
P 5 4 3 2 1

This book is printed on acid-free paper.

Library of Congress Cataloging-in-Publication Data

Rachleff, Peter J.
[Black labor in the South]
Black labor in Richmond, 1865–1890 / Peter J. Rachleff. — Illini Books ed.
p. cm.
Reprint. Originally published: Black labor in the South : Richmond, Virginia, 1865–1890. Philadelphia : Temple University Press, 1984. Originally published in series: Class and culture.
Bibliography: p.
Includes index.
ISBN 0-252-06026-1 (alk. paper)
1. Afro-Americans—Virginia—Richmond—History—19th century. 2. Richmond (Va.)—History. 3. Labor and laboring classes—Virginia—Richmond—History—19th century. I. Title.
F234.R59N47 1989
975.5'4510049607—dc 19 88-29432
CIP

"If God intended a part of the Human Race to be in Slavery (wage and chattel), why did He implant in his breast a thirst for Independence?"

—topic of debate organized by
Local Union No. 1 of the Co-Operative
Commonwealth of Virginia, 1898

Contents

Acknowledgments

The pursuit of a project like this is impossible without the support of many people. David Montgomery and Jeremy Brecher influenced more than the course of this study. Each, in his own way, has shaped my development as a historian. My fellow graduate students at the University of Pittsburgh—Jim and Jenni Barrett, John Bennett, Cele Bucki, Nora Faires, Dodee Fennell, John Gillie, Peter Gottlieb, Clare Horner, Horace Huntley, Betti Marconi, Mark McColloch, Peggy Renner, Rob Ruck, Steve Sapolsky, Ron Schatz, Shel Stromquist, Vic Walsh, and Steve Weiner—provided me with honest criticism of my work and a glowing example of the beauty of mutual assistance. They were instrumental in creating a unique learning environment based on a shared commitment to the collective pursuit of both working-class history and social change. Individual faculty members—David Montgomery, Joe White, Maurine Greenwald, Larry Glasco, Van Beck Hall, and Richard Blackett, among others—contributed both to this environment and to my own development. Edward Thompson, in a one-semester stint at Pitt, breathed a special life into this environment. He also played a special role in this study. Edward read and criticized my masters manuscript, put me in touch with an interested publisher, and encouraged my continued pursuit of this topic.

Among the things we did for each other, as graduate students, was the collective sharing of data and information. Whenever our research overlapped, we stayed on the lookout for information for one another. At times, this network reached beyond the confines of the University of Pittsburgh. In a competitive profession, in a competitive society, the unselfishness and mutuality of my colleagues will always stand as testimony to the possibility of something else. John Bennett taught me about the intricacies of the iron and steel industry in the late nineteenth century, worked up a preliminary index to the Powderly and Hayes Papers with me, and shared primary documents he had discovered. Vic Walsh alerted me to the importance of Irish-American nationalism and clued me in to the Irish world. Leon Fink and John O'Brien completed dissertations that overlapped mine. Graduate students at another institution they shared ideas and documents with me in an utterly unselfish fashion. James Tice Moore of Virginia Commonwealth University supplied me with primary documents he had uncovered in the research of his book on the Readjuster movement and eagerly discussed the ins and outs of local politics in late nineteenth-century Virginia. Joe Carvalho provided me with primary documents and his own notes from a study of the Knights of Labor boycott of 1886. Herbert Gutman provided me with statistical work-ups on the 1880 census, which had been done by his students. John Scattergood, secretary-treasurer of Richmond Typographical Union no. 90, generously let me use minutes of local union meetings that were still in its possession. Warren Chappell, the grandson of John Taylor Chappell, lent me his grandfather's ledgerbook, which included minutes of the Knights of Labor Co-Operative Building Association and of local socialist meetings in the 1890. More than any other person, Mr. Chappell made this study come alive to me, a contribution even greater than the ledgerbook itself.

Lee Krieger and Ingrid Glasco, of the Hillman Library of the University of Pittsburgh, went out of their way to help me with inter-library loans and searches for obscure materials. Floyd Merritt and Margaret Groesbeck, of the Robert Frost Library at Amherst College, were of similar assistance. I am also indebted to the staffs of the Virginia State Library, the Virginia Historical Society, the Amistad Collection at Dillard University in New Orleans, the National Archives in Washington, the Valentine Museum, and the Richmond Public Library.

The continued pursuit of this study has been possible only through the material and moral support of my family and friends. My parents, my grandmother, my brother—all have been there when I've needed them. Perhaps the biggest debt of all is owed to my uncle Marshall Rachleff, a fine historian in his own right, who has encouraged me in every possible way. My wife Meg has demonstrated interminable patience and has been a much-needed steadying influence.

Earlier drafts of this manuscript were read and criticized, in part or in whole, by a number of friends and colleagues. Along with the circle of my fellow graduate students, my friends in the Work Relations Study Group provided me with an informed and interested audience. Jeremy Brecher, Keith Dix, Robb Burlage, Susan Reverby, Laird Cummings, Joan Greenbaum, Jim Weeks, Rick Engler, Stan Weir, Rick Simon, Kathy Stone, and David Noble have all had a hand in this. Bruce Laurie and Milton Cantor have provided simply marvelous editorial assistance and much needed moral support. Whatever strengths this book has are a testimony to their skills and sensitivity.

Special thanks are due to Pat Dunleavy and Jo Ann Howlett for their care in typing the first version of this study, and to Tim Hodgdon, Juliette

Ramirez, and Dave Brady for their work—and sympathy—in preparing the final book manuscript.

My greatest debt, of course, is to the working women and men of Richmond, Virginia, whose trials and tribulations make the stuff of this study. I deeply hope that I have done justice to them.

Black Labor in Richmond, 1865–1890

CHAPTER 1

Race and Class in Richmond

Social and labor historians, over the last two decades, have reshaped and enriched our understanding of the post–Civil War working class. They have scrutinized the component parts of working-class life—the family, the neighborhood, the fraternal society, the church, the workplace, the fire company, the political organization, the trade union—as well as the relationships between them. As a result, a far more sophisticated and comprehensive picture can now be constructed.[1]

But the history of Afro-Americans in this period has remained peripheral to such developments. Innovative research in Afro-American history has tended to emphasize the slave experience or the period after migration northward.[2] The post-bellum period, the subject of W. E. B. Du Bois's brilliant *Black Reconstruction in America* a half-century ago, has been left to economic and political historians, sociologists, economists, and psychologists.[3] Our understanding of these decades has moved forward in two critical areas, following the paradigm suggested by C. Vann Woodward's *Origins of the New South, 1877–1913* in 1951. First of all, our attention has been directed away from consensus ("the solid South") toward conflict. Second, former slaves are now perceived as actors in their own right, rather than the dupes of evil carpetbaggers.[4]

This study seeks to step outside the confines of Woodward's paradigm and subject Afro-American history to the questions, concerns, and insights of the "new" labor history. Precious little ground has been tilled in such fields. Robert Starobin's *Industrial Slavery in the Old South* is a major inspiration. Herbert Gutman has also contributed, and his work has been imaginatively and productively pursued by younger scholars such as John O'Brien, Leon Fink, and Steve Brier. None, however, has traced the organizational and ideological developments of a single Afro-American community from Emancipation through the Knights of Labor.[5]

Richmond represented the most advanced economic development in the antebellum South. By the early 1850s, canal and rail connections with the rest of the South had been completed, creating new markets for its rapidly expanding iron, flour, and tobacco industries. All were firmly grounded in the processing of regionally available materials—coal, pig iron, wheat, tobacco, and the like. Their growing exploitation fueled locally based industries, from barrel making to building construction. Over the course of the 1850s, Virginia embarked on a frenzied campaign of "internal improvements" for the purpose of promoting industry. The impact was obvious: Richmond's factory workforce alone grew by 581 percent in one decade. By 1860, Richmond was the terminus of the South's major railroad networks, its leading port, and an industrial pace-setter.[6]

A self-confident, forward-looking bourgeoisie grew to maturity in the Richmond of the 1850s. The men were a strikingly homogeneous group. Ninety percent owned slaves, had been born in Virginia, and lived in Richmond for over a decade. Three-quarters of them owned more than $15,000 in property. Overwhelmingly industrialists, bankers, wholesale merchants, professionals—not one pursued a manual calling—they promoted economic growth, internal improvements, and regional self-reliance.[7]

An activist core among them provided the leadership for successive projects, organizations, and activities. Joseph R. Anderson typified this group; manager of the Tredegar Iron Works and director of the Richmond Branch of the Farmers' Bank of Viriginia, he was also a major stockholder in two internal improvements companies and a member of St. Paul's Episcopal Church, the House of Delegates, the Richmond City Council, and the executive board of the Richmond Board of Trade. Other activists had similar backgrounds. Barely two percent of Richmond's household heads provided the city with a coherent political, economic, and civic direction.[8]

Facing this bourgeoisie was a racially divided working class. Before the war, few blacks and whites had worked together. Most slaves and freedmen had been employed in tobacco factories or in domestic service; most whites had worked in skilled trades not practiced by blacks, occasionally with black helpers. While wartime labor shortages brought some erosion of these barriers, it was largely limited to the mills of the iron industry. Little direct interracial work experience existed; for that matter, little existed away from the workplace. Organized social activity—churches, temperance, fraternal, and benefit societies—tended to follow racial lines. While there was surely a considerable amount of informal interracial activity—children playing in the street, men drinking, gambling, and visiting houses of prostitution—it was generally seen as outside a broadly shared (across both racial and class lines) conception of proper social activity. While Richmond was not yet rigidly segregated, instances of shared interracial experiences were notable for their very existence.[9]

Race overshadowed all other features of the working-class experience. In the absence of black-white socializing, a range of preconceptions, prejudices, and ideologically shaped viewpoints determined attitudes. Race divided Richmond's working class, set limits to the expansion of the labor movement, and entered the collective self-images of each group of workers.

Thus, it is hardly surprising that white workers perceived slaves as a negative reference group: the antithesis of the "independent" white worker. "Independence" had to be earned through the demonstration of "integrity, virtue, and intelligence," and its absence indicated "unworthiness." In 1830, white workers explicitly excluded "aliens or slaves, . . . unworthy of a voice," from their quest for the suffrage extension. Denying entry of freedmen into certain skilled trades in 1857, they decried "the degrading positions which competition with those who are not citizens of the Commonwealth entails upon us."[10]

Afro-Americans, for their part, had a less than favorable image of white workers. When David Goldfield sampled ten percent of Richmond's white "non-elite" for 1850 and 1860, he found that more than half of the male heads of households were slaveowners. (This was more than double the percentage that even owned their own homes.) White nonslaveowners, meanwhile, did little to allay black fears and mistrust. They intermarried with slaveowning families, staffed the local militia, and agitated for restrictions on the employment of both free blacks and slaves. While Richmond's Underground Railroad could not have functioned without some white participation, those involved were perceived as mercenaries or as distinct exceptions to the rule. In either case, black respect for white workers was hardly encouraged.[11]

The emancipation of the slaves in 1865 brought no improvement to this relationship. To the contrary, the connection between black labor and "degradation" remained a cornerstone of white working-class perceptions, intensified by the fears attending federal military occupation, the abolition of slavery as a system of social control, the extension of suffrage to former slaves, and the persistence of unemployment. White labor's association of black employment with new machines and new divisions of labor fueled fears of being swept into a "dark sea of misery." With blacks organized in the GOP and allied with carpetbaggers, the bourgeois-controlled Conservative party posed as the defender of "white supremacy." Politics—and society—thus revolved around two poles: white Conservative and black Republican.

• • •

Richmond had been one of the few urban centers for industrial slavery in the antebellum South. Since the 1840s slaves had been employed, through either direct ownership or hire, in the city's tobacco factories, iron and flour mills, coal mines, and stone quarries as well as in the construction of buildings, canals, and railroads. The hauling, unpacking, and repacking of goods along the city streets and waterways, in warehouses, and on the docks had also been dependent upon slave labor. No other southern city boasted such a widespread system of slave labor before 1860.[12]

Tobacco manufacturing was the most labor-intensive industry in antebellum Richmond. It alone accounted for more than half the slaves employed in nondomestic labor. Richmond housed a multitude of processing plants, with no less than fifty-two in the 1850s. All shared almost total reliance on slave labor. Forty-two of the fifty-two employed over ten slaves, and sixteen of them had over ninety-five each. By the mid-1850s, 3,400 slaves worked in the city's tobacco factories.[13]

Slaves in the tobacco factories performed a great variety of work, both skilled and unskilled. There were processing manufactories that only stemmed, prized, and shipped the tobacco, usually to England. Stemming and prizing were semiskilled jobs, easily learned in a short time. Hogsheads of tobacco would arrive at the stemmery and prizery from the warehouse auction. They would then be unpacked and their contents taken to the roof to dry; the pickers, usually black women, would sort through the dried tobacco; the male stemmers would moisten the leaves to make them pliable and remove the harsh mid-rib; the leaves would then be returned to the roof for redrying. Once dry, they were taken to the prizers or screwmen, who would compress them with manually operated presses before repacking them in hogsheads for shipment.[14]

The largest number of the tobacco processing factories was devoted to the production of chewing tobacco—"plug" and "twist." The initial processes were the same as in the stemmeries. Once the leaves had been stemmed and dried, they would be flavored. Skilled black men would mix huge vats of a black, syrupy compound of licorice and sugar into which they would dip the stemmed leaves. The leaves were then returned to the roof to be dried and then sprinkled with rum or other flavorings. They would then be ready for the critical process, "lumping" or "twisting," that required considerable skill. In the lump-making room, two-man teams—the lumper (or twister) and his helper, usually a child—jointly labored. The helper would remove the stem from the wrapping leaf and hand it over to the lumper, who had already used his gauges and scales to achieve uniformity of size and weight in the plug. "With agility and skill, the workman moulded a quantity of tobacco, still pliable from the application of rum and flavoring, into a rectangular cake which he measured, trimmed, and weighed. Receiving a stemmed but unflavored wrapping leaf from his assistant, the lumper then encased the moulded cake of filler in a beautiful yellow leaf." If the product were to be twisted, a twister—again, a skilled black man—would form the filler leaves into a roll, equal in length to the wrapping leaf being used. He would then double the roll and twist it into compact form.[15]

The plugs went from the lump room to a press room, where they were placed in multidivided wooden molds and then pressed by men "as strong as the lumpers were nimble." "Heaving and chanting as they worked," the workers swung giant wing-screw presses with tremendous impact, forcing the plugs into proper shape and firmness. Hydraulic presses were introduced by the mid-1850s, replacing the wing-screw presses and making possible the employment of workers lacking the physical attributes of the earlier pressmen. Once pressed, the plugs and twists were labeled and packaged, usually by women.[16]

Some antebellum factories produced smoking tobacco. Here, too, work processes remained manual through the 1850s. The leaves were dried, stemmed, and dried again, as in all the factories. Black women and boys would flail the dry leaves until thoroughly pulverized. Black men wearing a single heavy glove granulated the tobacco by pushing it through a sieve. The tobacco was then weighed and packed, ready for shipment.[17]

Freed blacks, as well as slaves, had worked in tobacco factories. In the 1850s, the rapidly rising price of slaves encouraged tobacco manufacturers to seek other sources of labor—white women, on occasion, but usually free blacks. In Richmond, less than one-third of the latter held skilled jobs by 1860. Many of the others took temporary or permanent employment in the tobacco factories. There is no evidence that free men were accorded special status—skilled jobs or supervisory positions—within these factories. Rather, all accounts indicate, they worked alongside slaves.[18]

While freed blacks earned wages in the tobacco factories, slaves often earned "overwork" money. Employers had learned that they could get more production from their slaves through a bonus system than by driving them. Quotas were set in some factories, regular work hours in others. By exceeding either, individual slaves or work groups could earn between five and twenty dollars a week, which they could spend or save as they saw fit.[19]

So many slaves worked in the tobacco factories that it was impossible—or uneconomical—for employers to house them. Instead, they were provided with "board money" for lodging and food. The slaves found what they could, usually within walking distance of work. Some also found spouses among the local domestic servants and took up residence in their masters' quarters. Some moved in with free blacks, often resulting in marriages. Others drifted from place to place and spent their money on things deemed more important than housing—be they whiskey and gambling or savings toward eventual self-purchase. Some received clothing money instead of clothing itself; thus, they could purchase clothing suited to their own tastes rather than to their master's. The point, of course, is that these decisions were theirs to make.[20]

Like the overwork and board money systems, the organization of work in the tobacco factories left slaves with considerable latitude for decision making. Dexterity, strength, and a willingness to work kept production going. There were no machines to set the work pace. Manufacturers had learned from experience that incentive got better results than pressure or punishment. Foremen found work processes regulated by the songs of their operators and wisely left their cat-o'-nine-tails hanging on the wall. In the large tobacco factories, production revolved around the lump rooms; skilled lumpers and twisters, many of whom had learned the trade as helpers, emerged as song leaders and work-pace setters. One observer noted of the press room in Harvey's tobacco factory:

> In one very large room there were 120 negroes at work upon various stages of the manufacture. Those who were rolling the leaf, performed it with a regular see-saw motion, all in concert, not only of action, but of voice, singing in parts, a hymn or sometimes an impromptu chant, which at a distance produced a pleasing and somewhat plaintive harmony. Those who were pressing the rolls into little square cakes went through every motion in drill. Six or eight at a time, pulled a great iron lever to turn the screw press, and at each pull they uttered a simultaneous noise in their throats, a sort of half cough and half bark.[21]

Tobacco factory slaves exercised considerable freedom. While some—lumpers and twisters, for example—enjoyed more control over their work and commanded more social status than others, all black tobacco workers were seen as central to the vitality of black Richmond. They brought cash into the black community and therefore helped to support boardinghouse keepers, grocers, barbers, tailors, seamstresses, shoemakers, churches, beneficial societies, and gamblers, prostitutes, and grogshop owners. They also brought a sense of independence and an awareness of the factory into the community. William Still, an organizer of the Underground Railroad, later wrote: "No one Southern city furnished a larger number of brave, wide-awake, and likely-looking Underground Railroad passengers than the city of Richmond."[22]

The iron industry was second only to tobacco in its reliance on slave labor. It more clearly restricted both the employment and the social lives of its bondsmen. Few, for example, found any positions in Richmond's smaller foundries and machine shops. They labored in the larger iron mills, such as Tredegar. Only a few slaves held skilled positions; most performed the hot, heavy, and repetitive tasks around the furnaces. They had little control over the pace, conditions, or content of their work; they felt pressured by foremen, skilled white workers, and the demands of iron production. Similarly, their lives outside the workplace were more confined than the social existence of slaves employed in tobacco factories. Many were housed in company-owned and controlled "tenements," and enjoyed only limited freedom of movement around Richmond. If a bondsman were to marry, he rarely could live with his wife and children. Participation in religious and social activities was also limited. Nevertheless, the paternalistic system of the ironmasters had greater space within it than did the rural world. Much like the tobacco employers, the ironmasters learned that industrial slave labor responded better to incentive than to punishment. Overwork bonuses were offered, though usually smaller than in the tobacco factories. Slave ironworkers could also choose whether to work overtime and how to spend the cash they received. Though less central to the black community than the tobacco factory employees, they too were an important workforce.[23]

The employment of slave ironworkers skyrocketed during the war years. Tredegar, for instance, expanded its employment of slaves from 80 in 1860 to more than 1,000 by 1864. For the first time, they worked in the mill's foundry and machine shop, often performing tasks that had been the province of skilled iron molders. Operating within Tredegar's paternalistic system, they wrested improved food and higher overwork pay. However, some were not satisfied with these improvements and the material security they "enjoyed." In June 1863, one of Joseph R. Anderson's partners wrote to the owner of several slaves who had been hired out to Tredegar and had recently escaped together:

> The demoralization among the negroes here and at our furnaces is a source of much disquietude to us who have contracts with the government for iron on the faithful compliance of which the fate of the country may depend. We are sure that here and at all of our furnaces, the negroes are humanely treated, well-fed, and clothed as well as can be done at present and we know of no reason why they should run off except to get to the enemy. Recently, several have been captured nearly within the enemy lines.[24]

Slaves in other occupations also enjoyed a good deal of autonomy in their daily lives. Teamsters, boatmen, stevedores, carpenters, plasterers, shoemakers, and barbers chose and controlled much of their work, earning money for themselves as well as their owners. Most found their own lodgings, married, and raised families, despite the uncertainties of slave life. The systems of "hiring out" and "self-hire" often operated in unskilled as well as skilled work. Building trades laborers, ditch diggers, warehouse laborers, and even domestic servants (female and male) had some experience with bargaining over work conditions and selecting their own residences, spouses, food, and clothing.[25]

The Christmas–New Year season provided a holiday for slaves as well as whites. A wealthy white woman wrote in December 1857:

> This is the season for the servants holidays, all the mills and factories being closed for about ten days, during which the whole tribe of negroes are permitted to roam about at will. If any have fallen short in Christmas gifts, it is not the servants, and we are bound to confess, when we see thronging the streets and stores, well cloaked, cravated, and crinolined, that there is not much of slavery in their appearance, here at any rate.[26]

But this season was more than a holiday for many hired slaves, and their "roaming at will" was not without a purpose. It was the time to find new situations for the following year, with new jobs and new residences. Bargains were struck throughout the city. The *Richmond Dispatch* recounted a conversation between a slave and his prospective employer in December 1856:

> Judge Lomax negotiated with a young slave, whose appearance, qualifications and price suited him, about working as his dining room servant for a year. The two men agreed upon a price, but the slave asked for a delay before finalizing the deal in order "to inquire into the standing and character of the Judge."[27]

Owners and employers were frequently disturbed by the "ingratitude" of their hired slaves, who took advantage of their conditions and fled slavery. One white woman described the consternation of Richmond's elite in the autumn of 1863:

> There was unquestionably an underground agency to decoy away our negro servants, or to assist any who meditated flight from their owners. Thefts of the most provoking character were everywhere perpetrated, usually under circumstances which pointed to family domestics as the perpetrators. . . . The store room or pantry of the citizen, or a gentleman's or lady's wardrobe would be plundered and the articles mysteriously disappear and all efforts of the police to discover the thief or the destination of the missing goods would generally prove unavailing, to be followed in a short time by the singular disappearance of one or more of the domestics of the robbed establishments, to be heard of no more in Richmond.[28]

Even under the more favorable wartime conditions, most Richmond slaves did not flee to the Union lines. They had built families as well as religious and social institutions; in doing so, they had created a considerable area of freedom for themselves and their loved ones. Ties of kinship, love, friendship, and religious fellowship had developed. On the one hand, these ties made daily life more tolerable for slaves and gave them an opportunity to develop their personalities apart from their existence as human chattels. On the other hand, such ties could bind individuals, give them a stake in the status quo and make running away an unacceptable option.

Two critical social institutions were maintained by—and maintained—Richmond slaves: the family and the church, which tended to be linked. Between 1848 and 1857, for instance, the black deacons of the First African Baptist Church expelled 265 black members for adultery. They also mediated marital disputes, divorces, and remarriages. All evidence points to the centrality of the family in black life: the naming of children after parents, grandparents, aunts, and uncles; the efforts of free men and women to purchase the freedom of their spouses and children; the thousands of former slaves who sought to gain legal sanction for marriages in 1865 and 1866; and the recurrent lament about marriages broken by sale. It was through the family that values and knowledge were kept alive and passed on, that each generation drew from its past.[29]

No extrafamilial institution received greater attention than the church. By 1860, 4,633 slaves and free blacks belonged to the city's three African Baptist churches, and 340 belonged to African Methodist churches. The degree of autonomy granted to black congregations by the parent Baptist church made this denomination the most appealing. While whites retained ultimate control and selected the white minister, most daily business was conducted by a black board of deacons that was accountable to the congregation. John O'Brien has described the functioning of the First African Baptist Church, Richmond's most prominent black church:

> The church provided the only public forum for voicing opinions, taking collective action, taking active decision-making roles, and aiding the poor and helpless. The church provided the law and the institutional mechanisms for regulating conduct, which the secular government withheld entirely from slaves and, to a lesser extent, from free blacks. The church did not simply complement the law as it did for whites; the church board was the elected government of the blacks which executed a set of laws that were useful and not simply restrictive standards. Because it performed essential functions that no other institution did and because whites permitted blacks to govern most of their own affairs within the church, it became the most important institution in the black world, and its pronouncements resonated with particular strength within the black community.[30]

The church and the family provided space for the development and transmission of values and social relationships among slaves and free blacks. Some values like some social relationships, such as those between the sexes, mirrored those of the dominant white world. Others, like solving the problem of "remarriage" after the sale of one's spouse, were more specific to the needs of black life in Richmond. Extended kinship networks developed among blacks, both slave and free, especially among those who had been born and raised in the city. Many blacks, led by free men and women, organized beneficial societies to carry them through periods of illness or hard times, or to provide for their funerals after death. Such societies, "secret" in character and composition, were often connected with a specific church and built on extended kinship ties. Altogether, these relationships wove a social network that provided the foundation for a vibrant black community in antebellum Richmond.[31]

The character of the people who produced, and were produced by, such a community greatly impressed the white missionaries and teachers who flocked to Richmond after the war. Only two weeks after the city had been occupied by Union troops, one missionary observed:

> The colored people of Richmond are far more intelligent and thrifty than any I have met with in the South—and though the laws against learning have been so strict, many can read and a large portion know their letters and can spell a little.[32]

• • •

In the twenty-five years after Emancipation, black Richmond gave birth to several popular crusades. During Reconstruction, a mass movement waged a prolonged battle for "equal rights"—for dignity, respect, and recognition; full citizenship and its privileges; and a voice in the writing of a new state constitution. In the early 1880s, after a decade in which economic hard times and the local bourgeoisie had eroded the Reconstruction-era victories, another popular movement arose and renewed the struggle. This time, however, the new ideology of "race pride" emerged. Hardly had the fire of this movement died down when yet another broke out, one which represented the most serious threat to put "the bottom rail on the top." Infused with a class consciousness rooted in race pride, black workers organized themselves through the Knights of Labor and reached across the color line to white labor. The chapters that follow trace the developments that made the Knights of Labor possible, but its ultimate success unlikely.

CHAPTER 2

Community of Former Slaves, 1865–1873

RICHMOND AFRO-AMERICANS constructed a remarkably cohesive community directly following Emancipation. Their achievement appears all the more remarkable given the dreadful shortage of their material resources. Jobs were scarce after the burning of Richmond's business district, the significant loss of wealth by the city's elite and its financial institutions, the devastation of Virginia's agriculture and rail system, and the more general collapse of the regional economy. Black efforts were also opposed by the most powerful elements of society, indeed, by both the South's traditional rulers and the federal occupying forces.

With limited resources and in an atmosphere of continual social conflict, Richmond Afro-Americans built an impressive community. They wove together the formerly free and the formerly slave, the city native and the "country negro," dark-skinned and light-skinned, literate and illiterate, skilled and unskilled. The initial building block was the extended family, a resiliant, vital social institution. Linked with it was the church. Together, they nourished a common set of relationships. Built on this foundation, a broad network of social organizations called "secret societies" fulfilled a multiplicity of purposes: funerals and death benefits, trade organization, collective self-education and self-improvement, religious advancement, political expression, socializing, and the like. Woven together, and interwoven with extended families and church organizations, these secret societies were the circulatory system of the black community.

Barely two months after the fall of Richmond, a group of local black men drafted a petition to President Andrew Johnson, proudly citing what they saw as the accomplishments of their community:

> We represent a population of more than 20,000 colored people, including Richmond and Manchester, who have ever been distinguished for their good

> behavior as slaves and as freemen, as well as for their high moral and Christian character; more than 6,000 of our people are members in good standing of Christian churches, and nearly our whole population constantly attend divine services. Among us there are at least 2,000 men who are worth from $200 to $500; 200 who have property valued at from $1,000 to $5,000, and a number who are worth $5,000 to $20,000. None of our people are in the almshouse, and when we were slaves the aged and infirm who were turned away from the homes of hard masters, who had been enriched by their toil, our benevolent societies supported while they lived, and buried when they died, and comparatively few of us have found it necessary to ask for government rations, which have been so bountifully bestowed upon the unrepentant Rebels of Richmond. The law of slavery severely punished those who taught us to read and write, but, notwithstanding this, 3,000 of us can read, and at least 2,000 can read and write, and a large number of us are engaged in useful and profitable employment on our own account.[1]

The petitioners sought an end to the pass system that restricted black travel, demanded legal titles to their church property, and called for the removal of the "Rebel-controlled" local government. Its very existence, they claimed, confirmed a conspiracy between the "unrepentant Rebels" and the Federal occupying forces. Though they referred to themselves as "oppressed, obedient, and loving children," the petitioners bore witness to the growing self-consciousness and militancy of black Richmond.[2]

While the pass system was an indignity for all, it posed a particular problem for those black men and women who were entering Richmond in large numbers. In the summer of 1864, Lucy Chase, then teaching in a "contraband" camp outside Norfolk, had observed: "The multitude wait patiently for the gates of Richmond to open that they may rush therein. Here and there, as we move about the country, we find many freed people longing for Richmond. All who come from its neighborhood refuse to find a home elsewhere." The steady stream began as soon as the city fell in April 1865. In 1860, there had been 14,275 black people, slave and free, in Richmond. By May 1866, a white school principal could refer to "the usual estimate of 30,000." A black Baptist minister, once a slave and a migrant to Richmond himself, later recalled the oft-repeated scenes when groups of former slaves reached Richmond:

> The colored people from all parts of the state was crowding in at the capital, running, leaping, and praising God that freedom had come at last. It seems to me that I can hear their songs now [1893] as they rung through the air: "Slavery chain done broke at last; slavery chain done broke at last—I's goin' to praise God till I die."[3]

There were many reasons for coming to the capital. Some saw immigration as a celebration of freedom. Black men with skills or particular aspirations might pick Richmond as the site of greater opportunity than existed in the rural areas and small towns. Many had spent some time in Richmond as "hired" slaves and therefore had important social connections as well as a clear sense of how to proceed.[4]

Among those who had lived there before the war were men and women who had been sold away from their families and now sought reunion with them. The petition to President Johnson pointed out:

> A number of men who have been employed upon plantations have visited Richmond in search of long-lost wives and children, who had been separated by the cruel usage of slavery. Wives, too, are frequently seen in our streets, anxiously inquiring for husbands who had been sold away from them, and many of these people, who ignorantly supposed that the day of passes had passed away with the system which originated them, have been arrested, imprisoned, and hired out without their advice or consent, thus preventing the reunion of long estranged and affectionate families.[5]

Families were reunited, nevertheless. Husbands and wives, separated for years, along with those who had been able to remain together, legalized their vows in mass ceremonies before black ministers and Freedman's Bureau officials in 1865 and 1866. George Washington Drew's experience illuminates the processes. He had been owned by a family in rural King and Queen County and had been hired out in Richmond in the early 1850s. There he had married a free woman, Mary, and they had had a daughter. In the late 1850s, Drew had found himself restricted to the plantation, where he had also spent most of the war years. Mary and their daughter had moved in with another "single" mother and her two children, and the two women had sustained their families by taking in washing. After the war, Drew returned to his wife and daughter in Richmond and worked in tobacco factories and as a newspaper carrier. Their relationships with other black families rapidly expanded; Mary was elected president of the Sylvester Evening Star Society in 1871, while George served as its secretary. They both became active in the Children of Emanuel and the Sisters of Emanuel, and they joined the Second African Baptist Church, where they helped direct its Missionary Society. Through these activities, their network of associations multiplied, reaching old and new city residents, free-born and former slave, men and women.[6]

Some traveled a great distance to return to Richmond and pick up the fragments of their families. Charles Maho had been sold away from his wife and daughter in the late 1850s to a Mississippi cotton planter. Escaping to northern lines, he enlisted in a black regiment and returned to Richmond with the invading Union troops, only to discover that his wife had been dead for years. Maho did find his daughter, and they shared an apartment in the town's east end while he worked in a tobacco factory to support them. Olmstead Scott had been born in Stafford County and hired out in Richmond. His parents died while he was living and working in the city. In 1860, then thirty years old, he was sold to a Florida planter. It took Scott until 1869 to get back to Richmond, where he was reunited with his grandmother, his aunt and uncle, and his brother and sister. Family ties were a powerful magnet, drawing one-time Richmond residents back "home."[7]

The extended family, the church, and the rapidly growing network of secret societies provided institutions by which new residents integrated themselves into the black community. Material and emotional survival was often too great a struggle for the isolated individual. Single women and men shared lodging or boarded with black families. Many secret societies were open to both sexes, and young men and women joined as much to meet each other as to enjoy the sickness and funeral benefits. Churches—with Sunday and evening classes, suppers, socials, excursions, and services—brought young men and women together. Aged widows and widowers were more common in black Richmond than unmarried men and women in their late twenties and thirties.[8]

Marriage established new relationships with a spouse's entire family, which brought both new support and new obligations. Twenty-year-old George Woodson arrived in Richmond in 1865, leaving his parents and six younger brothers and sisters in Fauquier County. He found a job in a quarry and soon met Harriet Brooks, who had grown up a slave in Richmond. She lived with her mother and two sisters. Her older brother John, who had been the "man of the house" for some time, had recently married and moved into an apartment of his own. When Harriet married George Woodson, they settled into an apartment in the same neighborhood. Literate and some fifteen years older than his new brother-in-law, Brooks helped Woodson learn to read and introduced him to his friends, some of whom belonged to the Rising Sons and Daughters of the East. Woodson himself was elected an officer of the all-black Grand Lodge of Quarry Men in 1873. Over the course of the 1870s, George and Harriet Woodson had four children, one of whom died. They named their first son George, Jr., and their second son John. Extended familial ties did not end there. Harriet died early, before her thirtieth birthday. George, by 1880, a widower with three young children, was joined by his mother, two younger sisters, and his niece (one sister's child). Together, they constituted a family and created a functional household.[9]

For many, of course, the development of extended familial networks, or their inclusion in existing ones, took much time. But for those whose families had lived in Richmond since the 1840s or early 1850s, these networks were facts of daily life. Slaves and free blacks knew too well the destruction of marriages and families by the sale of a husband or a wife, a father or a mother. Under such circumstances, all blood and in-law relationships had been highly valued. Long-time Richmond residents, free-born and former slave, kept these relationships alive in the post-war years. They integrated a new generation—too young themselves to have experienced slavery as adults—into this social network. The continuing economic hardships of black Richmond created conditions in which mutual assistance remained an everyday necessity. Most black family units lived on the edge of subsistence, able to manage only by combining the wage-earning abilities of virtually all family members; even then they succeeded only in the best of economic times, periods that were few and far between. Given these conditions, members of extended kinship networks provided each other with much needed material and emotional sustenance.[10]

Support within an extended family could flow in many directions, across households and generations. Samuel Mayo was born in 1849 in rural Powhattan county; shortly afterward, he and his parents were sold to a Richmond slaveowner. In 1852, his sister Camilla was born. In the late 1850s, their father was sold again, this time to the Deep South, away from his family. Mrs. Mayo and her two children moved in with another "single" mother and her children, an arrangement that provided the emotional and practical support all needed.[11]

The Mayos were similarly engaged in the black social network that stretched beyond their household. In 1870 Camilla, at the age of eighteen, worked full-time as a cook for a white family, though she continued to live at home. Her new adult responsibilities received social recognition when she was elected an officer in the Daughters of Elijah. (This beneficial society was affiliated with the Second African Baptist Church and had a young men's counterpart, the Rising Sons of Elijah.) Samuel, who was twenty-one years old in 1870, had assumed the role of "man of the house." After the war, his mother had arranged for him to learn the plastering trade, one of the few "black" skilled trades in the city. Black artisans may have sought apprentices among the offspring of widows as an expression of the community's collective obligation to such children. By 1870, Samuel Mayo had completed his apprenticeship, was working full-time, and had learned to read and write. He opened a savings account at the Freedman's Bank for his sister, even though she earned her own wages as a cook and contributed to the family income.[12]

The Mayo family was transformed in the 1870s, but its bonds held firm. Mrs. Mayo died and both children married. Camilla married Joseph Jones, who had steady and respectable work as a porter in a grocery store. She quit her job, had two children, and devoted her time to raising them and keeping house. They took an apartment in a three-family tenement in the rapidly growing Jackson Ward ghetto. Keeping his job through the depression of the mid-1870s, he was able to earn enough to support a growing family without Camilla having to return to the labor market. However, the years were not so kind to her brother Samuel. He also married and became a father who looked forward to prospering as an artisan and raising a family, but in the depression of the mid-1870s, he found himself unable to support his young family as a plasterer. There simply was not enough work, especially in a trade where job opportunities were heavily dependent upon the expansion of black homeownership. Forced to give up the trade he had worked so hard to learn, Samuel Mayo took a job in a tobacco factory. Shortly afterward, his wife became ill and died, leaving him a thirty-year-old widower with a young son.

When an apartment became vacant in her tenement, Camilla persuaded him to move in. She cared for his son while he worked and cooked for both of them as well as her own family. While having separate apartments, they functioned as one household and one family.[13]

Parents provided for their children's future as well as caring for them in the present. Tony Myers had spent his youth and early adulthood in bondage, working in Richmond's tobacco factories. He had married in the 1850s, joined the First African Baptist Church, and started a family. By the early 1870s, though illiterate and still working in a tobacco factory, he had been elected an officer in two church-related secret societies: the Young Lambs and the Sons and Daughters of Noah. Each of his seven offspring, as they came of age, found a job and contributed to the family income. Mark, Joseph, and Charles followed their father into the tobacco factories, Julia became a nurse, and Sarah, a seamstress. As the children went to work and brought in money, their father opened savings accounts for each of them at the Freedmen's Bank. Other fathers behaved in similar fashion. Even though Henry Davis's daughter Caroline was married and over forty, he started a bank account for her. John Lee, a hackman and officer in the Young Men's Gold Key, the United Sons of Ham, and the Young Brothers of Friendship, and treasurer of Ham's cemetery, opened an account for his teen-aged son, who was working for him. Mothers were equally concerned with their children's future. Emily Jane Watkins took in boarders and washing to open bank accounts for her two young daughters. Agnes White opened an account for her twenty-one-year-old son, even though he already supported himself as a cook; this was not unusual. Fannie Johnson, a widow, opened an account for her twenty-year-old son, who worked in the Tredegar rolling mill. Thursday Hewlett opened an account for her daughter, who was eighteen at the time and still at home. Kitty Wiggins did not want to wait until her daughter reached maturity, so she opened a bank account for her when she was only five months old.[14]

As parents grew older, their ability to provide for themselves, let alone their children, usually waned. Elderly parents, especially widows and widowers, were frequently taken in by their grown children. Jane Green, an officer in the United Daughters of Ham, and her husband, a shoemaker, had one daughter. Jane's elderly mother lived with them from Emancipation until her death in 1871. Mariah Morton had lived many years as a slave in Richmond. She had married, raised five children, and been a member of the First African Baptist Church long before the war. Widowed after Emancipation, she faced a life alone, but kinship ties and community support remained. She moved in with two of her daughters, one already a widow herself and the other still single. The three women took in washing and boarders, and thus supported themselves. Mrs. Morton joined a beneficial society and became active in the Eureka Savings Society.[15]

Grown children offered support to their aging parents, even when the latter were still able to care for themselves. They might open bank accounts for them or guarantee them access to their own savings. John H. Smith, a huckster in the First Market, started an account and informed the bank officials that he wanted "this money paid to my mother in case of her requiring it." Beverly Woodridge, who had been working at Tredegar, put funds in the bank as he prepared to leave Richmond in search of work elsewhere. This money was "to be used by his mother if she needs it during his absence." George Barber, a railroad worker, left instructions for his mother and step-father to have access to his account. Although having a wife and seven children, George Robinson, a tobacco factory worker, opened a joint bank account with his elderly, widowed mother. Mutual support flowed back and forth between parents and children, tying them together for their entire lives.[16]

Such relationships often extended beyond two generations. Whether or not an intermediate generation was present, grandparents and grandchildren supported each other. Fifteen-year-old America Gregory, a "nurse" for a white family, lived with her widowed father, her brother, two sisters, and grandmother, who started a bank account for her. Richard Forrester, a successful contractor, opened an account for each of his grandchildren as they were born. So did Ann Singleton for her young grandson, William Graham Butler Lincoln Garrett. William Bingham, the year-old infant of a single parent, had an account opened by his grandmother. Harriet Gregory did as much for her thirteen-year-old grandson, who had moved in with her when his parents died. Frank Martin, a seventy-seven-year-old baker, left instructions that "if he dies, he wishes for his granddaughter to get an equal share with the rest of his children." Young Alfred Method, already contributing to the family income through tobacco factory work, opened an account for his aged grandmother, who lived with the family. Phil Burnett, a nineteen-year-old tobacco factory worker, opened one for his grandmother; she was his only family in the city.[17]

Support also flowed in lateral directions. Brothers and sisters greatly assisted each other. Continuing mutual assistance through various stages of life, like that of Samuel and Camilla Mayo, remained a common feature of sibling relationships and a prominent building block of the black social network. The Freedman's Savings Bank records abound with examples. Martha Williams opened an account for her younger sister, who was already married and the mother of two children. Sampson Starks, a drayman with a wife and two children, opened an account for his brother, who had remained in rural Hanover County to farm. Alexander Giles, a twenty-two-year-old tobacco factory worker, prepared to leave Richmond temporarily in 1871. He deposited some money in an account to be "paid to his sister Vina if needed during his absence." Henry Williams, an unmarried teamster, and his sister, a widow with two young children, opened a joint bank account. John Kersey, a railroad worker, lived with his sister Louisa Ann and her husband, when he worked in the city. John and Louisa opened a joint bank account, perhaps to make sure she got his savings if he were killed in an accident (a common concern among railroad workers). Rachael Johnson and Mary Jones were two middle-aged sisters who formed the backbone of a household. Rachael and her husband Abraham had no children; Mary was a widow with three children. The sisters opened a joint back account. Laura Gaines and Catherine Green were sisters who lived together on Twenty-seventh Street. Laura was single, thirty-five, and worked as a washerwoman. Catherine was a thirty-four-year-old widow with one son. While Catherine worked in a tobacco factory, Laura watched her nephew and labored in their home. They had separate bank accounts, but left instructions that each would have access to the other's savings.[18]

Sibling support reached step-brothers and sisters, as well as in-laws. John Stokes and Henry Johnson, step-brothers named for their respective fathers, had left their Halifax County home for rolling mill jobs at Tredegar in 1866. They shared an apartment on Broad Street with Henry's younger brother Elmer, a Tredegar worker, too. John and Henry shared a bank account; both were elected officers of the Young Men of Liberty, a politically oriented secret society organized by black Tredegar workmen. Charlotte Roy, a widow with no children, opened an account with her sister-in-law. Mary Robinson, a twenty-three-year-old widow with two small children, made sure her brother-in-law had access to her savings if anything should happen to her. Apparently, it was understood that he would take responsibility for the offspring in such a situation. The lateral bonds of step-siblings and in-laws were an important source of social cohesion and mutual assistance.[19]

Of course, husbands and wives offered mutual assistance to each other. It is interesting, however, to note some of the forms this could take, using only examples drawn from the records of the Freedman's Savings Bank. Men opened accounts for themselves and their wives; women, for themselves and their husbands. Husbands and wives opened joint accounts—marked on one couple's sheet: "This money is the joint property of husband and wife." These patterns had little obvious connection to work or wage-earning roles within the family. Rather, the elusive elements of husband-wife relations—the implicit and shifting balance between power and sharing in each relationship—must explain the variations.[20]

Bonds extended from aunts and uncles to their nieces and nephews. This happened most often when the particular aunt or uncle was childless, and the niece or nephew was parentless. While the material assistance tended to flow from the older generation to the younger, emotional support flowed both ways, as nieces and nephews became surrogate children. Nelson Morton, an orphaned eighteen-year-old tobacco factory worker, shared his bank account with his aunt. Julia Carter, a childless widow still working as a washerwoman at the age of fifty, shared her bank account with her thirty-nine-year-old nephew John, who was described as a "sawyer, lives with his aunt, single, no brothers and sisters, father and mother dead." Young Lizzie King came from Gloucester County to live in Richmond with her aunt. Each was the other's nearest living relative. The orphan and the childless widow constituted a household unit, hardly unusual in black Richmond. Sally Porter had been born and raised in Richmond. After her parents died, she moved in with her uncle, Washington Brown. He had no wife or children, and she had no brothers or sisters. Aunts and uncles added nieces and nephews to their own broods when the need arose. James Worsham, a rolling mill laborer at Tredegar, had four children of his own. When his brother and sister-in-law died, leaving their son (named for his uncle) an orphan, Worsham and his wife took in the eleven-year-old boy. Family income was too thin to spread very far, so the youngster went to work as a shoeblack. But his uncle wanted him to keep some of his meager earnings and opened a savings account for the boy. Aunts and uncles could assist nieces and nephews later in their lives, too. Peter Williams worked as a waiter. He and his wife were childless and had lived alone for years. In 1872, his wife's twenty-two-year-old niece Sally Willis left her husband and turned to them for help. They took her in and treated her as if she were their child. Williams opened a bank account for her and left instructions that his own savings be turned over to her in the event that he and his wife died.[21]

Aunts and uncles might also rescue a family unit facing particularly serious problems, usually by singling out one child for continued aid. The death of one parent, a debilitating injury to the breadwinner, the loss of a job, or the growth of an immediate family beyond its ability to provide for all its members could bring aunts and uncles into the picture. Jake Price was only two years of age when his father died. Elderly Stephen Scott, the boy's great-uncle, started a savings account for him. James Branch started one for his nineteen-year-old niece Francis Griggs, then supporting herself "in service," while both her parents were still alive. Thus he shared the burden felt by his sister and her husband, who were struggling to provide for their eight children. If Frances contributed to her family's income, she surely had little left to save for herself, so her uncle James helped her. Then there was John Mayo, a young blacksmith only recently married, who opened a bank account for his nephew Patrick Hughes. The boy's mother, Mayo's sister, had died in childbirth and left her husband with three children to care for, of whom Patrick, at twelve, was the oldest.[22]

At times, mutual support reached surprising lengths. In the absence of other familial relationships, cousins occasionally turned to each other for mutual economic and emotional relief. James and Mary Shepherd were first cousins who had been raised like brother and sister in Fluvanna County. They came to Richmond together after the war. James found work in a tobacco factory, while Mary moved in with a white family as their domestic servant. Though living apart, they opened a joint account at the Freedman's Bank. City cousins could provide special support for country cousins who moved to Richmond. Born and raised in Richmond, Dabney Elliott was named for his father, who had died before the war. His mother remarried and had four more children before she died. In 1870, Elliot was twenty-one, single, still illiterate, and lived with his grandmother and his four half-brothers and sisters. The oldest male in the household, his wages were the foundation of the family income. When his twenty-five-year-old cousin came to Richmond, Elliot took on the responsibility of helping her. He found her a position as a live-in domestic, and he opened a savings account in her name. In this and similar ways, extended familial relationships integrated new and established Richmond residents and further enlarged existing relationships among long-time residents.[23]

In certain circumstances, relationships extended beyond blood lines into the realm of fictive kinship. Childless widows and orphaned adolescents, for instance, frequently reached out to each other. Eliza Winston, still a full-time washerwoman at age sixty, took in a girl with no family of her own. She gave the fourteen-year-old an all too rare privilege—to attend school full-time rather than to work. Moreover, Winston, seeking to provide for the girl's future, left her savings account to the orphan. Rosetta Hunter and Mary Littlepage's relationship provides another example. Born a slave in Hanover County in 1815, Hunter had spent most of her life hired out in Richmond. In 1842, she had been baptized and joined the First African Baptist church. She married and raised a family, all while working as a slave. Emancipation found her alone, a widow, her children gone. She then became active in "society" life, was elected an officer of the Daughters of Zion in 1867, remained a member of the First African Church, and "adopted" an orphan, Mary Littlepage, who had been born on the eve of the war. They lived together in a small apartment on Canal Street, along the river. Fictive kinships often operated to the mutual support of everyone involved and at times wove Richmond blacks together beyond actual blood lines.[24]

Naming patterns bear witness to the centrality of familial relationships in black life. Both boys and girls were named for their parents, grandparents, aunts, and uncles. Unmarried mothers named their sons after their own fathers and brothers, as well as after the boys' natural fathers. Some names carried special meaning for the family. James Wetherless named his first son Daniel, after his own father who had been sold in 1830 and his older brother who had been sold in 1860. Samuel Randolph's first daughter was named for his mother to preserve her African name, Sinte. Biblical names—Moses, Ezekiel, Isaiah, and the like—were also transmitted from this adult generation to their children. But names associated with slavery—Orpheus, Titus, Primum—even though they were of loved ones, tended not to be passed on to the generation born after 1865. New names appeared, some of which represented the aspirations and appreciation of former slaves. One couple named their first two sons, born after Emancipation, Moses and Lincoln. Another named their two daughters Independent and Victoria. One child born right after Emancipation was named William Graham Butler Lincoln. Above all else, naming patterns affirmed familial loyalties and affixed a stamp of approval on the lines of mutuality and kinship.[25]

The family not only provided the critical channels of mutual assistance and the basic foundation of the black community, but also served as a prism through which members viewed social development. A twenty-one-year-old black father of two who was on his way home after a day at common labor was stopped by a journalist. The man had earned only $1.50 and had to admit, "It's right hard, these times, everything costs so high. I have to pay $15 a month rent, and only two little rooms." They managed, however, as his wife took in washing and even went "out to work" once in a while; her mother, who lived nearby, watched the children. Life was clearly a daily struggle. But when the journalist asked, "Were not your people better off in slavery?," the young man was quick to reply: "Oh, no, sir! We're a heap better off now. We haven't got our rights yet, but I expect we're go'n to have 'em soon. . . . We're men now, but when our masters had us we was only change in their pockets."[26]

• • •

The church was the most important extrafamilial institution in black Richmond. In critical ways, the church and the family were interrelated, reinforcing each other ideologically and socially. Families, more than individuals, joined specific churches, with the Baptist Church holding an overwhelming attraction. Children were introduced to it through Sunday school and evening classes, and they were taken on church excursions, outings, and picnics. While there were separate activities, organizations, and roles reserved for adults or children, the focus of membership and participation was familial. Inside Richmond's several "African" Baptist churches, the prewar tradition of seating men and women separately gave way to sitting by families.[27]

The church promoted family values. Members were punished for adultery, fornication, and other offenses; deacons adjudicated family disputes, and divorce was discouraged, becoming a rarity among church members. Husbands and wives joined church-affiliated secret societies together, or joined separate men's and women's societies; their offspring joined the children's version, like the Rising Sons and Daughters of the New Testament and its affiliate, the Young Rising Sons and Daughters of the New Testament. Clearly, then, the family was at the core of the value system promoted by the church.[28]

In black Richmond, the church—and religion in general—promoted much more than the family. The physical structure itself accommodated public mass meetings, day schools, night classes, and the like. The church also provided skills in self-government, from the deacons who managed the church on a daily basis to the men who elected them. The scope of self-government expanded as blacks replaced white pastors and congregations assumed ownership of church property. These actions, which severed ties with the "parent" white churches, culminated in the organization of the all-black Shiloh Baptist Association. Church congregations also assumed responsibility for supporting indigent members "Poor Saints' Funds," as well as the church-affiliated societies that blossomed. Their activities ranged from providing sickness and death benefits to Bible reading. The church remained the hub of these activities and organizations, all of which went beyond the expression of religious sentiment.[29]

More than anything else, however, religious commitment nourished the black church. One historian has pointed out what should be obvious but has often been overlooked: ". . . the South's lost cause was the fulfillment of a prophecy the slaves had been singing of for more than half a century. . . . The initial impact of Emancipation was a glorious confirmation of the sacred world view and the expressive culture the slaves had forged and maintained through their years of bondage." For those who had built their lives and self-understanding around such religious notions as the coming of the "Day of Jubilee," Emancipation only confirmed their beliefs. This generation, freed in adulthood, would be one of the most religiously imbued of any people in all of American history. Living a "Christian life" dominated their days, and the church, its precepts, and its leaders commanded their respect.[30]

Black parents socialized their children into this perspective, much as they integrated them into familial and social networks. Sermons, lectures, classrooms, folk tales, and secret societies echoed and reechoed the "sacred world view" that had been created by slaves, confirmed by Emancipation, and transmitted to their offspring. No longer did religion need to be tempered with the same "practicality" that had kept slaves from acting fully and openly. Now they could draw lessons from their religious views, strictures by which they might live. Religious goals and visions legitimated the struggle to improve social and economic conditions. Shortly after Emancipation, for instance, a group of black women domestics, who worked on a daily rather than live-in basis, expressed their concern over the dignity between their wages and their rent charges. This situation, they feared, "will tend to demoralization among them, and lead them into temptation contrary to good morals and conscience, in making bargains for rent that cannot, under the circumstances, be complied with."[31]

The church and religious ideas played important roles in everyday life. Organizationally and spiritually, they underpinned the mutual assistance practiced within extended families and justified its extension beyond blood lines. Being one's "brother's keeper" took on a special significance in black Richmond. Indeed, they were involved in virtually every instance of community activism.

• • •

Richmond Afro-Americans took pride in their ability to care for their orphans, widows, widowers, cripples, and those who were destitute. In June 1865, petitioners to President Johnson proudly asserted that "none of our people are in the Almshouse" and "comparatively few of us have found it necessary to ask for government rations." Indeed, Freedman's Bureau records bear them out. As a northern visitor to the city noted in late 1865, Richmond blacks "seem to look for an improvement in their condition more to their own exertions and to local action, and less to the general government and the people of the north."[32]

Secret societies provided the framework for collective self-improvement and mutual assistance. In January 1866, a local newspaper described a "quite imposing and very orderly" funeral procession conducted by the "United Sons of Love." The Sons were a "colored benevolent organization, whose principal features are to care for the sick, look after the poor and destitute, and bury their dead." It was a "secret society," so-called in antebellum Richmond because membership was kept confidential to protect all involved, both slave and free.[33]

Secret societies enlarged their social role, transcended their antebellum limits, and expanded their membership after Emancipation. By the early 1870s, black Richmond was honeycombed with more than 400 such societies, which reached into its every corner and touched every sphere of activity.[34]

Secret societies provided an institutional framework through which black people could help each other—and seek help—beyond familial and churchly ties. The continuously harsh economic situation they faced demanded a tremendous collective effort just to escape abject poverty. Few families, no matter how large or how extended, could withstand a serious crisis. The elderly and the infirm, moreover, were unable to provide for themselves and needed more than their family networks could provide. Richmond Afro-Americans built from preexisting relationships—of family, church, neighborhood, workplace, or even shared home county—to construct these secret societies.

Along with family networks, the church provided a major foundation for these societies. Through them, parishioners raised funds for the poor, sent out people to care for the infirm, found homes for the homeless. Such societies also organized bazaars, excursions, bake sales, and the like to raise funds for charity and for the church. The "Christian" purposes of their activities were reflected in the names of the societies—the Good Samaritans, the Baptist Helping Society, the Benevolent Daughters of the Young Army Shining, and the Christian Union Aid Society. Indeed, many of these were affiliated with a specific church.[35]

As Richmond's most prominent black church, the First African Baptist generated the greatest number of such secret societies. Tracing the activities of the Osborns, one active family within the congregation, provides an interesting angle on this process. Humphrey Osborn, a member of Richmond's black community since the 1840s, was a sexton at the church through the 1860s and 1870s. Over that period, he served as an officer in the Soldiers of the Cross, the First Star of Jacob, and the United Sons of Adam, and he was a trustee for the church's Poor Saints' Fund and Foreign Missionary Society. His wife Margaret was an officer in the Soldiers of the Cross, the Female Star of Jacob, the Female Soldiers of the Cross, and the Young Female Hope. His brother Charles was a tobacco factory worker who also joined, through the church, a number of secret societies: the Christian Union Aid Society, the Pilgrim Travellers, and the Benevolent Star. Charles Osborn's wife Elizabeth was an officer in Liberty Lodge, No. 104. This one family, then, illustrates the extent of the church's role in the organization of secret societies.[36]

These church-related societies directed their support towards others—for instance, orphans or widows without any local family—rather than themselves. Some probably offered benefits to their own members, but this was secondary. Raising funds for the church itself would often take precedence over "insurance" functions. Since both men and women were involved in such activities (attending church, providing for the needs of the poor, raising funds for the church), many of these societies had mixed membership. Both men and women served as officers, attended and voted at meetings, organized activities, and did the necessary work. Although all-male and all-female church-related societies existed, they were often paired together as "auxiliaries."[37]

The Golden Rule Society was organized in 1872 by a group of First African Baptist Church members. Born in Brunswick County, Nancy Taylor had come to Richmond with her daughter after the war to find her husband, but she never found him. She lived with another female-headed family in a tenement on Main Street between 19th and 20th and, while there, was elected president of the Golden Rule. Deliah Price was also a "single" mother; just forty, she had already been an officer in several other church-related societies—the Daughters of the Golden Rod, the Daughters of the Golden Band, and the Daughters of Jerusalem—when elected an officer of the Golden Rule Society. She supported herself and her daughter Susan (named after her sister) by taking in washing. Surely, all these society activities helped fill voids in their members' lives. The third female officer of the Golden Rule Society, Winnie Ann Scott, was in her mid-forties. She and her husband Fleming, a tobacco factory worker, were childless. Her mother, now alone, still lived in Richmond. Mrs. Scott joined the Young Rising Sons and Daughters of the New Testament and the Loving Sons and Daughters of Revelation, as well as the Golden Rule Society. The male officers in this society seemed to play secondary positions. William Mickens served as secretary, a role he fulfilled for six other church-related societies. It is doubtful if his involvement went beyond keeping records for the society. Mickens was one of several young black men in popular demand as secret society secretaries owing to their literacy and unmarried status. This was often the case in societies with women officers because few possessed the literacy necessary to fulfill their roles. There were other male officers in the Golden Rule Society, but they, too, appeared to play secondary roles. Robert Howlett, for instance, was also an officer in the Railroad Helpers' Society, an occupation that often might have taken him out of town. Thus, while the Golden Rule Society involved men and women, the latter were the prime movers.[38]

Some of the church-related societies seem to have developed a tentative equality between their male and female members. This was especially true among the societies composed primarily of church members. The Loving Sons and Daughters of Bethlehem, for example, had an identical number of male and female officers. All were teen-agers and the children of church members except Johnson and Lucy Gay; the recently married couple, in their early twenties, provided spiritual leadership to the youthful and mixed membership. For young parishioners, these societies existed in large numbers; their activities and functions were more social and educational than charitable or beneficial. Many were affiliated with adult societies, their junior status noted by the addition of "Young" to the title of the parent body. Male and female members, mostly teen-agers, held discussions, read the Bible, elected officers, and perhaps held some fund-raising events. Many husbands and wives, we may speculate, first met at such gatherings.[39]

Black adults organized to meet their insurance needs by creating beneficial societies. A family could be taxed beyond its abilities by a sudden crisis, and black people saw the need to prepare. They organized societies with clearly specified dues and definite benefits and an explicitly beneficial purpose. They provided respectable funerals and paid out death benefits to widows and children. As with all secret societies, members held meetings, elected officers, discussed commonly held interests, and collected dues. These societies tended to be all-male or all-female, and they were organized by everyone from unskilled laborers to successful contractors.[40]

In October 1865, a group of black men appealed to Richmond's local military authorities: "We are man of color desire to attend to our sick and bury our dead. We propose to have aprons as a signal of our society, and did not desire to perform such without your permission." A glimpse at the officers of this body—the Secret Sons of Love—suggests that it had been organized by long-time Richmond residents, adult men with families, former slaves who knew that no "master" would take care of their families after their death. Among the officers were forty-year-old Anthony Hill, a former slave who worked in a tobacco factory and belonged to the First African Baptist Church; Henry James, a wagoner in his late thirties who had been born and raised in Manchester and now had a family of five in Richmond; and William S. Owens, a Richmond native in his mid-forties who worked as a newspaper carrier. Black women, especially single mothers, could be equally concerned with the fate of their families. A group of them organized the Mutual Benevolent Society in 1872 and elected Ann Lipscomb their president. Born in the city and a single mother, she had tried to support her family as a seamstress since Emancipation. After abyssmally low wages, severe seasonal downturns, and a general scarcity of work had undermined her best efforts, she had turned to prostitution. Prompted by a desire for security for herself and her family that she had been unable to find on her own, Lipscomb helped to organize the Mutual Benevolent Society. Its women members demonstrated their trust by electing her president and putting their collective bank account in her hands.[41]

Trade-based societies, some of which called themselves "unions," also existed. They provided sickness and funeral benefits and, occasionally, unemployment payments; they participated in parades and held meetings at which conditions of their trade were discussed. As a rule, their membership was all male. They elected officers and collected dues that were deposited in the Freedman's Savings Bank. Officers held the same jobs as members, were often illiterate, and usually had short tenure in office. Such Richmond trade-based societies include the Warehouse Combined Industrial Society, No. 35; the Younger Twisters Aid of Shiloh; True Laboring Class, No. 1; the National Laboring Club; the Railroad Helpers; Laborer's Association, No. 55; the Bailey Factory Hands; Union Laboring Branch; the Union Laboring Class; and the Grand Lodge of Quarrymen. Trade societies that negotiated wages or conducted strikes in addition to their other functions include the Bakers' Union, the Hod-Carriers' Union, the Coopers' Society, the Stevedores and Wagoners' Association, and the Lincoln Union Shoemakers. The Coopers' Society and the Tobacco Laborers' Association even sent delegates to sessions of the National Labor Union and Industrial Congress in the early 1870s. Other bodies spawned "auxiliary"-type societies: the Teamsters' Benevolent Society-Star of the East and the Mechanics' Union Society.[42]

The officers typified the membership of the societies. Philip Banks, Thomas Haskins, and John Henry Dixon were three officers of the National Laboring Club. Born in New Kent County, Banks had come to Richmond as a slave child with his parents in the 1840s. In 1851, he joined the First African Baptist Church. His family had held together through the ordeals of slavery and war. When elected an officer in the National Laboring Club, Banks, then twenty-seven, still lived with his parents and his younger siblings and worked in a tobacco factory. Thomas Haskins had come to postwar Richmond as a teen-ager, leaving a sister back in Middlesex County. Though able to read and write, he, like Banks, was an unmarried tobacco factory worker. John Henry Dixon had been born to a free family in Richmond in the 1840s; they were members of the First African Baptist Church. He and his brother George led similar lives as tobacco factory workers who never learned to read or write. Both married Richmond women, started families, and opened joint accounts at the Freedman's Savings Bank. In the early 1870s, they served as officers in tobacco factory workers societies: John Henry in the National Laboring Club and George in the Union Bengal Aid. Both men also opened bank accounts for their children. John Henry also served as an officer in a religious society, the Travelling Companion. Such experiences were common to members of these trade-based secret societies.

The Tobacco Laborers' Association, which appears to have been more like a trade union than the National Laboring Club, was particularly interesting. Isaiah Doyle had been born a slave in Chesterfield County in the 1840s. His father was sold away and his mother "re-married," which provided him with five step-brothers and step-sisters. Doyle came to Richmond in his early twenties, right after the war, went to work in a tobacco factory and joined the Rising Sons of America, a politically oriented secret society. Able to write, he became its secretary in 1869; in 1870, a young women's society, the United Daughters of Love, asked the young, eligible bachelor to serve as its secretary. Soon afterward, Doyle married a member of the society. They named their first child Isaiah, Jr., and their second child James, after Doyle's step-father. In 1872, Doyle was elected an officer in the Tobacco Laborers' Association. John Bannister was another officer. After he, his brother Winston and his sister Susan had been sold to a Richmond owner in the early 1850s, they left their childhood home in rural Henrico County, where their parents were already buried. The two young men were put to work in tobacco factories, while little Susan labored in their owner's house. While still slaves, they joined the First African Baptist Church as a family in the late 1850s. John and Winston learned to read and write and started families of their own. After the war, they continued to work in the tobacco factories and became active in the local Republican party. John's community involvement stopped there, but Winston became an officer in the Secret Sons of Love, a beneficial society, and in True Laboring Class No. 1, another tobacco workers' organization. Susan was later elected an officer in four women's societies. Warwick Reed, the elder statesman among the officers of the Tobacco Laborers' Association, was well into his fifties by the early 1870s. Born in Amherst County, he had labored as a slave in Richmond tobacco factories since the 1830s. In the 1840s, he married the slave of a wealthy local man. Warwick and Amanda Reed both joined the First African Baptist Church in the 1850s. They had three sons, all of whom followed their father into the tobacco factories. After Emancipation, Reed left the tobacco factory to become a self-employed whitewasher and plasterer; then he joined the Savings Club, a society of black men who, in 1869, hoped to get ahead. When young tobacco factory workers started to organize a union-like society, they turned to him for guidance and elected him to office. In 1873, they sent him to the national Industrial Congress in Cleveland where, the only black man present, he became vice-president.[43]

Leaders of the Bakers' Union were not all that different from the activists among the tobacco factory workers. Nathaniel Mitchell had been born and raised in Richmond and had learned to read and write in the postwar years. Only twenty when elected the secretary of the Bakers' Union, he still lived with his mother, his two brothers, and his sister. After the war, Nelson Turner, a grown man, had come to the capital from King William County. He and his wife shared a house with another black baker and his family, and she took in washing to supplement his wages. Later they augmented their household with his young niece from back home. Turner opened a joint bank account with Bakers' Union officer Henry Harris, who had also come from King William County. Harris, less than half Turner's age, boarded for several years at a white-owned establishment that catered to single black men. By the late 1870s, he had learned to read and write, had married and started a family. Christopher Gordon, the president of the Bakers' Union, had come to Richmond as a child in the 1840s. His father worked as a carpenter as did his older brother. The late 1850s were hard times for free black craftsmen, and when Christopher came of age, he turned away from carpentry to the baking trade. After the war, he married and started a family, but times were not easy for bakers; in 1870 they lived temporarily in his brother's household.[44]

Political activity was a major concern for Richmond Afro-Americans, and they organized a large number of secret political societies. Such societies promoted the political education of their members and provided activists with a vehicle for organizing political expression. The all-male membership was linked in one way or another to the local Republican apparatus. Several lodges of the Rising Sons of Liberty were joined by the Young Men of Liberty, the Rising Sons of America, the Sons of the Union, the Star Union Sons, the Union Association of Richmond, the Union Benevolent Star, the Union Bengal Aid, the Union Branch of the First District, and the Union Liberty Protective Society, among others. Such groups often depended on elaborate ritual as a way of expressing political ideas. One, for example, thus described its ceremony:

> The altar is draped with the flag, on which lies an open Bible, the Declaration of Independence, a sword, a ballot-box, sickle, and anvil or other toy emblems of industry. At first, the room may be in darkness with sounds of groans and clanking chains issuing from corners. The chaplain calls the League to prayer, invoking Divine vengeance on traitors. From a censer (sometimes an old stone vase) upon the altar blue flames, "fires of liberty," leap upward. The Council opens ranks to receive novitiates; joining hands, all circle round the altar, singing "The Star-Spangled Banner" or other patriotic air. Novitiates lay hands on the flag, kiss the Bible, and swear: "I will do all in my power to elect true and loyal men to all offices of trust and profit."[45]

Men active at their workplaces or in the churches were often prominent in these political secret societies. Most or all of the members of some societies came from one workplace; in others, they were drawn from several levels of black Richmond. Thus, the Union Laboring Branch was composed of workers at Patterson's tobacco factory. Jordan Reed, Warwick Reed's son, was one of its officers. He also had been born and raised a slave in Richmond and had joined the First African Baptist Church shortly after his parents in the late 1850s. By his early twenties, Jordan Reed had learned to read and write; he assisted the Young Home Secret Daughters as their secretary and also worked at Patterson's. While he still lived with his father, Reed was elected an officer in the Union Laboring Branch. Fellow officer George W. Johnson had similarly deep roots in black Richmond, where he had grown up a slave, worked in the tobacco factories, and started a family. In addition to serving as an officer in the Union Laboring Branch, he was active in the Young Men of Liberty, another political secret society; the United Sons and Daughters of Love, a beneficial society; and the Morning Pilgrims, a religious society. In his early forties, Johnson, like Reed, was literate. The third officer of the Union Laboring Branch was not educated. A tobacco factory worker at Patterson's, like the others, Benjamin Braxton had reached the age of forty without learning to write. But this did not prevent his fellow workers from looking to him for political leadership. Richard H. Johnson was a more likely officer. Literate and still single in his mid-twenties, Johnson served the Young Men's Self-Interest, the Young Female Hope, the Young Men's Gold Key of Richmond, and the Loving Sons of Galilee, as well as the Union Laboring Branch. He, too, worked at Patterson's, and he supported his widowed mother. The example of the Union Laboring Branch demonstrates the extent to which workers from one factory, organizing a political secret society, were tied into familial, church, and beneficial networks within the larger community.[46]

Shared political concerns brought together black men with a wide variety of work experiences. The Union Liberty Protective Society was led by an interesting mix of men. William H. Gwathmey had grown up a slave in Richmond, joined the First African Baptist Church in 1849, and transferred to the Third African when it opened in 1858. He was one of the former slaves who took charge of the Fourth Church Sabbath School Society after the war. Lewis H. Carter became a successful barber, one of the few blacks in this trade who were ardent Republicans in the late 1860s. Unlike the mostly free-born (and politically conservative) Richmond barbers, he had been born and raised a slave in the city. He was a widower, although only in his late thirties; his elderly mother lived with him and helped to care for his son and the two young apprentices who also resided under his roof. Carter owned his own shop and was a prominent Mason, but his success did not mute his political concerns. Another fairly successful man, Elijah W. Dabney was born and reared in Richmond and served as an officer in the Union Liberty Protective Society. He had developed two marketable skills: music and carpentry. Dabney's Band was prominent in every black parade in the city. Like Lewis Carter, Dabney owned property by the early 1870s and built a good-sized house in Jackson Ward. Binford Anderson, another officer in this political society, had nowhere near the success of Carter and Dabney. Also born and reared in Richmond, he had learned to read and write and, in the 1870s, as in the 1850s, worked in a tobacco factory, struggling to support his wife and children. By the mid-1880s, he would be a prominent black activist within the Knights of Labor. The cast of characters at the helm of the Union Liberty Protective Society suggests how political views united blacks from several layers of the social structure.[47]

Black women also played an organized role in political activity, even without the right to vote. They also organized political secret societies, often as auxiliaries of men's societies. The Rising Daughters of Liberty, for example, was affiliated with the Rising Sons of Liberty. Such groups were important in generating enthusiasm in campaigns, fund-raising, getting out the vote, and enforcing the black community's political consensus. Organization and activity were hardly limited to the city. Black coal miners' wives from the pits outside Manchester organized themselves as the United Daughters of Liberty. They cooperated with both the United Sons of Liberty, founded by black coal miners at the nearby Midlothian pits, and the United Laboring Men's Society of Coalfield, founded by their husbands.[48]

• • •

In the late 1860s and early 1870s, the leadership of the black community emerged from those families that had deep roots in Richmond. As slaves and as free men and women, they had built extended kinship networks, organized churches and secret societies. They set the pace for the postwar black community as they expanded and integrated their social networks, absorbed and socialized newcomers, and built new organizations out of the relationships they had already established. Secret society officers were usually enmeshed in local familial and social networks. As new societies emerged, they further elaborated and extended the existing associations. An increasing number of new residents were drawn in, often finding their places in existing kinship networks only after joining one or more secret societies. Others were introduced to extrafamilial social organization by new in-laws. The ties were inescapable; by 1873, few but determined loners lived outside this web of social relationships.

Within the identifiable core group of long-time Richmond residents, other interesting patterns may be found. Tobacco factory work and domestic service were the two most common occupations for black men and women. Of those men and women elected officers in secret societies, tobacco factory workers held leadership posts out of proportion to their share of the population. Few live-in male or female domestics were elected, although most of them joined one or more secret societies. Whatever their occupations, men married to live-in domestics (so that they and their families resided in the employer's house or the old quarters) were rarely elected society officers. When it came to managing their own affairs in secret societies, black males and females clearly believed that working and living in a daily paternalistic context was inappropriate for a society officer. Male tobacco factory workers were functionaries in every sort of society: workplace, political, beneficial, and religious. The black community, as it relied on its wages for day-to-day survival, was dependent on its experience, its sense of collective strength, and its well-developed organizational ties for self-improvement, whether through collective self-help or collective struggle.[49]

The network of secret societies enveloped black Richmond. By the early 1870s, virtually every part of the black community was linked through a series of social relationships. Kinship, the church, the neighborhood, and the workplace were interwoven with these societies. Through them, black workers increased their ability to help themselves, one another, and the indigent of their community. These societies further provided the necessary social foundation to address black issues collectively. Religious, political, social, and economic concerns meshed like the people who brought these societies to life; something greater than the sum of its parts—a vital, active collectivity, striving with dignity for equal rights—was created.

CHAPTER 3

The Development of Black Popular Political Activity, 1865–1870

RICHMOND AFRO-AMERICANS, free-born and former slave alike, learned two very important lessons in the immediate period after Emancipation. Each family's quest for self-improvement, they discovered, could not be separated from the struggle for the improvement of black Richmond as a whole. The rapidly spreading network of secret societies tied families together throughout the city. Racist forces promoted economic, political, and social conditions aimed at limiting blacks' spheres of work and life and circumscribing their opportunities. Richmond Afro-Americans realized that any rights and improvements they might be accorded would be the result of their own efforts and determination. Though they knew that some white allies were needed, each twist and turn of political events drove home to black activists their ultimate responsibility for their own rights and dignities.

The first years after Emancipation witnessed the emergence of a popular movement grounded in the social network that honeycombed black Richmond. This movement reflected the strength of these social ties, and the ease with which they could adapt from mutual aid and self-help to more overt forms of political organization and social struggle. The movement relied heavily on popular forms of organization and expression—parades, mass meetings, secret societies. While more privileged blacks in the community (e.g., the free-born, the literate, mulattoes, skilled artisans, and the like) initially provided political direction, by 1870 working-class activists emerged from the social network to assume leadership within black Richmond.[1]

The constant narrowing of black Richmond's social, political, and economic space set the context for these developments. The Republican party quickly proved unsatisfactory for black political expression when its local white bosses and their friends in Washington denied blacks a decision-making role in party policy. And, by the early 1870s, the Republican party had lost its grip on political power across the state as well as in Richmond.

The local black vote was contained through clever gerrymandering, which created Jackson Ward as a political as well as a social ghetto. Meanwhile, whites guarded skilled trades and respected occupations as zealously as they did their neighborhoods. Afro-Americans found their opportunity to learn and practice new skills severely restricted. Every step of black accomplishment must be measured against this backdrop.[2]

• • •

In the first months of freedom, Afro-Americans pressed, above all else, for the repeal of laws and executive measures designed to restrict their movement. Federal military authorities, state legislators, and white employers agreed on the need to restrict their mobility. These authorities perceived the restoration of a social stability based on the availability of cheap labor as more important than the search of blacks for separated family members or for new homes. Barely two weeks after Emancipation, the local commander of the Union forces wrote General Stanton: "There are thousands of colored people flocking into town and roaming throughout the country. They should be sent to work." Laws and military edicts established a "pass" system, and Federal authorities enforced it with a vengeance.[3]

Richmond Afro-Americans were quick to organize and protest. In June 1865, a group of former free men wrote to the *New York Tribune*, decrying the "daily mounted patrol, with their sabers drawn, whose business is the hunting of colored people." Federal authorities had also reinstated pro-Confederate, antiblack Mayor Joseph Mayo, his administration and police force. Black Richmonders knew them well.

> During the whole period of the Rebellion, Mr. Mayo, as the chief magistrate of the city, and as a private citizen, exerted all his influence to keep alive the spirit of treason and rebellion, and to urge the people to continue the contest. The cruelties perpetrated upon sick and defenseless Union prisoners, at Libby Prison and upon Belle Isle, were openly and shamelessly approved by him. For a long series of years he has been the Mayor of Richmond, and his administration has been marked by cruelty and injustice to us, and the old Rebel police now again in power have been our greatest enemies. It was Mayor Mayo who in former days ordered us to be scourged for trifling offenses against slave laws and usages; and his present police, who are now hunting us through the streets, are the men who relentlessly applied the lash to our quivering flesh; and now they appear to take special pleasure in persecuting and oppressing us.[4]

The pass system, applicable to all blacks, promoted a hasty alliance between former freedmen and former slaves. Both discovered that the system was designed to confine them to a permanently dependent status. Once able to follow their own trades, they were now "required to get some white person to give us passes to attend to our daily occupation, without which we are marched off to the old Rebel Hospital, now called the negro bull pen." For them, the "present treatment is worse than we ever suffered before." Albert R. Brooks, a respected member of Richmond's free black community had bought his freedom long before the war; his experiences with the indignities of the pass system were typical. While having a license to operate his hack stable, he lacked a formal "pass." Arrested at his place of business by a Richmond policeman, Brooks was informed that "all niggers that did not have a paper from their master, showing that they were employees, must be taken to jail and hired out for 5 dollars per month." The policeman turned Brooks over to a Federal cavalry soldier who took him to jail, where he was locked up by the jailer, "the same one who has kept the jail for many years." He was eventually released after obtaining a formal "pass" from a Union officer, "which I am obliged to show to Mayo's police, who stop me on nearly every corner of the street, and make it nearly impossible for me to carry on my business." That, of course, was the intention. The pass system was designed to make sure that the lives of black men and women would revolve around wage-labor.[5]

The pass system, however, had unanticipated results. It made activists out of those who might have stayed on the sidelines. John Oliver is an interesting case in point. He had worked in Boston as a carpenter and had been active in the American Missionary Society. Having come to Richmond simply to observe the situation of local blacks, he would spend the rest of his life there. One day, the black "bull pen" caught his attention, and he soon found himself a resident in it, rather than an observer. Oliver gave this account:

> We stopped to look at it, when I was hailed by a Provost Guard, who without asking for a pass, demanded to know why I was walking in the street. I told him I came to see Richmond. Then he said you will stop here with me. I asked him how long? "Longer than you think for," he replied. He continued to address me in vulgar and abusive language. I showed him my protection from Massachusetts, which I told him "ought to protect me in any part of the world." But he said he did not care for that, and contemptuously spurned it.

Five years later, Oliver would be elected president of the Richmond chapter of the Colored National Labor Union. His experiences had prompted him to remain in the city and fight for black rights.[6]

The universal applications of the pass system promoted a unifying process within the black community, for all black men and women faced the same pressures, whether born slave or free, whether from Boston or Richmond. Policemen did not restrict themselves to harassment on the streets. Not uncommonly, they entered a workshop, demanded to see the passes of all blacks, and arrested those without them. For those who had come to Richmond in search of lost family members, the pass system created a special tragedy. "We saw women looking for their husbands, children for parents, but to no purpose—they were in the bull pen." Richmond Afro-Americans bitterly informed President Johnson that "many . . . who ignorantly supposed that the day of passes had passed away . . . have been arrested, imprisoned and hired out without their advice or consent."[7]

In early June 1865, Union forces and local police arrested 800 blacks, including children, for violations of the pass system. On June 7, a group of free-born men met and drafted a letter of protest, which they forwarded to the *New York Tribune*. "All that is needed to restore slavery in full is the auction block as it used to be." The next day, they were joined by a group of former slaves "for the purpose of taking some action." They appointed a four-man committee to document complaints, take depositions, draft a statement to President Johnson, and report to an "adjourned meeting" of the group.[8]

This "adjourned meeting" proved to be a public gathering on June 10 at the First African Baptist Church. Those in attendance concurred in the committee's findings, elected a seven-man group to visit President Johnson, and then voted to raise travel funds through local black churches. Their action brought results; Governor Pierpont removed Mayor Joseph Mayo from office, and President Johnson ordered the transfer of Union Army officers Halleck, Ord, and Patrick, putting General Alfred Terry in charge of Richmond. Terry immediately abolished the pass system and publicly extended his hand to Richmond blacks. These events thus taught them that they did have the power to address their problems, that they could organize and struggle for what they wanted.[9]

Throughout the summer and fall of 1865, Afro-Americans followed similar procedures. Common grievances were raised, mass meetings were held, and committees were elected. These committees then called on public officials, presented their case, and made clear the mass support that stood behind them. In July, similar mass meetings had elected delegates to the Convention of the Colored People of Virginia in Alexandria, which adopted a "Declaration of Rights": "As citizens of the Republic we claim the rights of citizens; we claim that we are by right entitled to respect."[10]

• • •

Economic conditions placed severe strains on black families and imperiled the emerging social network. A restricted base of resources can be stretched only so far. The chaotic condition of the local economy and the extraordinary influx of blacks suggested to local employers that they could reduce wages with impunity. In October 1865, Baptist minister Peter Randolph expressed his fears for the first winter of freedom: "Those who are at work scarcely get enough to keep body and soul together, while the old slave-holders make them pay high for the houses they live in. It seems to me impossible for the poor here to live through the coming winter." A group of female domestics called attention to the disparity between the "rents asked for houses and rooms and the prices paid for our labor." Poverty, they feared, "will tend to demoralization among us, and lead us into temptation." A society of tobacco factory workers declared:

> The whites say we will starve through laziness. That is not so. But it is true we will starve at our present wages. They say we will steal. We can say for ourselves we had rather work for a living. Give us a chance.[11]

Richmond blacks tried hard to give themselves that "chance." Within a month of Emancipation, some 2,000 children were attending day schools established by northern-based missionary societies. Many more were eager for education, but lacked teachers. A local agent complained to his national office: "Much more would have been done had we a working force to meet the demand. I have no doubt the number would have been 4,000 to 5,000." Where 2,000 had been literate in 1865, more than 7,000—over a third of the adult population—could read and write by 1870. Such numbers were a testament to what former slave Joseph Wilson called "this longing of ours for freedom of the mind as well as the body."[12]

While "freedom of the mind" began with reading, writing, and arithmetic, it went much further. The Reverend W. D. Harris, black pastor of the Third Street American Methodist Episcopal (AME) Church, described a typical session in his night school:

> I open the remarks by singing and prayer and close by Remarks, Singing, and Benedictions. I try to keep the school informed as to the prominent bills before Congress and at present we are reading the Constitution of the U.S. in concert. I then explain it to them as best I can and have them spell and define the important words.[13]

Richmond Afro-Americans tried collective self-help in their efforts to improve economic conditions. A group of tobacco factory workers, led by veteran twister and community activist Stephen Jones and the northern-born Reverend William Troy, organized the American Tobacco Manufacturing Company. They pooled their savings and sold subscriptions, with the hope of opening a producers' cooperative. It was the dream of home ownership that motivated the tobacco factory workers who organized a Building Aid Society, to which each paid his weekly dues.[14]

Reality, which spawned these aspirations, continued to undermine them. The American Tobacco Manufacturing Company never opened a cooperative factory; the Building Aid Society never awarded a house; and being literate hardly earned a salary increase. The history of the Freedman's Savings Bank itself bears witness to the futility of collective self-help. Despite adverse economic conditions, more than 7,000 Richmond blacks opened accounts, an incredible effort to put aside savings. One depositor later recalled: "I can remember that I used to walk up to the bank and put in the few pennies that I could rake and scrape together." In its nine years of existence, the bank held some $166,000 in accumulated black savings, all of which was lost when the bank failed in 1874, sweeping away individual and family savings along with secret society treasuries.[15]

• • •

On April 3, 1866, local blacks celebrated the anniversary of Richmond's fall to Union troops. Although white Republicans insisted that January 1 was the proper "Emancipation Day," the anniversary of Lincoln's Emancipation Proclamation, the city's Afro-Americans preferred to emphasize the date of their actual release from bondage. The only local account of the black parade that marked this "holiday" was in the *Citizen*, a paper published on a cooperative basis by striking printers. Despite its scornful tone, this account does offer us a glimpse at the appearance of the parade:

> An immense cavalcade of black horsemen led the van, preceded by a dusky son of Ham tooting on a worn-out bugle, and sounding original calls ever and anon. . . . Then came a Patriarch with a stick, with a gourd on the top of it, all covered over with ribands; this individual was decorated in an apron of black and gold, and a gold stripe down his legs. . . . A chapeau on his head was gracefully festooned with a black feather. . . . After the band there marched a long string of unsentimental, unbleached, some with aprons, some with rosettes, and some with sashes. There were two banners in the line, one of which, composed of silk and bullion, was of commendable appearance; the other seemed to be but a piece of white domestic streaked all over with red letters . . . finally climaxed with a parcel of field hands in jeans walking in squads, without commander, uniform, or decorum.[16]

The marchers were organized by secret societies, walking together in ceremonial garb and bearing symbols. Observers noted "a banner with a concentric tobacco plant and an eccentric inscription"; one group wore striped sashes; another group was decked out in broad black scarves tipped with white, carrying a banner with the inscription: "Union Liberties Protective Society, organized February 4, 1866—Peace and Goodwill Toward Men." Religious, benevolent, and trade societies marched alongside political societies. Farmhands from out of town joined in the celebration; so, too, did the Humble Christian Benevolents of the Chesterfield Coal Pits.[17]

The parade, two thousand strong, proceeded to Capitol Square. There, on the grounds of the former confederate capital, joined by fifteen thousand observers, the former slaves concluded their celebration. The Reverend J. W. Hunnicutt, spokesman for the "ultras," the most extreme of local white radical Republicans, and the publisher of the *Richmond New Nation*, was the featured speaker. His evangelical style was particularly appropriate to the politics of this period. He called for racial equality, and hard work, and expressed his—and their—hope of success, themes echoed by several of the black speakers who followed.[18]

On July 4, 1866, Richmond blacks again took to the streets. A black Methodist minister reported to his northern associates:

> The 4th of July was celebrated by the colored people in Richmond for the first time . . . and with an enthusiasm never realised before; what was once a mockery to them, has now become a reality. They make a demonstration very similar to the ones on April 3rd, with an addition of three or four military companies, everything passed off very quietly and respectably. The southern whites did not seem to observe the day as they seemed to desert the streets entirely.[19]

But disgruntled whites did not stand by quietly. At times, they tried to undermine black activities. On the eve of the controversial Emancipation Day celebration in April 1866, the Second African Baptist Church burned to the ground in a mysterious blaze. The congregation's response was quick and to the point—they would rebuild what had been destroyed, based on their own efforts. And by late May, a parade of fraternal orders and secret societies had commemorated the laying of a cornerstone for a new church building.[20]

White resistance sometimes took the form of organized violence. Gangs of white youths harassed, stoned, and shot into crowds of black churchgoers, especially in the Chimborazo area of Richmond's east end. Black "militia" units appeared in this district, in the black Navy Hill neighborhood, and throughout the city by mid-summer 1866. The Navy Hill "Irrepressibles" were the most prominent of these groups, with more than 200 members. They outraged white public opinion by marching around the city dressed in full regalia, with rifles and cavalry sabers. By late July, the *Richmond Dispatch* complained that these defiant gestures occurred nightly. It is hardly coincidental that no white gang attacks on blacks were reported over this period. Yet General Terry banned these musters, though not outlawing the militia units themselves. By December, five companies of a black militia regiment had been formed, though now they were apparently controlled by the Federal authorities.[21]

Black political activity expanded in the fall of 1866, encouraged by radical Republican victories in congressional elections and by passage of the Fourteenth Amendment. In January 1867, the Reverend Hunnicutt organized a petition campaign calling for the removal of the Pierpont government and its replacement by "true and loyal men." It was signed by 2,400 Richmond residents, most of them black. Nearly 4,000 black men and women packed the First African Church, with another 500 outside, on the night of March, 7, 1867, to voice their support for the Federal Sherman Bill and their opposition to the reelection of Mayor Mayo. Similar meetings followed at the Ebenezer Baptist Church and the Manchester African Church.[22]

This growing assertiveness marked the April 3 Emancipation Day celebration that came during a month of intense popular struggle in black Richmond. The day before, General Terry had suspended all local elections because Congress was going to assume control of Reconstruction. Blacks were now confident that the right to vote would soon be theirs. After the parade, with marchers again organized by societies, the assemblage heard several addresses that stressed their coming responsibilities as voters. Hunnicutt and his white political associate Burnham Wardwell, the first white power brokers within the local Republican party apparatus, were on the stage. (Their reign was brief, as men with greater polish and political shrewdness would push them aside.) They were joined by Peter Randolph, a popular black minister, who urged his listeners to register to vote, and Lewis Lindsay, formerly the servant of John Minor Botts, the best-known Unionist in prewar and wartime Virginia. Lindsay, now a bandleader, would soon become Richmond's most renowned—and reviled—black orator. He urged his audience to "be steadfast, fight the good fight, be strong, get your diplomas. Be peaceable and wait until you get to the ballot-box before you proclaim your political sentiments. Then vote for a good man without regard to color. But whatever you do, don't cast your vote for a rebel."[23]

This April 3 celebration created a momentum that carried over to the Republican party's state convention, held in Richmond two weeks later. Of the 210 delegates, two-thirds were black. Richmond's delegates included Lewis Lindsay and John Oliver, as well as Joseph Cox, a free-born tobacco factory worker who had once worked at Tredegar and now served as president of the Union Aid Society, one of Virginia's largest secret societies. They were joined by two free-born lay preachers, Fields Cook and Cornelius Harris, a barber and a shoemaker, respectively. These men, and others like them, emerged as the political spokesmen for the black community in these first years of political activity. They had enjoyed greater opportunities to learn to read and write; to earn, save, and spend; to travel with some freedom; and to live somewhat removed from the daily paternalism of the slave system. In the immediate postbellum years, these more privileged blacks served as the popular leaders.[24]

Relations between them and the broader movement they sought to lead were a constant give-and-take, within a context of widespread participation and open-ended debate. This first Republican convention, for instance, was held outdoors at Capitol Square, before an audience of thousands of local blacks. When delegates disagreed among themselves, the audience actively took sides. The most heated argument revolved around confiscation of the property of prominent former Confederates. Cook and Harris took opposite positions, the former calling for moderation, the latter stressing the black need for property in order to build an independent life. According to a local reporter, Harris "repudiated all idea of the colored men submitting to the white aristocracy of the South, as though the blacks were a helpless race."

The gathering cheered his speech, as well as that of a black Petersburg delegate who proposed that former slaves seize the land themselves if Congress refused to give it to them.[25]

Richmond Afro-Americans were unwilling to leave the solutions of their problems to the delegates. When it came to gaining access to the local streetcars, for instance, they took matters into their own hands. They gathered inspiration from the Reverend William Brown of Baltimore who, on April 11, lectured to a packed house at the First African church. He spoke of the social equality of the races and the successful efforts of Charleston blacks to gain access to city streetcars in late March. A plan for direct action developed in early April, when individual blacks tested the streetcar company's "whites-only" policy; they would leave the platforms where they were supposed to remain, take seats inside, and refuse the order to vacate. When they did so, the first four were arrested.[26]

Militants then devised a more complex strategy. On April 23, three members of a militia unit, the Lincoln Mounted Guard, "with ribbon and badge on their coats," climbed aboard a car, paid their fares, sat inside, and refused to get up. One said that "he had paid his money and he's be damned if he wouldn't ride." The police were summoned, but by the time they arrived,

> . . . negroes were seen flocking from every direction to the point, and before the car had reached the place where the arrest was made, a large crowd, numbering several hundred, had collected. The eager desire which many of them exhibited showed that it had been a subject of thought with them; and the threats and utterances of the excited crowd proved that they were ready for any emergency. . . . The excited crowd of negroes shouted, "Let's have our rights!" "We will teach these damned Rebels how to treat us!" "We have petitioned General Schofield about it, and he won't do anything. We must take the matter into our own hands."

This crowd followed the police and their prisoners to the station house, threatening en route to free them. A week later, the streetcar company gave in and announced that from then on there would be six streetcars, two of them being reserved for white women and children. Through the networks established by the secret societies, with militia units at the forefront, Richmond's black community had won access to the city's streecars.[27]

Meanwhile, another black secret society moved into action. The Stevedore Society of Laboring Men of the City of Richmond struck the city's docks on Saturday, April 27. They posted a handbill, explaining their action:

> The undersigned having organized themselves for protecting the laboring men, stevedores, and horse-hoisters, of the city of Richmond, having agreed to strike for higher wages, they warn all members of this society to abide by the constitution, and any member violating said constitution will be fined not less than fifty dollars, to be paid in advance. The regular wages allowed

> by the society are as follows: Foremen, $3 a day; laboring men, $2 per day or 25 cents per hour; horse-hire, $4 per day for working on board of vessels, 25 cents per ton for coke, 25 cents for discharging guano; 25 cents for plaster, 25 cents per ton for railroad iron. All other prices will be charged in proportion. The stevedores will be held responsible for these wages.

Such wage demands appear aggressively high compared to the average seventy-five cents to one dollar per day for most unskilled labor. Though the docks were a focal point for casual labor, and therefore difficult to organize on a permanent trade union basis, Richmond's black stevedores felt that they were up to the task: "the stevedores will be held responsible for these wages."[28]

This stevedores' struggle illustrates the resolve and determination of black workers in these years. The irregular ship traffic and the freezing of the James River in winter created a large, casual labor market on the docks, especially in the first peacetime years when many men without marketable skills sought employment in Richmond. But before and during the war, a large group of free men and slaves had worked on the Richmond docks, many of them for years. Their jobs called for some know-how, if not actual skill, and brought them into contact with free workers, black and white, of all kinds—sailors, shipwrights, teamsters, coopers, and others. These experienced dockworkers made up the core of the Stevedores' Society. Through their own organization, and through their ties of kinship and organization in the black community, they hoped to prevent other black men from taking their jobs. Though the available pool of unskilled black labor was substantial, the black community was clearly in movement; networks were drawn into action through the Emancipation Day parade, the state Republican convention, and the streetcar struggle.[29]

The experienced members of the Stevedores' Society believed it to be an ideal time to strike; their ties to the community provided the foundation for this struggle. The depth and breadth of these ties can be gauged by examining the background of the union's treasurer, Valentine Griffin. He had arrived in Richmond at the age of twenty-three in 1853, a free man from Charles City County with a wife and two young sons. He brought a letter of introduction from his church to the First African Baptist Church, and the Griffins became members of the congregation. Like many other free blacks, Griffin had to turn to a number of pursuits to support his family. In addition to stevedore work, he took jobs in tobacco factories, casual labor, and even an occasional stint as a grain measurer. Meanwhile, there were three more children, and his wife took in washing to help support them. When the oldest boys, Malachi and Joshua, reached working age, they also turned to the tobacco factories. Griffin had been active in the Independent Order of the Messiah, as well as the church, when selected as treasurer of the Stevedores' Society. Already forty-seven at the time of the strike, he would live to see two of his sons distinguish themselves within the black community—one as a city councilor and a deacon in the First African Baptist Church, the other as a schoolteacher.[30]

The sort of turmoil that marked the streets around Richmond's docks during the strike reappeared elsewhere in the following month. On May 9, at an exhibition by Richmond and Delaware firemen, a riot resulted when a black man who had refused to move when asked struck the fire captain who had pushed him. When he was arrested, the spectators—estimated at 2,000—surged forward in an attempt to free him. They were led by a barber who had "raised a portion of his barber pole over his his head, and waving it, exclaimed: 'Come on, freedmen! Now's the time to save your nation!'" Twice they momentarily succeeded in rescuing the prisoner, first, from the police on hand, and later from reinforcements. But social order and the end to stone throwing waited on the arrival of General John Schofield and a group of Union soldiers. Two nights later, another crowd fired on the police in a vain effort to free a black man arrested for drunk and disorderly conduct. Only the intervention of Federal troops turned back the crowd. After these incidents, General Schofield warned "that the time had come to teach the negroes that they could not be a law unto themselves." He issued a special order that disarmed the Lincoln Mounted Guard, and he threatened to disband all black militia units.[31]

Black workers found it difficult to sustain an effective trade or workplace organization, despite the high level of street activity in 1867. The swollen number of unemployed and of casually employed labor provided employers with a pool of strikebreakers from both races. The stevedores' strike failed when, despite community support, strikebreakers were found to replace them. Black coopers faced similar problems in their strike a month later. Though they were able to shut down every tobacco factory's barrel shop in one day, they were unable to prevent their employers from hiring white coopers to resume production.[32]

Despite these failures, the popular movement surged ahead. Outside political figures stepped in to try to regain control over this explosive situation. Senator Henry Wilson of Massachusetts and Union League officials from Boston, New York, and Philadelphia came to the city in mid-June to meet with leaders of the two local GOP factions: the mass of blacks around Hunnicutt and Lindsay, who called for the disfranchisement of former Confederates and the confiscation of their property; and the moderates, a small group of blacks, some native white "Unionists" led by John Minor Botts (Lindsay's former owner), and a growing contingent of carpetbaggers. The black radicals' response to these appeals was to launch a massive voter registration drive. At a mass meeting at the First African church, the radical faction, by their overwhelming strength, demonstrated that any fusion would have to be on their terms.[33]

• • •

When Congress took over Reconstruction in early 1867, its members required each Confederate state to rewrite its constitution before readmission to the Union and restoration of political rights. The new constitutions were to reflect the changed status of black people in the aftermath of Emancipation and of the Thirteenth, Fourteenth, and Fifteenth Amendments. There were no formal limits on the potential scope of constitutional revision; all concerned wished to shape Virginia's new legal foundation toward their own ends. The Republican state convention in August 1867 became critically important to blacks, since it would decide the party's platform going into the constitutional convention. Richmond blacks met in their Republican ward clubs and elected GOP convention delegates. Many also chose to attend. Tobacco worker societies informed employers that their workers would not work on August 1, the opening day of the convention, and the manufacturers had no choice but to close their factories.[34]

These tobacco workers, and the other black men and women who joined them, did not intend to be passive observers. On the morning of the GOP city convention, a line started to form outside the First African church by 7:00 A.M.; so many local residents crowded in when the doors opened four hours later that even many delegates could not attend. A group of dissatisfied delegates, led by Botts and his "co-operator" faction, withdrew from the church to hold a meeting of their own in Capitol Square. Several thousand local blacks, unable to get into the crowded church, gathered about this group. They saw this impromptu meeting as an opportunity to air their opinions, much as their friends and neighbors were doing in the church. Things started smoothly enough. Fields Cook, respected despite his moderation, assumed the chair and entertained comments from the audience. The dissatisfied delegates, speaking first, attacked the domination of the convention by Richmond's radicals. However, when Cook turned the meeting toward a formal stand, they were out-voted. The black crowd elected John Hawxhurst (a white radical) chairman, and they voted down a proposal to let Botts speak. Instead, a thunderous voice vote reaffirmed support for the radical "April program," including disfranchisement and confiscation; the "official" convention inside the church did as much.[35]

Political observers—and national Republican leaders—were aware that the continued dominance of the "ultras" rested on the strength of Richmond's black popular movement. The "ultras" maintained that important issues should be settled by mass meetings rather than by delegates, even though it meant that Republicans from outside the capital city, both black and white, would have little say in the making of party policy. This critical link between radicalism and mass activity would bring anguish to white GOP leaders all the way to Washington.[36]

As the constitutional convention met, from late 1867 to the spring of 1868, popular participation marked its proceedings. When an important issue was on the agenda, mass absenteeism shut down tobacco factories and crippled white households as black workers filled the gallery. A *New York*

Times reporter noted: "As is usual on such occasions, families which employ servants were forced to cook their own dinners, or content themselves with a cold lunch." Voting at mass meetings was by voice, he added, and women and children also took part.[37]

Five Republicans represented Richmond at the constitutional convention. Three were white: Rev. Hunnicutt, a moving force behind the "ultras"; Judge John Underwood, a northern-born farmer who had lived in Virginia for twenty years and had presided over the trial of Jefferson Davis; and James Morrissey, an Irish-born plasterer and long-time Richmond resident who had opened a grocery-liquor store at the end of the war. Perhaps sensitive to his own immigrant roots, Morrissey urged the disfranchisement of every foreign-born Richmond resident who had supported the Confederacy. Two black men, both recognized as radicals, were also chosen: Lewis Lindsay and Joseph Cox. Both were experienced in political affairs, Lindsay as a popular orator and Cox as president of the powerful Union Aid Society and the Lincoln Mounted Guard. Cox was "in favor of disfranchising all rebels except poor whites." Lindsay's acceptance speech indicated the great extent to which social equality now figured in the black vision of the society's future:

> I go there to say all public buildings and places of amusement must be open to the whole people, not to the s'clusion of any. I go to raise up the public schools for everybody.[38]

The delegates reflected the militancy and extremism of their constituency. A northern reporter had commented on Lindsay before his election: "He is very violent in his views, and preaches miscegenation and social equality. He will be elected, for such ideas are very popular with the majority of his color." Indeed, it was becoming difficult to maintain any other position in black Richmond. For instance, when Fields Cook and his moderate allies tried to elect an alternate slate of delegates, many angry blacks disrupted their meeting.[39]

The Constitutional Convention opened in Richmond on December 4, 1867, and immediately became the focus of public attention. Black delegates sought to provide models of behavior for local Afro-Americans. Thomas Bayne, a runaway slave who had returned from New Bedford, Massachusetts, to his native Norfolk, and Lewis Lindsay raised black perspectives to new levels. The local press reported their addresses to the opening session. Bayne told the delegates and the packed gallery:

> The cullud race, Mr. President, has allus been leaders in all de great rebolutions of history. And dey do say dat it was a black man what druv Jeff Davis out of dis here Richmond. Certain it is dat a negro, so-called, led—now he didn't follow, you mind dat—now he led de attac on de British sodjers on State Street, dat's in Boston. Dis was de beginnin' of de Rebolution and if dat

> blackman hadden't led de white men on to victory, I specs dat dere wouldn't have been no Rebolution-War, and you would all be still a-groanin' under de British yoke.

Lindsay placed black activity in a world-wide context, when in a speech filled with references to Ethiopia, Egypt, and Othello, he exclaimed: "Tell us de black man ain't got no history, when de Coffeeginians made Rome trimmel, when Sesoretus made de world trimmel, and who can say dey was white!"[40]

The demand for dignified treatment reflected the example provided by black delegates. It wasn't simply what they said, but how they said it. Bayne, for instance, was enraged by the local press rendition of his above-quoted speech. "Do not the proprietors of those papers know that it is them and their people who have robbed the black man of his education, who have taken the money and labor of the black man to support themselves in grandeur, and now they curse the black man because he is not a grammarian?"[41]

Black delegates quickly demonstrated an independence from their white "allies" that was grounded in the realities of both race and class. Even before substantive constitutional debate began, black delegates had challenged white radicals over the size of their per diem (Willis Hodges: "Many of us have no incomes. A great number of delegates here are poor and unable to meet expenses . . .") and over the firing of black voters by their employers. Lindsay, with the support of the other black delegates, would also push the constitutional protections against the garnishment of wages, and for constitutionally mandated paupers' burial grounds in every city.[42]

Delegates also clashed over a number of other issues: the disfranchisement of former Confederates (including all police and corporation owners, Lindsay suggested), the confiscation of their property, equal access to all public facilities, and the development of an integrated, free public school system. Through it all, black delegates were pushed forward by the momentum of black popular activity. Peter Jones, a delegate from Sussex County, argued that discrimination on public conveyance should be illegal, and introduced into the record a petition signed by over 500 residents of Elizabeth City and Warwick counties. They demanded "that no 'white ball street cars' shall insult us when in Richmond; that there be no separate schools." Lindsay himself pointed to the popular pressures behind his demands:

> Now, unless you give equal rights before the law to all the people of this state, unless you do away with all those distinctions which have been made in past times on account of the existence of slavery, the people declare that they will vote down your work. When I say the people will vote it down, I mean that class which enables me and every other gentleman of my race to sit here and speak here.[43]

Not surprisingly, black delegates retained a particularly close relationship with the Richmond black community. They addressed parades, rallies, and mass meetings, and they secured considerable feedback from those in attendance. They stayed in black boardinghouses or hotels, attended local black churches and numerous social functions. Richmond Afro-Americans debated every issue that appeared before the convention and also made their opinions known. They pushed for disfranchisement of leading rebels, confiscation of their land, a decrease in poll taxes and in taxes on trades, and a shift in the tax burden to the landed in an effort to force large landowners to break up their plantations and sell land to blacks. They sought integration of public facilities such as railroads, streetcars, hotels, and restaurants; opposed a conservative proposal to ban laborers and mechanics from holding state offices; demanded the right of suffrage for all males over the age of twenty-one who had lived in Virginia for six months; and proposed voting by secret ballot. A minority even argued for the extension of the franchise to women.[44]

Mass participation remained the foundation of the "ultra" position, and the convention gallery loudly engaged in the debates. Nowhere was this clearer than in the clash over the school system, an issue that found black delegates, deserted by their white "allies," supported only by those in the gallery. Bayne, Lindsay, and Hodges were the leading advocates for integrated schools. After a conservative proposal for segregation was defeated, Bayne moved that children be admitted to schools regardless of color. White radicals, however, joined with conservatives in overwhelmingly defeating this motion. Charles H. Porter, a leading white northern radical who had settled in Norfolk, then proposed a compromise motion. It urged that the constitution be silent on school integration. Lindsay, replying to his proposal, turned to the crowd:

> I say, dout speakin disrespectfully of carpetbags, dat if you carpet-baggers goes back on us, woe be unto you. You had better take your carpet-bags and quit, and de quicker you leave de better. . . . I'll say to you, colored men in de gallery, if dey don't give you your rights, down with 'em!

He then pointed out that the white radicals had seated their wives in the "white" section of the gallery. Porter's compromise motion carried, though the gallery pressed loudly for its defeat.[45]

The Constitutional Convention (in session from December 1867 to April 1868) gave black Richmond an intensive political education. Thousands attended convention sessions, keeping the gallery permanently full and predominantly black. Each day's newspaper was filled with information from the convention. Parades, rallies, and mass meetings afforded many opportunities to learn about current issues and express opinions on them. So did black delegates, who usually stayed among local black families, and visiting convention speakers, who spoke to large local crowds. For example, Senator Pomeroy of Kansas addressed a mass meeting of the First African Baptist Church on January 3. Ten days later, Ben Butler, from the same lectern, called

called for the redistribution of land to black families. Later that month, even General Grant put in a brief appearance. Such speakers boosted black morale, which otherwise might have sagged under the weight of continuing economic problems. These were important and powerful national figures coming to visit them. Though they listened carefully, local blacks—like their delegates at the convention—continued to think for themselves. Despite advice to the contrary, they pressed for equality and integration. And they continued to rely on direct action to address critical issues.[46]

Black militants provided a public demonstration of such reliance and their independence of white "radicals" in early April 1868, just as the Constitutional Convention entered its final stages. They remained firmly committed to the celebration of the fall of Richmond (April 3) as Emancipation Day, despite the entreaties of Grant and Butler. And in 1868, they had something special in mind. With black unemployment high and wages low, the toll on Mayo's footbridge joining Richmond and Manchester discouraged close relations between the two black communities. When the Emancipation Day parade neared the bridge, some 200 marchers, led by Ben Scott, a militia captain, detoured from the main body, crossed the bridge, and collectively refused to pay the toll.[47]

White radicals had had nothing to do with these demonstrations. They were waiting on the podium when part of the parade turned to confrontation at the bridge. When the paraders had reassembled to listen to speakers, they provided further evidence of their independence. The Rev. Hunnicutt's son made the mistake of speaking against mixed schools and was unceremoniously booed off the stage.[48]

• • •

As the Constitutional Convention wound down in mid-April, black popular activity reached peaks in organization and self-confidence. With adjournment, however, the movement's unanimity began to dissipate. Over the next two years, the shifting character of political conflict increasingly offered black working people a succession of choices between lesser evils. The draft Constitution voted on publicly, for example, did not include black radical views on school integration or property redistribution, and the disfranchising and test oath clauses would soon be excised. Yet, the alternative of unqualified opposition would delay Virginia's readmission into the Union and the extension of political rights to black, as well as to white, Virginians. Within the Republican party itself, blacks experienced a steady narrowing of their influence, while a sophisticated group of white politicos used money and national connections to tighten their control over the GOP.

At the same time, a nucleus of experienced and respected activists began to emerge from the working-class base of the popular movement. Most of them were long-time residents of Richmond and officers in secret societies. Two examples are typical, suggesting the sort of men involved and the sort of experiences from which they emerged. William Taylor and Stephen Jones, one free-born and one a former slave, both life-long Richmond residents, were two leading activists in Monroe Ward's insurgent Republican organization. A twenty-eight-year-old bricklayer, Taylor had also worked in tobacco factories. Both he and his wife were members of the First African Baptist Church. He was an officer in the Loving Christian Society, and she was one in the Benevolent Daughters of Weeping Mary Society. Jones, thirty-three years old, worked as a skilled tobacco twister at Patterson's Factory. In early 1868, with many tobacco factory workers unemployed, Jones had led the campaign to establish a cooperative tobacco factory. He also was secretary of the powerful Union Aid Society, headed by popular activist Joseph Cox. Jones also presided over a lodge and occupied a position of public trust on the Ebenezer Baptist Church's bank committee. Taylor and Jones—and other black workingmen like them—not only led their black neighbors and fellow workingmen in political affairs, but also were linked to them through bonds of kinship and of social organization.[49]

Despite their popular base, these men were unable to influence Republican party positions or candidate selection. Instead, railroad men like William Mahone and William Wickham and patronage brokers like James Humphreys of the Customs House dominated. Powerfully connected to the Republican party machine in Washington and to the Federal military director of Virginia, the white political bosses had ample resources to maintain their control. In early May 1868, they assumed control of Richmond's municipal government using General Schofield's appointment powers, and they secured the third district congressional nomination for Charles H. Porter, the northern-born lawyer who only two months earlier had led the opposition to integrated schools at the Constitutional Convention.[50]

The restrictive nature of formal political channels frustrated the black popular movement. The continued disfranchisement of black women, for example, cost the movement some of its most valuable resources when the time came to cast ballots. Moreover, independent political campaigns demanded material resources beyond black Richmond's reach. A new political uncertainty swept over black Richmond. For the first time in three years, there was no parade to celebrate the Fourth of July. A Grant-for-President demonstration in late August drew a small number of marchers and made a generally lackluster appearance. The spring, summer, and fall of 1868 passed with little mass activity, a pronounced downturn from the heated 1867 struggles.[51]

The day-to-day fervor that had marked the spring and summer of 1867 could not be maintained. A severe economic recession, beginning in the late fall, strained black Richmond's resources. The growth of formal political activity and structures had also played its part in sapping popular political energy. The creation of official ward committees, the election of delegates to conventions, the GOP's internal hierarchical structure, the disfranchisement of women, and the presentation of voting itself as the proper channel of political expression all combined to distance politics from mass participation. Popular desires expressed in mass meetings stood little chance of emerging at the end of the political process as the official GOP stance.[52]

Black Richmonders played little role in the reorganization of the Republican party and the nomination of a new gubernatorial slate in the spring of 1869. The nominating convention was held in Petersburg, railroad magnate William Mahone's base of operations, rather than Richmond. Mahone and his allies—northern and southern businessmen and lawyers—employed a devious strategy. They supported the black delegates' push for a black candidate for lieutenant governor, Dr. J. D. Harris, believing it would effectively doom the Republican ticket. They then promoted the formation of an opposition caucus, seceded from the convention, and nominated Gilbert C. Walker, the director of Mahone's Norfolk and Petersburg Railroad, and John F. Lewis, a respected spokesman for small white farmers, for governor and lieutenant governor, respectively. Calling themselves the "True Republicans," they looked to an alliance with the leaders of the newly organized Conservative party. They also announced their opposition to the disfranchisement of former Confederates. Mahone himself had been a much-decorated general in the lost cause. In April of 1869, under his leadership, the two white movements formally merged.[53]

April 3, 1869, came and went with no Emancipation Day celebration, for the first time since the fall of Richmond. Over the next two months, local party chairman James Humphreys and his "ring" concentrated on breaking the power of black militants and their "ultra" faction. For instance, he invalidated all ward committee votes taken by "rising and sitting," a form conducive to popular pressure in an open meeting, and instituted "secret ballots," a form conducive to manipulation by the ballot-counters.[54]

Humphreys and the "ring" continued their project of isolating the "ultras." None was elected in the July 6, 1869, state election, nor was the Wells-Harris ticket. The new constitution was ratified, but without the disfranchising clause. The True Republicans and Independent Conservatives had carried the day. Walker defeated Wells, even in Richmond, by a slim edge of 6,215 to 6,143. Over the next months, Humphreys offered Customs House and Post Office jobs to several of the activists, who accepted them. After all, they had argued that more of these openings should be awarded to black men; in the midst of continuing hard times, steady well-paid work looked attractive. Thus did Robert Hobson leave his barber shop and William Lester and Joseph Cox, the tobacco factories. Lewis Lindsay even took a post as "janitor" at the Customs House. All seemed unaware that these positions would further distance them from their only source of political strength—the black community.[55]

• • •

Quiescence gave way to disarray and pessimism in the latter half of 1869. The failure at the polls, confusion within party ranks, and another economic downturn—even before the local economy had recovered from the earlier one—spread demoralization within the black community. Lewis Lindsay's arrest in August for public drunkenness suggests the depths to which the popular movement had fallen. Local newspapers reported large numbers of blacks leaving Richmond in the fall to find work in the Deep South. The city only sent four black delegates out of their total of twelve to the Republican state convention of November 21, 1869. This convention nominated an all-white slate of officers, to which two token blacks were added after black delegates complained.[56]

In early December, the historic first convention of the Colored National Labor Union was held in Washington. Richmond's formal nonparticipation bears mute witness to the condition of its popular movement. Only ninety miles from the convention, and the home of the largest concentration of black industrial workers in the country, it failed to select any official delegates. William H. Lester and Fields Cook attended some of the sessions, but not in any official capacity. Toward the end of the convention, Lester, once a leading "ultra," proposed a resolution drenched in the defeat:

> Whereas the Legislature of Viginia is now largely under the control of a rebel majority, a result accomplished largely by intimidation on the part of the rebels towards the loyal voters, and especially the colored electors; and whereas there can be no liberty for our race in that state much less any safety for the interests of colored and white labor, unless said Legislature is under the control of loyal men . . .
>
> If not enforced, loyalty will be lost, and the colored people, more than 600,000 in that state, will be reduced to a condition as deplorable as when they were fastened in the chains of slavery.

Lester's resolution was little more than a cry in the darkness. Nothing changed in the Viginia legislature and the U.S. Congress sanctioned the status quo.[57]

Black activists tried to adapt to the changed circumstances, but to no avail, as seen in the celebration of Emancipation Day. The black popular movement had faded to such a point that 1869 had passed with no formal celebration whatsoever on April 3, the date blacks had stubbornly held to, opposition from their white Republican allies notwithstanding. By 1870, however, black activists dropped their resistance to the January commemoration of Lincoln's Emancipation Proclamation. While this revised date was marked by a parade, it was but a bare shadow of the mass events of 1866 and 1867; only a few secret societies participated. One local newspaper observed: "The procession was rather smaller than usual, there being hardly over two or three hundred in it." Nor was there the harmony that once existed. For the first time, resolutions introduced from the speakers' stand, including some made by Lewis Lindsay, were not greeted with unanimity. Many in the procession simply marched on, ignoring the speakers' platform altogether.[58]

Renewed efforts to gain access to streetcars also reflected the continuing demoralization of the black community. The very tactics now employed documented the general decline of mass activity. Ben Scott, who had led the march over the toll bridge in April 1868, got on a "ladies" car—"designated as such by the white ball on the roof"—on January 26. He was immediately thrown off by the driver but, being alone, could not effectively challenge the rules. He went to the police station and swore out warrants against the driver and the conductor. Joined by three friends, he then tried another "ladies" car. It was driven to the stationhouse, where Scott and his friends were arrested. A small angry crowd gathered but was easily dispersed. The following day, more than five hundred black men and women packed the mayor's courtroom for the trial. Evidence presented suggested the deterioration of the black accomplishments. In 1867, only two of Richmond's six streetcars had been adorned with white balls. By 1870, ten of twelve cars had them. Moreover, white men, even "badly dressed and vulgar-looking ones," were allowed on the "ladies" cars according to one black witness. The Republican mayor George Chahoon, presiding over the court, found against Scott and his friends and ordered them bound over for inciting to riot and for perjury. The black community mounted no response.[59]

Fragmentation grew within the black working-class community. "Colored Walker Republican" clubs appeared and held meetings without incurring black protests. One such club met on February 25 under the chairmanship of Abram Hall, a tobacco factory worker, and adopted the following resolution: "We . . . most respectfully petition the Congress of the United States to remove the political disabilities of all the white citizens of this Commonwealth." For the vast majority of black workers who still rejected such a concession, the Republican party was no help. An all-white state GOP meeting, held in Richmond on March 12, appointed committees to plan a convention to reorganize the party yet again, and included no blacks.[60]

A sudden political crisis exploded on March 15, 1870, when Governor Gilbert Walker appointed a new city council for Richmond. All were white conservatives. In closed session the following evening, they elected Henry K. Ellyson, publisher of the *Baptist Religious Herald* and prominent Conservative, as the city's new mayor. Ellyson went directly to the police station to take command but found Chahoon there, together with much of his police force. They flatly refused to turn over the building to the incoming administration. Five hundred white men immediately volunteered, and Ellyson swore in 200 of them as special officers. The city council met in an emergency session and promised to "uphold his [Ellyson's] hands by all the means within their control in the effort to maintain the peace of the city and to punish the acts of lawless men now conspiring in arms against it."[61]

In the face of such an organized force, Chahoon turned to the black community for support. He appointed twenty-five black men as special police officers and placed Ben Scott in command. While Scott and Chahoon had locked horns over the streetcar issue, Chahoon recognized the importance of the community backing that Scott enjoyed, and he was aware of Scott's experience as commander of a militia unit. Scott, for his part, knew what unchecked Conservative rule in Richmond could mean, and he was prepared to give his life to prevent it. In the course of the conflict, he would be seriously wounded and accused of the murder of one of Ellyson's policemen. Chahoon's partisans barricaded themselves inside the Old Market Police Station and rejected the governor's demand that they give up. They found themselves under siege, since all food, gas, and water to the building had been cut off. On Thursday night, March 17, a large black crowd encircled Ellyson's forces that had surrounded the building, threatening to forcibly break the siege. They threw bricks at the police, who fired on the crowd, dispersing them. Ellyson went to General Canby, the head of the Federal garrison, who promised to send troops to keep order.[62]

By 8:00 A.M. the next morning, another large crowd of blacks appeared and attacked the police, who again fired into the crowd. This time Daniel Henderson, a black porter, was killed. General Canby's troops arrived early in the afternoon, and the police withdrew. As they left, they were set upon by a brick-throwing crowd, which was again despersed by gunfire. Finally, General Canby imposed a truce and created a temporary stand-off that left Chahoon in control of the police station and Ellyson, the city hall, until the courts could make a decision.[63]

Five years of continuous effort—massive self-education, the accumulation of savings accounts, the reconstruction of families, the elaboration of an extensive social network, the development of political organization—had brought black Richmond to yet another crisis. This time, in the spring of 1870, the community appeared shorn of the resources needed to hold out. Even some of its most respected leaders appeared to have compromised themselves. Still, blacks had waged an impressive struggle in the mayoral conflict, with the future of their community hanging in the balance.

CHAPTER 4

Working-class Activism, the Republican Party, and the Colored National Labor Union, 1870–1873

BLACK WORKERS had been propelled into a new wave of direct action by the high stakes of the mayoralty race. Hundreds had risked their lives in the mid-March street confrontations, less for George Chahoon than for the protection of their collective accomplishments. Were they to allow Chahoon's undemocratic removal, they would condone a precedent for future depredations. Moreover, racial reactionaries would then control every major political institution in Virginia, from the council and the mayor's office to the legislature and the executive branch. Such terrible prospects reawakened black Richmond.

Black militants saw this burst of activity as an opportunity to revitalize the movement. But this situation—and the popular response to it—proved to be distinctly different from 1865–1867. By 1870, a new group of activists joined the veteran core that headed popular organizations. More clearly rooted in the working class by upbringing and occupation, these younger men had developed their talents since Emancipation and gained recognition through the black social network. They had already served one or more secret societies as officers, were enmeshed in the community's web of mutual assistance, and were active in organizing the community's resources to meet its needs.

This new group gave voice to an emerging shift in popular opinion. Developments since the Constitutional Convention adjourned in the spring of 1867 had shaken the political allegiances of black Richmond. Distrust of the white GOP bosses was rampant. Frustration was everywhere. Here and there, calls to abandon the Republican party could be heard. These new activists promoted mass-based organization independent of the Republican apparatus. Some felt that such an organization could gain control of the GOP; others thought it might displace the old vehicle altogether. All shared an awareness of the importance of an independent base.

The Colored National Labor Union (CNLU) was the embodiment of their efforts. Its founding convention had been held in Washington in January, and its ideas swept down the Potomac like a breath of fresh air. The CNLU was built on the twin pillars of class and race consciousness among black workers, especially artisans in larger commercial cities like Baltimore and Philadelphia. It would have an appeal in Richmond, where newly developing activists would appropriate it in their search for an organizational vehicle that could focus renewed popular struggle.[1]

• • •

Following the mid-March 1870 street clashes, activists put their new strategy to work. They promoted the Colored National Labor Union throughout black Richmond. On the evening of April 11, more than 1,200 black workingmen crowded Metropolitan Hall to hear Isaac Myers, the national president of the newly organized CNLU. Veteran leader Lewis Lindsay called the meeting to order and immediately turned to the election of officers. John Oliver was elected president amid enthusiastic applause. Oliver "came forward and, after a graceful bow, said that he esteemed it an honor to have been elected president of the first laborers' meeting ever held in Richmond." Oliver continued, according to a local reporter:

> He felt honored not only because it was a laborers' meeting, but because he himself was a laborer, being a carpenter. If there was anything he could do, it was build a house. He believed sincerely that this meeting would meet with fruitful results. It was proposed, as he understood the purport of the call for this reunion, to exclude politics. The colored people have had political meetings since the War and nothing good has been achieved. Let us now, said he, learn how to make home comfortable by associating ourselves upon a firmer basis than politics. We should hold meetings for the purpose of exchanging our views and devising the best means practicable for the protection of our labor.[2]

After Oliver took the chair, the meeting elected twenty-four "vice-presidents," largely honorific and symbolic offices. These officials tended to share common organizational and social experiences—in politics, work, secret societies, and the church—that differentiated them from the first group of local black activists. Unlike them, few of these new activists had enjoyed a privileged status in the slave South. They were motivated not by a sense of something lost, but of something yet to be gained. They were fundamentally products of the years of mass activity that had followed emancipation. Some had only come to maturity, become literate, and started a family after 1865. All had become officers in the black community's network of secret societies.[3]

The selection of vice-presidents reaffirmed the mutual support that had existed between slaves and free blacks in antebellum Richmond. Among these officers were representatives of both. John Adams, for example, was an elderly plasterer and contractor with real estate worth $4,000; his family had been prominent among free blacks in Richmond since the 1840s. They had maintained an extensive city-wide network of kinship and of societal relationships in postwar Richmond. Adams was an officer in the Mechanics Union Society, while his sons were officers in the Union Association of Richmond, the United Daughters of the Holy Temple, and the Ebenezer Sabbath School's Tree of Life. The Adams's household included husband and wife; two sons and two daughters; and an apprentice plasterer, a fifteen-year-old girl, and her eight-year-old brother, neither of whom were related to the Adamses'. They had probably entered the household through a de facto adoption, as fictive children. Like Adams, a few other vice-presidents had tasted success, yet never thought to remove themselves from the working-class network in which they had prospered.[4]

Two Baptist ministers were selected as vice-presidents. One represented the traditional self-taught preacher of the older generation, and the other typified the formally educated, professionally oriented new generation of ministers. The selection of the Reverend James Holmes of the First African Baptist Church and the Reverend William Troy of Second African reflected the ongoing centrality of the church and the continuing flow of religious ideas and values into "political" concerns. Holmes, once a slave in Richmond, had been sold to a New Orleans slaveholder and had lost his family; he eventually returned to Richmond and purchased his own freedom during the war. While a slave, he was elected a deacon in the First African Baptist Church in 1856; he personified its moral perspectives and devoted his life to it. In the postwar years, he served as secretary to five different church-affiliated secret societies, taught in the church's Sunday school, managed the church's affairs with the board of deacons, and did an extraordinary amount of personal counseling. He also served on the Advisory Board of the Freedmen's Savings Bank. Despite his community standing, Holmes had neglected secular affairs, politics in particular. Indeed, his CNLU involvement, which seems out of character, points to the importance of this organization. William Troy was very different from Holmes. Northern-born, formally educated, and aggressive, he devoted most of his time to nonchurch activities. He had organized the tobacco producers' cooperative (which never got off the ground) and had stood for the state senate (unsuccessfully, but with widespread black popular support) in 1869. He had played a prominent role in organizing the May 1869 State Colored Convention in Richmond, and he was elected its first vice-president. The differences between these two ministers demonstrate the breadth of experience that could be encompassed within the Colored National Labor Union.[5]

Most of the black vice-presidents were drawn from the older generation of building trades and crafts and from the younger generation of skilled ironworkers. Black artisans in the construction trades had learned long ago that their fortunes dependend directly on the economic condition of the black community. They were employed by black contractors or became subcontractors themselves, and their work was usually limited to the construction of black homes. In these circumstances, most black building artisans became active "joiners," members of many secret societies, to build the reputation and associations needed to secure work. Skilled black workers in the metal trades had somewhat different problems, though they, too, were active "joiners." In the years after the war, the chaos of the local industrial economy destabilized their employment. One week there might be ample work; the next week there was none. The growing back social network provided the mutual assistance they and their families needed during periods of unemployment. For different reasons, then, both groups were deeply enmeshed in the social network.

Thomas Hewlett represented the older generation of building trades artisans. He learned carpentry as a slave in Richmond, became an active Methodist, and served as treasurer of the Virginia Home Building and Loan Association, a cooperative building society. He was also an officer in the Friendly Sons of Temperance and the Odd Fellows. The Hewletts—Thomas, his second wife, and his three daughters from his first marriage—rented a house in a black neighborhood. All single and in their early twenties, his daughters helped to support the household by working as washerwomen. One found time to serve as an officer of Ruth Council, No. 11, of St. Luke's. Hewlett's young apprentice lived with them, as did two people from opposite ends of the life cycle who had no blood ties in the city: a seventy-one-year-old widower and a ten-year-old orphan. The elderly man still worked as a gardener, and the young boy had already left school for tobacco factory work.[6]

Robert Shelton typified the younger generation of iron tradesmen who were represented in the CNLU. A skilled blacksmith in his early twenties, he supported his wife, their two children, and his mother-in-law. Unable to find enough work in his trade, he often had to turn to the hot, heavy, dangerous unskilled labor available to black men in the furnaces at the Tredegar works. Shelton and his family lived in an apartment in a black neighborhood and belonged to the First African Baptist Church. He and his brother were involved in church-related activities, and both were officers in the Loving Charities Christian Tabernacle Society. Times were hard for young black metal tradesmen like Robert Shelton, and they needed the support of the black social network in order to survive.[7]

CNLU officers came from other trades as well. Robert W. Johnson represented shoemakers; he was an officer in the politically oriented Lincoln Union Shoemakers' Society, and he served seven social and religious societies in a leadership capacity. The coopers were represented by Richard Carter, an officer in the newly organized Coopers' Union. Interestingly, no CNLU officers were tobacco factory workers, despite their centrality in popular activism.[8]

Whether of the older generation or the new, the CNLU officers had developed from within the black social network. Those among them who had enjoyed success since Emancipation had done so on the basis of community support. Others had gained recognition as activists struggling within and on behalf of the community. Through their extended kinship ties and secret society affiliations, they were linked with thousands of other Richmond blacks. Leadership positions in churches, secret societies, political and workplace organizations had grown phenomenally between 1865 and 1870, and with them had grown the opportunity to develop the related skills. These black vice-presidents were but the tip of the iceberg: hundreds, if not thousands, of their fellow workers were undergoing the same experiences.

Veteran political activists Joseph Cox and Landon Boyd were among the vice-presidents. Both had been artisans who followed a political path to a patronage job. Their presence suggests the continuing role of "politics," CNLU references to its exclusion notwithstanding. How else, other than the influence of politics, can the election of five white men—all Republican party stalwarts—as "vice-presidents" of a black "labor" organization be explained? Their participation reflected the linkages between black organization and the Republican party, links that vexed some black men but were inescapable in 1870. For most, the Republican party was the "ark" in which they rode, and everything else became the turbulent sea. The CNLU had to remain within the safety of the Republican "ark" or face destruction on the shoals of discrimination and victimization. Though they might build an impressive independent base, their goal remained the control of the Republican party.[9]

Lewis Lindsay, Robert L. Hobson, and William H. Lester, all long-time activists, were elected to a "committee on resolutions." The resolutions, adopted by the mass meeting with little debate, demonstrate the extent to which black workers saw political issues, the Republican party, and social-economic issues in an interconnected fashion.

> Whereas, By the Blessing of Divine Providence, through the agencies of war and the great Republican party of the country, the colored men of Virginia have been released from long and cruel oppression, and invested with full civil and political rights; and, whereas, it is the solemn duty of freemen to be grateful at all times to their deliverers, as is exemplified in the devotion of the American people to the illustrious Washington and his compeers; and whereas, all history has proved that the rights of individuals can best be secured and protected by thorough organization, either political or industrial; therefore, be it—
>
> Resolved, That the thanks of the people of Richmond are due to President Grant, his cabinet, and the Congress of the United States for the prompt legislation tending to complete the work of reconstruction in the South, without which the War and the constitutional amendments would have been absolute failures.

Resolved, That we endorse the National Labor Union of colored men, and appeal to the colored mechanics and laboring men of Richmond to call meetings of their respective branches of industry, for the purpose of immediate organization.

Resolved, That we believe that labor can only secure its rights and the respect due it, by organization, and that all men, of whatever color, who oppose the systematized organization of labor, are enemies to the best interests of the working people.

Resolved, That we denounce all agents or agencies who have for their object and inducement of colored men to leave the State; and that we regard such persons as Democratic agencies, whose object is to reduce the Republican vote of the city, and give ascendency to the Democratic party.

Resolved, That we advise, with a proper application of its importance, the colored men of Richmond against such dangerous demagogues; that their promises are false is evident from the testimony of the large number who have returned penniless from imaginary goldfields.

Resolved, That we advise the colored men of Richmond to be industrious, sober, honest, and true, and peace and plenty will soon enter within our borders and bring joy to the barren fields of this State, when labor and good wages will be found for the whole working people, without regard to race, color, or previous condition.[10]

After the work of the resolution committee, Isaac Myers was called to the podium. The CNLU president opened a lengthy address with references to how far they had all come over five years. "But yesterday we were in chains, deprived of the shadows of the rights of a man. Today, not a cord binds our limbs, and by the authority of . . . the constitution . . . , we are authorized to say, each man to his neighbor, we stand equally before the law as American Citizens." Myers stressed that "equal rights" entailed equal responsibilities:

What we will be in the future depends entirely upon how we train and apply our minds, in everyday life, to the industrial, moral, religious, and political duties as free men and as citizens, having an equal proportion of the responsibilities of preserving and perpetuating free institutions and a republican form of government.

Each one of these duties which we owe to ourselves, our God, and our country, is a mill through which each man, woman, and child must be ground, and our market value depends on how fine we come out at the other end. It is said that "the mills of the gods grind slow, but they grind very very fine." So it necessarily must be with us as a class, who have been for the last two hundred years deprived of all the rights and privileges of education, and the advantages of accumulating capital. And as it must be slow, let it be extra fine, and when it comes out of the mill, let there be no necessity for it going back in again.

Individual responsibility was the touchstone of improvement, Myers declared, but only through collective organization could these goals be attained.

> How can labor be made respectable and productive and protect its rights? We answer, by being organized. By organization, men can accomplish almost anything; but without organization they can accomplish comparatively nothing. Is there a necessity for the colored mechanics and laborers of the United States organizing? My answer is, there is the greatest necessity; and unless you do organize, in a few short years the trades will pass from your hands—you become the servants of servants, the sweeper of shavings, the scrapers of pitch, and the carriers of mortar.[11]

Myers offered examples of successes achieved through black working-class organization elsewhere. He praised frugality, hard work, temperance, and "particularly enjoined upon his hearers to have confidence in, and respect for each other, in proportion would the white people of Richmond respect them." Stressing the connection between black organization and the Republican party, he urged his listeners to "let by-gones be by-gones, and each and every man walk to the polls in May and cast a solid vote for the Republican nominees." Underlying this support for the GOP, however, there had to be an autonomous black organization able to exert a strong influence. "He advised the [black] Republicans to stand united, and to make their leaders stand united; and if they did not, why throw them all overboard and lead yourselves."[12]

The Colored National Labor Union embodied a new outlook, that black workers should organize themselves on a permanent basis as an independent force. It melded race and class awareness into a social, political, and economic vehicle that, in turn, was interwoven with the black social network. It reached deep into religious, beneficial, educational, political, and trade secret societies, into iron mills and workshops, building sites, brickyards, quarries, and tobacco factories. It offered a vision of dignity, respect, and mutual assistance.

• • •

The spring of 1870 seemed to bring economic "good times"; the ratification of the Fifteenth Amendment at the same time provided a firm legal foundation for black political rights. Indications suggested that former Mayor Chahoon would win his court battle, thereby vindicating the massive black struggle that had erupted in March and keeping Richmond out of Conservative hands. Despite the recent disappointments, the future looked especially promising in spring 1870, and optimism infused the CNLU.

John Oliver, in his new capacity as president of the local CNLU, became chairman of the April 20 mass celebration of the passage of the Fifteenth

Amendment. The "committee of arrangements" was drawn entirely from the Union's "vice-presidents." And what a celebration it was! Fifty different secret societies from Richmond and Manchester marched; religious, charitable, educational, beneficial, trade, and political societies all participated. CNLU members did not march as a body. Some CNLU "vice-presidents" led their secret societies: J. Anderson Taylor (the Gold Key), Landon Boyd (Lincoln Aid), Peter Woolfolk (Home Building Society), Richard Carter (Mechanics' Union), and William Johnson (Reformed Sons of Love). Other CNLU "vice-presidents" were on the podium or with their societies on parade. The procession was over a mile long; most of the marchers wore the "uniforms" of their societies and carried colorful banners. Lindsay's and Dabney's bands provided the music. Six thousand spectators, some having travelled from rural districts, lined the parade route and waved handkerchiefs. John Oliver and six parade marshals led the procession. Three of the marshals were CNLU "vice-presidents" Landon Boyd, J. Anderson Taylor, and Joseph Cox; others were Republican activist Richard Forrester, and Warwick Reed and Stephen Jones, the two leading spokesmen for tobacco factory workers. The procession ended at the City Springs, where more than 5,000 people assembled to listen to speeches and participate in the ceremonies.[13]

Oliver opened by leading the crowd in a popular hymn, "Blow Ye the Trumpet, Blow":

> Blow Ye the trumpet, blow,
> The gladly solemn sound, Let all the nations know,
> To earth's remotest bound, The year of the Jubilee is come,
> Return, ye ransomed sinners, home.

The featured speaker was Sella Martin, associated both with Isaac Myers in the CNLU and Frederick Douglass on the *New Era*. He gave a rousing address that touched on many facets of black activity: support for the GOP, and struggle for equal access to public facilities, and the quest for better living and working conditions. Martin urged his listeners to learn from "the example of the laboring men of the North, who, by co-operative associations, could strike at any time they chose, having money enough in their treasuries to feed every idle man." Their workplace organization, he argued, provided the necessary foundation for political independence. "Thus, with their bread in one hand, their ballot was safe in the other."[14]

Several local activists followed Martin to express their agreement. Then, under Oliver's guidance, the gathering unanimously passed a series of resolutions of gratitude to the Republican party, allegiance to the flag, belief in education as "the bulwark to freedom and independence," and the state's responsibility to provide for it, so that "the children of laboring and poor men be educated." The black popular movement appeared to be revived, reunited, and reorganized.[15]

Black militants rode the crest of this revived movement and employed the network of the CNLU to launch a series of assaults on the machine's control of the GOP. Time and again, their efforts proved futile. In April 1870, they were unable to influence the contents of the Republican platform: The GOP remained officially silent on the right of black men to serve on juries; the low wages black workers received; the lack of municipal services for black neighborhoods; equal access to public facilities and transportation; and the victimization of black workers for the exercise of their political rights. In May and November, the black activists were unable to secure a single position on the GOP ticket for a black candidate. Nor were they able to block the renomination to Congress of carpetbagger Charles H. Porter. Formal political channels remained the bane of the black popular movement.[16]

Black working-class activists continued to promote the Colored National Labor Union as an independent force outside the Republican party. Union chieftains had drawn twelve hundred workingmen together in early April 1870 for the founding of the new organization. Later that month, five to six thousand men, women, and children joined in the Fifteenth Amendment parade and celebration directed by CNLU organizers. In early June, the Richmond CNLU hosted a three-day statewide convention. In the past, rural delegates to Richmond conventions had often complained of being ignored. This time, urban deputies paid special attention to their issues. The convention asked Congress to set aside $2 million to buy land for black freedmen, who then would repay the loan gradually. Resolutions called for an end to discrimination and urged blacks to abstain from alcohol and save their money. The convention organized a state "Bureau of Labor," intended "to devise ways and means by which our children may learn the various branches of trade and commerce."[17]

The CNLU also stimulated trade organization among black workers. In June, shortly after the state-wide CNLU convention, black coopers launched a new project—the organization of an interracial coopers' union. Their May 1867 strike, as seen in the previous chapter, had failed when employers replaced them with white strike-breakers. To effect a successful union, black coopers had to draw in the white workers who constituted a significant minority of the trade. The white coopers themselves had been unable to better their own conditions, since employers could threaten to replace them with blacks. The improved economic climate of 1870 reduced job competition between the races. Coopering, linked to the transport of agricultural and manufactured products, rose and fell with the fortunes of Richmond's major industries. As the tobacco, iron, and flour industries rebounded in 1870, the local demand for barrels also jumped. By July, Richmond's coopers' union sought affiliation with the growing Coopers' International Union. William Gittings, the black president of the local organization, sent thirty dollars in aid to No. 4 of Pennsylvania (whose members had just completed a lengthy strike) and asked for assistance in gaining recognition for his union. The request was passed along to No. 1 of Pennsylvania, one of the the most prominent locals in the international organization. Its secretary wrote in the *Coopers' Monthly Journal*: "The idea of colored and whites forming a subordinate union in that section of the country, if agreeable to them, in my opinion we cannot object to it." Richmond No. 1 was accepted.[18]

Black activists pursued other routes in expanding their social network. With improved economic conditions and a widening social base, many of Richmond's secret societies organized "excursions" in the summer of 1870. These were brief (two- or three-day) vacations, by train, for society members and their families. Because the tickets were bought in bulk, they cost less; thus a small profit went into the society's treasury. Unlike the summer vacations of Richmond's wealthy whites, who went to the "country" or to White Sulphur Springs, these excursions were usually to other cities. Those who went observed the social conditions of black people elsewhere, discussed common problems and activities, learned from each other's successes and failures, and developed a racial solidarity that went beyond Richmond's boundaries.[19]

As the second CNLU convention neared, Richmond activists planned to participate. J. Anderson Taylor represented them. A widowed blacksmith in his fifties, he lived with his old friend Warwick Reed and his family. While active in the affairs of the First African church and the Republican party, Taylor's first real public exposure had come with his election as a CNLU vice-president in April 1870. The *New National Era* praised him as "a very bright man,"

> cut out by nature for important parts—one of the few black men whose mind slavery itself could not extinguish. This Mr. Taylor is without education, in the technical sense of the word, but, if a knowledge of men and the possession of the power to wield his knowledge to wise be education, then Mr. Taylor is quite a liberally educated man.

Taylor was elected to the committee on cooperation, which was the core of the CNLU's planned future activity.[20]

Taylor brought a clear message of "cooperation" back to black Richmond. Isaac Myers had emphasized it in his opening address; he placed it above strikes, independent political action, or even the Republican party as the proper focus of future black activity. Only "cooperation" could emancipate the "millions of laborers [who] are the absolute slaves of capital, receiving a pittance of the wealth their labor produces." For Taylor, too, it was the key to the black struggle for equality and dignity. Surely, the extent of self-organization already achieved in black Richmond must have encouraged those who shared their views. The network of secret societies could provide the necessary foundation for cooperative ventures of all sorts—the investors, the workers, the customers, all were already tied together. Some cooperative projects had already been attempted by 1871 among tobacco factory workers, aspiring home-owners, and eager savers. Unions and mechanics' societies had discussed cooperation as both a strategy and an ultimate goal. But never before had cooperation been articulated as a priority. However, the problems that had limited it remained. Low wage rates made saving difficult, and the costs of opening a factory or a workshop appeared prohibitive. Building trades craftsmen were doing well as individuals and felt little need to organize their work. Coopers were proceeding with their interracial union and placed organization of all the city's coopers above establishing cooperatives among the existing members. "Cooperative production" held little meaning for the thousands of Richmond's domestic servants and casual laborers. It gave no more hope than did attempts to reform the Republican party; its major institutional advocate, the Colored National Labor Union, would itself fade from view by the end of 1871.[21]

• • •

By mid-1871, Richmond's black community was extremely well-organized. Yet the strength represented by the network of secret societies remained an unrealized potential, a gathering force that could find no structural channel or organizational vehicle through which to improve its position in society. The ironic conjunction of two events in April 1871 indicated a continuing frustration.

On April 20, Afro-Americans took to the streets to celebrate the first anniversary of the Fifteenth Amendment (in place of the original "Emancipation Day" of April 3). A wide range of secret societies participated. George Downing of Rhode Island, a leading figure in the Colored National Labor Union, was the featured speaker; he shared the podium with Landon Boyd and William Lester, both of the local CNLU. Despite its inability to achieve a genuine breakthrough, the CNLU continued to wear the mantle of leadership and to provide the central structures of the black popular movement.[22]

While thousands of Richmond blacks celebrated their political rights and potential power, the city council met to discuss how to contain them. They gerrymandered the city's political districts into six wards, one of which—Jackson—would be largely black, while the other five would have white majorities. Beyond the reach of the black paraders, white politicians were already restricting their future exercise of power under the Fifteenth Amendment. Official political channels would continue to thwart black self-expression and collective action.[23]

Black activists became particularly frustrated with the lack of help forthcoming from white GOP leaders. "The most shameful feature of our condition is," John Oliver complained, "we are still kept as the hewers of wood and drawers of water to as mean a class of white men—calling themselves Republicans—as live in any one of these reconstructed states." Lewis Lindsay objected to the all-white composition of the Republican slate for the House of Delegates:

> If adopted, if would exclude colored men entirely from the ticket, and if there wasn't a colored man on it, a howl would come up from the tobacco factories all over the city. He couldn't go back to his ward and tell them that the African race had again been slighted, not withstanding nine-tenths of the party was of that race.

Landon Boyd supported Lindsay: "The negroes were getting tired of voting for white men only, and being told to wait, and if they are asked to do it again, they will demand of us delegates what we mean by it."[24]

Though continuing to lead the popular movement, CNLU activists had little success. Even the old method of mass meetings and petitions no longer brought results. For example, on October 22, a mass meeting was held on Navy Hill in Jackson Ward to protest recent incidents of police harassment. Landon Boyd and William Lester chaired the meeting. The assembly elected a resolution committee that drafted a preamble and a set of resolutions, all adopted after full discussion:

> Whereas, the primary object of all law should be to secure and preserve inviolate the recognized and inalienable right of all men to life, liberty, and the pursuit of happiness, thereby compelling security to each member of civil society and insuring the preservation of peace, quiet, and order in communities; and whereas it is the boast of our laws that they grant a remedy for every wrong and secure the enforcement of all just rights; and whereas it is the painful, the deliberate opinion of this meeting that the laws intended to accomplish these beneficient ends have been perverted and distorted into instruments of oppression and wrong, by reason of their enforcement being committed to the hands of ignorant and vindictive potentates in many cases, resulting in such unwarranted and despotic abuse of their powers as those recently disgracing the pages of justice in this city, to wit. The illegal and unjustifiable ejectment of our citizens, male and female, from the cars of the Richmond City Railway Company; the worse arrest and brutal dispersion of a large number of our people at Ham's Hall on the 9th instant, where they were assembled in furtherance of a charitable and Christian cause—attempting to do good to all men and injury to none—which should have been encouraged and protected rather than molested, by the city authorities; and the more aggravated, because more illegal and brutal, arrest of a female, who was seized without a cause, shamefully dragged through the streets, and bruised and beaten in a manner as cruel and fierce as it was cowardly, by a policeman of Richmond. Therefore, be it
>
> Resolved, That in the name of law, of right, of justice, and lastly of humanity itself, we appeal to our authorities to grant us their aid in the suppression of such scenes, outrages, and wrongs, and to use the powers vested in them to bring all parties guilty of such abuses of their authority to immediate justice.[25]

A committee of three was elected to lay these grievances before the city council, but it totally ignored their demands. Local authorities no longer felt pressure to yield to black demands, especially those presented outside formal political channels; and with the city gerrymandered, they had little to fear through formal political channels either. The black popular movement, though it had entered an important new phase through the Colored National Labor Union, appeared limited and contained by late 1871.[26]

• • •

Disintegration stemmed from containment. Assimilation into the political system was a pretext for a dual subjugation: Blacks had been gerrymandered, their political strength restricted to one ward; they were subsumed within a political party structure that thwarted their efforts to represent themselves or to articulate their own positions. Pressures on every side defined formal political channels as the only acceptable ones for the redress of black grievances. Within these channels, the alternative to the GOP was the Conservative party, with its clearly racist record. It is little wonder that political uncertainty and confusion were widespread in the black community.

In November 1871, Conservatives swept to victory on the state and local levels. Richmond blacks felt their prospects dim indeed. Thus, a letter to the *New National Era* stated: "This city . . . is controlled by the Democratic party, and the civil rights of the negro, as well as the great mass of the members of the Republican party, are equally at its mercy." Two weeks later, another correspondent termed the elections a "terrible defeat" and expressed the fear that all "dissenters" from the status quo faced the unchecked power of the Conservative party. This defeat could wipe out the hard-fought accomplishments of the past six years. "The Constitution of the State adopted in 1869 was mutilated by the last Legislature in all its sections, and the upcoming one, with its more than two-thirds majority, will send what remains of it in the waste-basket."[27]

By the winter of 1871–1872, in addition to the adverse political situation, the black community's economic condition had taken a decided downturn, all the more disturbing after the rising expectations of 1870 and early 1871. More was involved than economic cycles. After the normal seasonal shutdown in the fall of 1871, many of the city's tobacco factories had failed to reopen in January 1872. Their owners, so it was claimed, were waiting to learn the level of congressional taxes on tobacco. By March, even fewer factories were operating. More than 4,000 black men, women, and children worked in these factories, supporting themselves and their families, and a prolonged shut-down imperiled the entire community. It threatened the treasuries of secret societies and the livelihood of black contractors, barbers, and shopkeepers. Factory owners, meanwhile, sought to use this occasion to build a paternalistic political relationship with their employees. This endangered independent workplace and political organization alike. The manufacturers, already organized among themselves for lobbying purposes, called a mass meeting in the First African Baptist Church on the evening of

March 11, 1872. Its purpose was for joint employer-employee sponsorship of a memorial to Congress, petitioning it to remove the present taxes on tobacco. The head of the manufacturers' association chaired the meeting and explained the issue. He was less than fully effective, as the *Richmond Dispatch* reported:

> Mr. Burwell's remarks were received with approbation by many of the better class of the audience, but others received them with that suspicion and blind prejudice characteristic of ignorance. They could not or would not see how an equal taxation could be of mutual benefit to employer and employee, and interrupted the speaker with many foolish questions not at all pertinent to the subject, one fellow desiring to know if the government reduced this tax from 32 to 16 cents whether "he was gwine to get any part of it." The speaker explained that the tax being lower it would enable the manufacturer to lower the price, thereby increasing consumption and demand, and consequently pay higher wages for labor.
>
> A voice: "Promises like pie-crust. You all done gone back on us once before." Here some confusion ensued, and the tendency of the discussion was evidently taking a political turn.

After heated debate, the chair called for a voice vote on the memorial, which he then declared approved.[28]

While the manufacturers got their resolution through, they had achieved nothing in terms of their workers' attitudes. These workers demanded their right to express themselves independently, even if they supported their employers' position. A mass meeting at the Ebenezer church three nights later convened under the leadership of John Oliver, still the titular head of Richmond's Colored National Labor Union, and of Stephen Jones and Warwick Reed, the two most active and respected spokesmen for tobacco workers. The assembly discussed the issue, voted to seek a tax reduction, drafted a memorial, and appointed Jones, Reed, and F. W. Jackson, another tobacco factory worker, to present it to the Congress. They made no mention of their employers, not did they seek a joint presentation. They were able to get their point across without making any political concessions to the manufacturer. Their insistence upon autonomy reflected the continuing resolve of the larger black community.[29]

Black activists adapted to changing conditions. They sought to capture the Jackson Ward Republican organization, and turn it into a base for independent black activism. In the spring of 1872, black activists successfully lobbied for the nomination of three black men for city council from Jackson Ward. Stephen Jones and Joseph Cox led the Jackson Ward campaign. They organized the April 29 Fifteenth Amendment celebration, which drew an estimated ten thousand participants. A month later, the three blacks were elected to the city council—a milestone in Richmond's political history.[30]

But it was only three votes out of thirty, and thus a symbolic victory of little practical value for black Richmond. Though activists had the power to elect men like John Oliver and Landon Boyd councilmen, they could not expect such successes to have any great impact on municipal policies—nor had their power inside the GOP increased. Instead, a new group of white politicos, led by "native" Virginians John Ambler Smith and William C. Wickham, took over the party machine from the less sophisticated James Humphreys and brought the GOP more directly into the service of national railroad and financial interests. Their attitude toward black political power was little more enlightened than that of their predecessors. A statewide spokesman for these "native" Republicans, Robert W. Hughes, boasted:

> We have the best system of unskilled labor in the world. Why can we not induce all classes of our people to treat as a blessing the presence among us of the most amiable, stalwart, teachable, and faithful race of laborers possessed by any country? It is a treasure worth annual millions to the State, if we but do our duty in educating, elevating, and fostering as men and citizens these people.[31]

Despite the waves of popular activism that black Richmond had generated between 1865 and 1873, no institutional vehicle, which could adequately express and focus mass black activity, had yet been found or created. The Republican party, the Colored National Labor Union, and local trade unions had all been tried, but none had offered consistent or permanent success. The black community had achieved an impressive organizational accomplishment: The network of secret societies had spread its web of relationships throughout the community and provided a wide range of "services" as well as a deep-seated racial solidarity. Both activists and working people had shown an ability to adapt to changing conditions and to develop new ideas. But no one had yet discovered a method to translate social organization into an influential political force.

CHAPTER 5

The Depression of 1873–1878: New Problems and New Paths

THE BLACK popular movement reached a peak in 1870–1871 and, before receding, displayed a new perspective and new organizational form. These developments remained interwoven with established organizations, like the Republican party, and with traditional ideas, like the pursuit of "equal rights." The independence of the Colored National Labor Union, its awareness of both race and class, had seized the imagination of black working-class activists across the nation. For them, the CNLU remained a source of inspiration in their struggle to create a society where blacks might live with respect and dignity.[1]

The "panic" of late September 1873, and the prolonged depression that followed in its wake, dealt a severe blow to their quest. As families or as individuals, most Richmond blacks lived so close to the margin of survival that their losses would not be significant. But, collectively, the community stood to lose many of its recent gains, from the accumulated treasuries of the secret societies to the free public schools. The depression threatened the future as much as the present.

The scale of the problems that threatened was such that black energy and confidence seemed, at first, to be on the wane. A deep-seated spiritual depression spread through the community. In the longer run, black workers bestirred themselves and responded in new ways to the new problems posed by the depression. Activists explored the twin branches of popular Afro-American consciousness—class and racial awareness. The ideas that had first received attention in the days of the Colored National Labor Union were elaborated, refined, and popularized by the late 1870s. During the worst years of depression, this ideological activity nourished a renewed popular movement.

Like the rest of the nation, Richmond's economy was quickly drawn into the vortex of depression catalyzed by the failure of Jay Cooke's financial empire in September 1873. Despite assertions by the press and business leaders that the city would escape, the bottom had fallen out of the local economy before October 1. Massive layoffs and plant shutdowns swept Richmond's industrial district, then crossed the river into Manchester for more of the same. Women, men, and children, regardless of race, found their livelihood imperiled. Short-time work and wage cuts threatened the living standards of those able to keep their jobs.[2]

Black workers sensed that their community was eroding. By October 1, fewer than half of Richmond's and Manchester's five thousand tobacco factory workers remained on the job. Many had still not recouped losses suffered during the lockout of the previous spring, when manufacturers had pressured the federal government to reduce tobacco taxes. Now, some had been asked to wait indefinitely for wages due them, as employers blamed a shortage of liquid funds and an inability to borrow from local banks. Black workers in other spheres—iron, flour, and barrel manufacture, transportation, and even services—faced similar problems. Economic conditions in black Richmond deteriorated progressively for the next year and a half.[3]

Workers were now thrown back upon resources accumulated since Emancipation. When needs overwhelmed kinship networks, they turned to the secret societies. Hard times had existed since the war, but secret societies had been adequate. They had carried a significant portion of the community through the erratic 1865–1866 period and the recession of 1868–1869.

The collapse of 1873–1874 was far more severe, and it placed a much greater demand on the community's shared resources. Black Richmond was then dealt another cruel blow: The Freedman's Savings Bank, entrusted with the lion's share of their collective resources, closed permanently on July 2, 1874. When the economic difficulties had begun in September 1873, the Richmond branch held over $166,000. White national bank officials used respected black activists Frederick Douglass and John Mercer Langston to forestall a run on the local branches by black depositors. In Richmond, as in most other cities, they were successful. Despite the high unemployment, black depositors withdrew only $26,000 of their collective savings over the fall and winter of 1873–1874. That left $140,000 to lose altogether, when the bank closed in April. In one day, the material foundation of the extensive black social network, the product of nearly a ten-year struggle, had been summarily destroyed. James Hayes, a teen-ager at the time, later reflected that "that little failure in 1874 did more to rob the Negro of hope . . . than any other occurrence."[4]

Since the day that Richmond fell, it had been obvious that Afro-Americans were determined to avoid any dependence on public relief or charity. Indeed, they trumpeted their ability to care for "their own" as a prime feature of their community. In the difficult days of 1865 and 1866, none but the residents of refugee camps, and surprisingly few of them, applied for assistance from Federal authorities. In the summer of 1874, suddenly bereft of their resources, Richmond Afro-Americans swallowed their pride and applied to the city government for relief. And the white, conservative administration offered little material recompense. Between July and December, they doled out only $2,205 in "out-door relief" to blacks, an average of less than fifty cents for each person out of work. Some turned to the almshouse as a last resort. Between December 1873 and March 1876, over 500 blacks entered the almshouse. Over half were widows or widowers. Few ever left. Their fate was an embarrassment to black Richmond—public acknowledgment that it could no longer care for its own.[5]

• • •

The depression highlighted black Richmond's insecurity in a particularly stark manner. The community faced its greatest challenge since obtaining the right to vote, while its collective resources had been reduced to little more than it possessed during the first days of freedom. Black working-class activists explored new ways of thinking and acting. Some pursued a number of variations on the theme of "class." The same depression, it was perceived, buffeted both black and white workers. Hence, black activists considered an alliance with the reform-minded segments of the white labor movement in the North; they promoted the organization of trade unions and the struggle against deteriorating wages and working conditions; they advocated regional "labor" organization, which would also operate as an independent political force. The severity of the economic crisis, the extent of the disruption of daily life it occasioned, and the patent bankruptcy of the Republican party encouraged popular experimentation along new lines and freed new ideas from deference to the old.

Late in the summer of 1873, Coopers' Union No. 1 and the New Light Lodge, Tobacco Laborers' Union, sent delegates to the Industrial Congress in Cleveland, Ohio. Prominent white labor reformers from all over the North were present. Independent labor politics and social reform were the main topics of discussion. Richmond's William Bailey and Warwick Reed were the only black men present, and they were quickly drawn into the Congress's committee structure. Bailey was appointed to the Committee on Correspondence, the Committee on the Rules and Order of Business, and the Committee on Bonds, which he chaired. Reed served on the Constitution Committee and, before the Congress adjourned, was appointed to the Executive Committee and elected first vice-president of the organization. Thus, black Richmond's delegates to this national labor reform convention were well-received, which encouraged the cause of labor organization and class awareness among Richmond's black workers.[6]

Even though they were the nominal delegates of two small trade unions, Bailey and Reed represented much of black Richmond. Bailey was never an officer in the Coopers' Union; his prominence rested on his role as captain of a black militia unit. Reed hadn't worked in a tobacco factory in almost ten years—with Emancipation he had become a plasterer and whitewasher—yet he was the delegate of the Tobacco Laborers' Union. Younger tobacco factory workers had sought his leadership time and again—to be an officer in a factory-based beneficial society, to be secretary of a mutual savings society, to marshal parades, and to represent them before Congress on the 1872 tobacco tax issue. Reed's family shared their apartment with widower J. Anderson Taylor, Richmond's delegate to the 1872 convention of the Colored National Labor Union. Reed's son, a tobacco factory worker, was an officer in a political secret society organized by tobacco factory workers, and the secretary of a predominantly female charitable society. William Bailey and Warwick Reed thus typified the community-based, working-class activism still alive and maturing in black Richmond.[7]

In depression conditions, activism and organization at the workplace level took a beating. On November 29, 1873, for example, 200 black common laborers employed on the Chesapeake and Ohio Railroad's Church Hill tunnel project went on strike. Their work was particularly dangerous—nearly one man a week had been killed on the job since the project had begun. Their pay had never exceeded one dollar a day, and since the depression began, several pay-days had been missed. The men had worked for three months without receiving salaries. On November 28, they were given pay packets for September, and nothing but promises for work completed in October and November. Now with some money in their pockets, they refused to return to work until the back wages were paid. In a matter of days, the Chesapeake and Ohio had contracted for a crew of 200 newly landed Italian immigrants. All the black strikers were replaced, and they lost the two months' wages due them along with their jobs.[8]

Black workers in more skilled and better organized trades soon felt the brunt of the depression, too. In early July 1874, black brickmakers shut nearly every yard on both sides of the James River in resistance to a twenty-five percent wage cut. Even though this was the peak of their season, construction work had slowed considerably owing to hard times, and the demand for building materials had plummeted; brick manufacturers found themselves with large inventories on hand. They could outlast their employees, they thought, and they were right. So they simply shut down and waited. By the end of the month, the striking brickmakers had returned to work—at the new, lower wage rates.[9]

Tobacco warehouse laborers had also maintained a multiworkplace organization. The mobile nature of their trades—frequent seasonal layoffs, and moving from warehouse to warehouse in search of work—helped shape their organization. These men had been among the first to organize secret societies, dependent as they were on occasional benefits to tide them over irregular bouts of employment. "Combination" Nos. 1, 14, 20, and 22 had opened accounts at the Freedman's Bank in 1870, followed soon after by the Warehouse Combined Industrial Society, No. 35. The majority of officers of all these societies were illiterate common laborers. Like the brickmakers, their organization was both industrial and citywide. Seeking to protect the interests of all black warehouse workers, it petitioned the governor:

> We take this opportunity to write you a few lines to inform you of the conditions under which we tobacco warehouse laborers are. The best hands who are coopers only get $1.25 per day. It is not enough to support our families and pay our house rent, which is from $10 to $12 per month; and we make this restatement to you hoping that during the time you are appointing tobacco inspectors if it is in your power we would be thankful to you to demand higher wages. We labors hard and know that they can give us higher wages than they do. This is not from one warehouse but from all the warehouses in the city of Richmond combined.

There is no evidence that Governor Kemper gave any attention to this request.[10]

The early 1870s had seen a growing interest among black workers in racially based "labor organization"—at the workplace, the trade, the industrial, and even the community levels. The depression years of 1873–1875 further stimulated this trend by giving priority to economic issues. But economic conditions also sapped the effectiveness of black labor organization. No matter how well-organized, black workers experienced one defeat after another. Their organizations, though woven into the broader black social network, were still unable to defend their members in hard times.

Notwithstanding the decline of self-help and labor organization, a return to the Republican fold remained unpalatable. In the summer of 1873, the state party chose R. W. Hughes, a Confederate officer and a leading opponent of the "test oath" in 1867, as its gubernatorial candidate. A mass meeting at Ham's Hall denounced the "professed Republicanism which is but Feudalism in disguise . . . and foreign to the best interests of this people." In the fall and winter of 1873–1874, with depression threatening black Richmond, no assistance had been forthcoming from Grant's administration. And in the summer of 1874, the local GOP had refused to assist the petition drive behind the Sumner Civil Rights Bill. More than 3,000 Richmond Afro-Americans signed. Local sentiments were articulated by one activist's complaint that blacks "exert themselves to the utmost and become the beasts of burden for the benefit of white men who reward them with insignificant places and contempt."[11]

In April 1874, the tobacco factory workers' organization sent Charles W. Thompson as a delegate to the Industrial Congress's convention in Rochester, New York. Thompson had fled Richmond before the war, but had returned from Detroit in 1865 to pick up the pieces of his family. He resumed tobacco factory work and helped organize several secret societies among young Manchester tobacco factory workers. He was also an officer in the Cadets of Temperance, and his son and namesake was an officer in the

Manchester Band of Hope. Sixty-one years old in 1874, Thompson surely commanded a good deal of respect on both sides of the James River.[12]

Thompson did not travel to Rochester alone. The Grand Lodge of Quarrymen raised fifty dollars to send Thomas Claiborne. The Government Granite Works had shut down in March, throwing 700 black and white employees out of work. Many of the white skilled granite-cutters left Richmond in search of work elsewhere. If their prospects were slim, those of unskilled black quarrymen were virtually nonexistent. The Old Dominion Granite Company remained open, but its unskilled labor force comprised 275 black convicts. The company paid the state penitentiary twenty-five cents a day for each, and provided room and board of questionable quality. Indeed, thirteen convicts died there in 1873 alone. Black quarrymen, being in dire straits, allotted fifty dollars in travel funds to Claiborne, a sum that reflects the seriousness of their situation, since it might have gone towards much-needed out-of-work benefits.[13]

Claiborne had just turned thirty when he left for Rochester with Thompson. Born and raised in Richmond, he had learned to read and write since the war. He and his wife rented an apartment from an Austrian-born cigarmaker in a racially mixed neighborhood. Claiborne, who had started out by breaking rocks for paving in a contractor's yard, took a better-paying job at the Government Quarry in the early 1870s. In 1873, he had been elected an officer in the Grand Lodge of Quarrymen. That same year, his wife was elected an officer in a women's lodge of the Good Samaritans. As with Reed and Bailey a year earlier, both delegates represented more than their trades.[14]

Thompson and Claiborne played active roles at the overwhelmingly white Industrial Congress. Thompson, a temperance activist, served on the Committee on Vice and Immorality, was selected as state representative on the Executive Committee, and was also appointed to the Committee on Amalgamated Unions. The last brought in resolutions advocating secrecy in organization and the establishment of regional unitary locals, rather than craft or even industry-based ones. Claiborne, for his part, devoted much of his attention to the Committee on Brickmakers, seeking solutions for the black tradesmen who would strike Richmond's yards soon after this Congress adjourned. Two themes raised in convention debates would later resonate in black Richmond: a Greenback-type demand for a national currency rather than the issuance of currency through banks and the recommendation that political parties be ignored and candidates be supported who endorsed specific measures.[15]

In March 1875, black tobacco factory workers sent Charles Thompson to the national convention of the "Industrial Brotherhood," which claimed the mantle of the Industrial Congress. It proved to be a small meeting of "reform-minded" activists from different backgrounds, eager to organize a national "labor reform" party independent of existing parties. Thompson had seen a growing interest in independent politics among black workers in Richmond and Manchester and had observed political restlessness within the white working class. Thompson was elected a vice-president at this convention, and he served on the Committee on the Platform, whose planks led to calling this gathering the "Greenback Convention."[16]

Thompson returned home and, with fellow activists, laid plans for a secret statewide organization embodying the precepts of the Industrial Brotherhood and serving the needs of black popular activity. This Industrial Brotherhood would be based on regional units, reaching black workers throughout rural and urban Virginia. It would operate on several levels, as a secret beneficial organization, a political vehicle, and a labor organization. While these were ambitious goals in such hard times, they offered the sort of vision that might capture the popular imagination. Perhaps fearful of being left behind, perhaps sympathetic, the small group of black state legislators issued a call in April for a state "labor convention" to convene in Richmond.[17]

The Initiation Ritual of the Industrial Brotherhood

> Should you become one of us, you will be required to work with all your strength and energy to secure the ends therein enumerated. You will be required to lay aside all selfishness and personal motives as we have all agreed to do, because labor can only be elevated by concerted action on the part of all concerned. The condition of one part of our class can not be improved permanently unless all are improved together. From this you will see that the task before us is not an easy one, and in consideration of this fact we will admit none to membership unless they agree to work with heart and hand, and with might and main to secure the amelioration of the producing classes.
>
> The great aim and object of our organization is to secure for the industrial classes that position in the world and in society to which they are entitled as the producers of the necessaries and comforts of life. It is a strange state of affairs that those who produce nothing, but live on the labor of others, hold the highest positions, are most respected, and can live in easy and luxury, while those who earn their own bread, and the bread of others, in the sweat of their faces, are often suffering from poverty and destitution, and in many cases in old age have no alternative but starvation or the poorhouse.
>
> That such a condition of things is manifestly unjust none will deny, and for this reason we demand that worth, and not wealth, shall be the standard of greatness; that individuals shall be treated and respected according to their industrial, moral, and social worth, instead of measuring their value by the length of their purses.
>
> Let your guides be truth, justice and charity. By truth, deceit and hypocrisy will be banished from our midst, sincerity and plain dealing will distinguish us, and the heart and the tongue join in promoting each other's prosperity. Justice we should be willing to give all, as we demand it for ourselves.[18]

• • •

Class consciousness had deepened and spread in black Richmond since it first surfaced in the Colored National Labor Union in 1870–1871. Hard times had promoted the development of class awareness and its expression through a variety of "labor" organizations. Such consciousness had logical implications for alliances, but reality put the lie to logic. Black affiliation with white labor reformers in national organizations, which certainly had provided significant experiences and ideas as well as a collective sense of importance, had not produced a single practical accomplishment. Local white labor reformers showed no interest in black workers. In 1875, class consciousness in black Richmond was articulated within racial perspectives. The call for the black labor convention began:

> Your own hands, your own energies, and your own genius must eventually lift you from the difficulties and embarassments with which you are surrounded. It is clear as sunshine that you yourselves, and not others, are competent to offer a beneficial and natural solution. You will at once see the wisdom in reflecting your own views and your own policy, to the end that human rights may be secured and preserved, and the glory and prosperity of Virginia enhanced by the labor and sacrifice of its citizens.[19]

Delegates from forty counties streamed into Richmond for the August 19, 1875, opening session of the black labor convention. The gallery at the First African Baptist Church was packed. State legislators held the podium, and their concerns and perspectives dominated the initial discussions. Keynote speakers criticized the GOP's patronage policies and its statewide disorganization. They denounced the Conservative party and warned the audience of plans to disenfranchise blacks through the poll tax and the use of petty larceny laws. Such concerns were hardly new, nor was the notion of trying to take control of the Republican party. One new idea was raised by the opening addresses: scaling down or "readjusting" the state debt to prevent the closing of schools that were endangered by a lack of state funds. This position clashed with that of the national GOP, which was "opposed to repudiation in every form."[20]

Two alternative strategies, each with a significant number of adherents, were proposed from the floor. Both stepped outside the formal political channels, and both ignored the opening speakers' suggestions. While these strategies were neither mutually exclusive in principle nor contradictory in practice, their proponents evinced little interest in working out a joint strategy. Meanwhile, experienced politicians manipulated the debate, used the rules of procedure to their advantage, isolated each of these proposals, and thereby controlled the convention. Victory would come only after the new ideas had received a full hearing in a popular forum and would mature over the next decade.[21]

Veteran activists and close friends Warwick Reed and J. Anderson Taylor proposed from the floor that the convention turn its immediate attention to the organization of a "trades-union in every county, with a supreme union in Richmond." Similar notions had been proposed at the 1874 Industrial Congress and the 1875 convention of the Industrial Brotherhood, both of which had been attended by black working-class activists. Though their resolution was now defeated, Reed, Taylor, and a number of others continued to push the issue. On the second day, a Committee on Labor and Organization was created; it recommended the same basic plan, but with significant modifications. Richmond would be the headquarters of an "advisory committee" rather than a "supreme union," and the organization would be governed by an Executive Committee composed of two members from each congressional district. This alteration eased rural delegates' fears that Richmond would control the organization and made the influence of white Republican bosses in the state capital less likely. The amended plan was approved. It called for the organization of a "Laboring Men's Mechanic Union," recognized the need for independent black labor organization, and sowed the seeds of further developments in this direction.[22]

The second challenge to the politicians' control came from Joseph T. Wilson of Norfolk, who stood for president of the convention. He and his supporters called for racial "independence" and organization.

> . . . he only desired that his race should take the same independent stand taken by other races, and, in unity of purpose and action, secure that consideration which would not be accorded while the colored people were the political serfs of unworthy white leaders, and were at discord among themselves both as to men and measures.

Wilson failed to win election to the convention presidency, but his ideas had been aired, and their time would come.[23]

Joseph P. Evans defeated Wilson for the presidency. Born a slave, Evans was both a shoemaker and a minister who had played an active role in black Virginia politics since 1865. He typified the first wave of black leaders that had emerged in the struggle for equal political rights. He had attended the first Colored National Labor Union convention in January 1870 and was elected to represent the Petersburg district in the House of Delegates in 1871 and in the State Senate two years later. As a state legislator, Evans had an impressive record. He had introduced bills to make education compulsory, to seat blacks on juries, and to require landlords to give ten days' notice before evicting a tenant. He was a spokesman for the venerable "equal rights" tradition.[24]

But this was no longer enough in 1875. In order to capture the presidency, Evans had to recognize the legitimacy of the new ideas expressed by both the labor and race organization advocates. In his acceptance speech, he gave an immediate priority to the problems of black workers: "The first thing to be done is to make a fair day's pay for a fair day's labor. The colored people need labor organization." Similarly, Evans stressed the need for blacks to organize on a racial basis and minimized the importance of the Republican party.[25]

This black labor convention signaled a new stage in the evolution and articulation of black consciousness. First of all, with delegates from forty counties and an organizational structure that did not revolve around Richmond, rural blacks had clearly been accorded a new role. Urban and rural activists now exchanged ideas. "Labor" organization interested some; "race" organization interested others. No single approach had gained dominance; no fresh synthesis had been devised, but the new approaches had clearly supplanted the traditional outlook by late 1875.

Charles W. Thompson and his fellow activists continued to promote the cause of black labor organization. In mid-September, they announced the formation of the State Assembly of the Industrial Brotherhood. Almost all the officers were men from Richmond who already had experience with workplace or trade organization. None had been prominent politically. Their backgrounds provide a perspective on the Industrial Brotherhood: It was the product of ten years' experience with self-organization.[26]

Thompson himself was "Grand Master," a suitable post for the sixty-two-year-old veteran of three decades of black struggle. Abraham Binford was "First Vice Grand Master." A Richmond native with two children, he had worked both in tobacco factories and in warehouses. In 1870, though illiterate, he had been elected an officer in Combination No. 20, one of the secret societies that linked black laborers who worked in warehouses across the city. His wife, who was a washerwoman, served as an officer in the Good Samaritans. They had been doing well enough in 1872 to open savings accounts for their two children, but in 1873 their nine-year-old son left school for work in a tobacco factory. By late 1875, the father, in his mid-forties, was ready to put his experience and relationships to work on behalf of the projected black labor organization.

"Second Vice Grand Master" James H. Williams, though fifteen years younger than Binford, was equally experienced with labor organization. In 1868, though only twenty-two, he had been elected an officer in the Rising Sons of Liberty, No. 2, a political secret society organized by young tobacco factory workers. Williams, a lifelong tobacco factory worker, became president of the Young Laboring Sons of Virginia, a beneficial society of tobacco factory workers, in 1871. Illiterate like Binford, he came from a large Richmond family and still had eight siblings in the city. His oldest brother was an officer in three secret societies. Thus, the entire family was integrated in the black social network.

Thomas Claiborne, the quarryman who had accompanied Charles Thompson to the 1874 Industrial Congress, served as "Grand Secretary." He was the natural choice for this position. Like thousands of Richmond blacks, he had learned to read and write after Emancipation. His recent involvement with labor organization on the local and national levels suited him for the secretary's critical position. William W. Bufort, a tobacco factory worker in his early thirties, served as "Grand Treasurer." In 1869 and 1870, he had been president of the Young Twisters' Aid of Shiloh, a tobacco factory workers' beneficial society; a year later he was elected an officer in Young

Sons of Jerusalem, a religious society. In their early thirties, both Claiborne and Bufort were capable, respected black workingmen, experienced with black labor organization and committed to its promotion.

James H. Washington was "Grand Guard." Raised a slave in Richmond, he was a long-time tobacco factory worker and the head of a growing family. In 1870 he had been elected an officer in the Star Union Sons and their affiliate, the Star Union Daughters. Over the next decade and a half, he would grow in prominence and eventually become an organizer for the Knights of Labor. Giles Willis, the "Grand Sentinel," was an officer in the Grand Lodge of Quarrymen, the body that had sent Thomas Claiborne to the 1874 Industrial Congress.

Together, these men represented a wealth of knowledge about workplace and trade organization, far more than most historians would expect to find in a southern black community in 1875. They were well situated within the network of social relationships that encompassed the black community. Within this network, where these men served as officers in secret societies, their abilities had already been recognized. Here, in late 1875, we find surrogates for the accumulated black working-class experience of the first decade of freedom.

• • •

The hopes of working-class militants, however, were shattered when the economy suddenly plunged into the second trough of the depression. The especially severe winter of 1876–1877 took a terrible toll. Several times a week, the press reported the death of a black woman or man who had gone to sleep by the lime kilns and been overcome by fumes. The Industrial Brotherhood had little more public presence than providing funeral ceremonies and death benefits for members. Black and white workers alike appeared defenseless.[27]

In April 1877, the Richmond middle class spoke with one voice—"austerity" was its response to this new wave of economic troubles. The city council led the way, urged on by the local press. It economized at labor's expense, allowing streets in black and white working-class neighborhoods to plunge into darkness. It approved the proposal of the privately owned City Railway Company to discontinue its Poplar Street route, which linked the Rocketts area of the East End with the center of the city. It refused to extend a gas main on Nicholson Street, also in the Rocketts, far enough to reach the neighborhood schoolhouse. The wages of all City Gas Works employees were slashed, and private employers wre encouraged to follow suit. The Government Granite Works, the Old Dominion Iron and Nail Works, the railroad shops, major print shops and building contractors, and many smaller employers announced similar wage cuts.[28]

The Powhattan Company, a shipping firm, was one of the first local employers to get on board the wage-cut bandwagon. On Saturday, April 21,

1877, their agent announced that stevedores' wages were to be reduced from twenty to fifteen cents an hour, a twenty-five percent cut. Black stevedores had already lost much during the depression. Ten long years before, in April 1867, they had struck for a two-dollar, eight-hour day—now surely a utopian fantasy, since few could even find steady work. They had maintained their fraternal organization, the Stevedores' Society, which had continued to participate in black parades during the depression. The very day before this wage cut was announced, the Stevedores' Society had joined in the parade marking the anniversary of the Fifteenth Amendment. Because the workers could not endure the threatened pay cut, they decided to strike. They organized community support by speaking to church groups on the Sabbath. The company agent announced that he had hired forty white men, none of them experienced longshoremen, to begin work on Monday morning for fifteen cents an hour. A large black crowd "collected in the neighborhood of the wharf" that morning, in an effort to enforce the strike. The municipal government quickly demonstrated how else it might support the "austerity" campaign. Police chief John Poe arrived with "a posse of officers to preserve order." They escorted the white strikebreakers to work, and dispersed the black crowd.[29]

In July 1877, with local newspapers full of accounts of the national railroad strike and the "Great Upheaval," black coopers revived their union and renewed their relationships with white coopers. "Machine" coopers of both races had submitted to a series of wage cuts during the depression, punctuated with bouts of unemployment and underemployment as the demand for barrels mirrored the ups and downs of Richmond's economy. By mid-1877, few earned even $2.50 a week, hardly enough to support one person, let alone a family. Some 110 men had joined the revitalized Coopers' Union by fall.[30]

Like the stevedores, the black coopers had considerable experience with self-organization. They founded a secret society soon after the war, struck for higher wages in 1867, and organized a formal trade union in 1870. White "machine" coopers had been brought into the union, and a close tie with a union of white "tight" coopers had been established, as well as an affiliation with the Coopers' International Union. Black coopers also joined, even led, organizations of warehouse laborers and other working-class political and fraternal secret societies. In 1873, they sent a delegate to the Industrial Congress. Led by experienced, lifelong Richmond residents, black coopers had consistently shown themselves open to new ideas and new strategies, tried out from their position deeply rooted in the black community.

On Monday, September 24, 1877, an estimated 200 coopers struck the barrel shops of Richmond's major tobacco factories, warehouses, and flour mills. The strikers presented a "list of prices" for "turned heads," "rough heads," and "dressed flour barrels," and demanded that the penitentiary close its cooperage shop, where more than forty convicts were leased to manufacturer Samuel Fairbanks for the standard twenty-five cents a day.

With his shop inside the prison, Fairbanks did not even have to provide shelter or food for his workforce, and his inexpensive barrels, made with the most up-to-date equipment, flooded the local market and provided Richmond employers an excuse to depress coopers' wages.[31]

The initial unanimity of the striking coopers was most impressive. Black workers had overcome the potential problem of cross-racial strikebreaking. The men were still holding firm a week after the strike began and had started to see some results. Tobacco factories and flour mills were running short of barrels, and some had to curtail production at a time when overall prices began to improve. One hundred strikers held "a large and enthusiastic meeting on Monday, October 1, and "resolved not to make a barrel unless they get the price demanded."[32]

But the striking coopers found themselves unable to match their employers' resources and power. In the short run, they could do nothing to block the transfer of even more orders to the penitentiary shop. Meanwhile, the ongoing depression limited the ability of other workers to help. After two impressive weeks of unanimity, coopers began to trickle back to work, shop by shop. In some cases, improvements had been agreed upon; in others, there were none. And Samuel Fairbanks was unimpeded in the expansion of his penitentiary-based shop. Putting him out of business would be a major concern of the Knights of Labor eight years later.[33]

The failure of these struggles—and the absence of others—pointed not only to the inherent problems of depression-era labor activity, but to particular weaknesses in the evolving strategy of black working-class militants. The stevedores' failure indicated the serious weakness inherent in the absence of a formal relationship with white working-class organizations. Without such connections, cross-racial strikebreaking could only be addressed through intimidation. The stevedores' close ties to the black social network ensured a popular turnout in their cause, but it was no match for the police. And it was black Richmond's lack of political power that allowed the police to place their forces at the manufacturers' disposal. This lack of political power undermined the coopers, the group that had shown the most initiative in interracial organizing. The black and white coopers, even with the support of the black community, were no match for the power of men like Samuel Fairbanks. Legislative control seemed to be a prerequisite for improving the coopers' conditions. Interestingly, the path forward in the late 1870s seemed to lead back in the direction of politics.

• • •

"Independent" politics was popular across the nation in 1877–1878. "Workingmen's," "Greenback," "farmers'," and "reform" parties mushroomed. Virginia—its state treasury nearly exhausted, its school system in chaos, its economy faltering—was no exception. Black working-class activists watched with interest as former Confederate general and railroad baron William Mahone galvanized small business and small farmer dissatisfaction into a political movement for the "readjustment" of the state debt.

This debt had grown over the 1870s, its amortization made all the more difficult by the depression. The Conservative regime had turned to an austerity program rather than scaling down the debt. Party leaders were committed to the repayment of the debt for several reasons. Many were bondholders themselves and were not about to give up their own claims. Others had close ties to northern and British financiers who were major bondholders. Still others accepted an ideology of southern "honor," which dictated the full repayment of all debts. Many of the manufacturers within the party felt that repayment was necessary to maintain credit ties with European and northern sources of capital.[34]

The depression of the mid-1870s made it difficult to raise revenues by increasing taxes. Many small tradesmen already felt themselves over-taxed, landowners were in severe financial straits, and large industrial and commercial interests opposed any increase in their tax burden. The Conservative administration redirected funds from some areas for purposes of debt repayment. Thus, some $526,000 intended for education was used for debt repayment in 1877, though nine-tenths of Virginia's families were then making use of the public school system. By March 1878, the Richmond school board was considering a shortened school year. The state had given it only $5,188 in educational funds for some 5,656 students; two years earlier, it had received $20,754 for 700 fewer students.[35]

Mahone's commitment to the preservation of the public school system won him an audience among white and black workers. White working-class activists, fearful that the notion of debt readjustment would hurt the credit standing of the state's businesses, had initially rejected it. But they placed great emphasis on the public school system, "education being the keystone of the arch that supports the whole superstructure of society." In the fall of 1877, a group of white workers adopted as part of their "independent" platform: "that the proportion of taxes set apart as the school fund should be held sacred from all encroachments."[36]

Black working-class militants were similarly committed to free public education. Thousands of black children and adults had achieved literacy since Emancipation. Access to schools was an important part of their social perspective. In 1878, for example, seventy-seven black East End residents petitioned the Board of Education for the establishment of a school in their neighborhood. They lived quite a distance from the existing, already overcrowded black schools. The Board denied their request due to "lack of funds." Meanwhile, operating expenses for the schools went unpaid. Richmond's black and white teachers volunteered to work for thirty percent of their wages, with the balance to be paid when expected state funds arrived. School conditions deteriorated quickly—some were threatened with closing—and promised appropriations failed to materialize by the end of 1878.[37]

Black workers, given their concern for public education and their interest in "independent" politics, appeared a potential voter base for Mahone's new movement. Moreover, they felt no obligation for the state debt, much of which had been contracted while they were still slaves. But Mahone and associates held back from an appeal for black support, even as their departure from the Conservative party seemed inevitable. They had carefully nurtured a fragile white base among farmers, small businessmen, and workers, and they feared losing it.[38]

In the short run, the local Greenback movement provided a transitional vehicle. In the fall of 1878, some black militants were drawn to the Greenback party in their search for an independent political voice. White and black Greenback clubs were formed, each led by men experienced in labor organization and independent political action. For the first time, working-class activists of both races cooperated on a shared project, in separate but parallel units of the same organization. Greenback clubs also appeared among both races in Manchester and in rural areas as the congressional campaign of fall 1878 opened.[39]

The overall structure of the Greenback party provided new opportunities and experiences for black militants. It was similar to the sort of organization that they promoted earlier in the Industrial Brotherhood, while it offered new opportunities to the advocates of independent racially based political organization. Outside of "ring" and "anti-ring" factions, it structured an alliance with "reform-minded" whites. It explored the common interests and outlooks of black and white working-class leaders. Popular enthusiasm for the Greenback campaign was low, however, and there was little the militants of either race could do to rekindle it. Virginia's black workers, according to one observer, "have, as a class, been suspicious of the Greenback movement, and not nearly so ready to enter into it as was expected. This is particularly true of the tobacco operatives and more intelligent laborers in and about Richmond and other large cities."[40]

Greenbackers failed to promote any of the issues that concerned black workers. Their campaign, despite the involvement of respected activists, failed to generate any appeal for black Richmond—or anyone else, for that matter. Their third district candidate, a wealthy planter and one-time Conservative state legislator, hardly aroused enthusiasm among urban blacks. Many of them ignored the election altogether. The Greenback candidate received only 641 votes in all of Richmond, most from Jackson Ward. Even there, however, it had not been a contest.[41]

The Greenback campaign did offer black labor militants a bridge to the local Readjuster movement. Ideologically, currency and taxation schemes, they concluded, could provide a common foundation with white "reformers." Organizationally, they had adopted a new creative form: autonomous, racially based units, linked structurally with white units in the pursuit of common goals, and expressed in the language of "labor reform." Black working-class activists had developed a new series of relationships with both

Richmond's white working-class "reformers" and with "readjusters" statewide. Ideologically and practically, they had begun to apply and adapt the notions of "race" and "class" that had begun to take shape in the early and mid-1870s.

CHAPTER 6

Readjusterism and the Rebirth of the Black Popular Movement, 1879–1883

BLACK ACTIVISTS' efforts paid off in the early 1880s. As the economic and political climate changed, broad-based popular activity revived. This new movement bore the marks of the campaigns for both independent racial and black labor organization, yet was also uncomfortably linked to William Mahone's Readjuster party. The latter shook the political status quo from the "New South" to the halls of the Congress. So did black workers throughout Virginia.[1]

The benefits of the postdepression economic recovery were slow to reach Richmond Afro-Americans. Though tobacco manufacturing achieved some stability in the early 1880s, it offered them a constantly shrinking number of jobs. Cigarette manufacturing, the most rapidly growing sector of the industry, was based on the labor of white women. Several manual operations in chewing tobacco manufacture were mechanized, at the cost of many skilled jobs. The Scales Automatic Lump Machine, for instance, displaced twisters and lumpers in one factory after another. Still, close to 5,000 black men, women, and children were employed by the tobacco industry, and their earnings provided the primary foundation for Richmond's social and economic development. Compared to the privations and losses of 1873–1878, the early 1880s opened a range of new possibilities.[2]

The political climate held even more promise. The Readjuster movement split the traditionally unified white camp and handed the balance of power to the black electorate. Suddenly, black working-class activists enjoyed new leverage in their struggle for social and economic improvement. Their efforts were greeted with popular enthusiasm, as a political reawakening swept not just black Richmond, but all of Virginia.[3]

• • •

In March 1879, black delegates from all over the state gathered in Richmond for a public discussion of the relationship between black Virginians and the white Republican leadership. A group of experienced local activists, including Cornelius Harris, Lewis Lindsay, W. J. S. Bowe, Stephen Jones, and some younger tobacco factory workers, had issued the call for this convention. William Roane, an organizer of "equal rights" campaigns in the 1870s and former local correspondent for Frederick Douglass's *New National Era*, was elected chairman. A former schoolteacher, he had just become Richmond's first black lawyer.[4]

This one-day meeting closed with a call for a more formal statewide convention on the first Monday in May, again in Richmond. The delegation also established a "permanent" organization, to promote local discussion and coordinate the planned convention. Cornelius Harris, whose activist credentials dated back to the Constitutional Convention of 1867–1868, was chosen president. The vice-president's post went to Joseph Brown Johnson, a young Manchester barber with extensive local connections. Born and raised a slave in Richmond, he had been in his late teens when the city fell to Union troops in 1865. His parents dead, he had assumed the primary responsibility for his siblings. He learned the barber's trade, learned to read and write at the local freedman's schools in the late 1860s; in 1871, he was elected assistant secretary of the Young Richmond Blues, a militia unit composed largely of tobacco factory workers. Soon afterward, he moved to Manchester to open his own barbershop. Johnson's sister, Caroline, went to work as a domestic servant in the household of former governor Henry A. Wise. With the move to Manchester and the establishment of his own shop, Johnson increased his participation in black popular activity. By 1874, he was an officer in the Faithful Lodge of Good Samaritans, as were community activists J. Anderson Taylor and William Roane. That spring, Johnson was chosen to lead the entire Manchester contingent in the Fifteenth Amendment celebration parade. Devoting an increasing amount of his time to black militia organization, he became the "major"—the highest rank available to blacks—of the First Battalion of the Colored Infantry in 1882. He would later become an organizer for the Knights of Labor and the first black delegate to a General Assembly of the Order in 1885.[5]

The honorific post of convention sergeant-at-arms went to James D. Allen, a respected deacon of the First African Baptist Church. A Richmond native, he, too, had been educated in the freedmen's schools. Now in his early forties, Allen had served as an officer in several church-affiliated secret societies, including the First Star of Jacob and the First Association, with tobacco factory workers as well as small businessmen among the members. A widower, he supported himself and his two children as a delivery wagon driver for John A. Belvin's woodworking shop. Belvin, interestingly, had been a candidate of the "Workingmen's Ticket" of 1877. Thus Allen, like Joseph Brown Johnson, had a personal relationship with white "independent" politicians. The three leading officers of this ad hoc organization,

Harris, Johnson, and Allen, were well-respected in the community and recognized as leaders in nonpolitical affairs, precisely the sort of men who could direct black popular activity as it emerged from the political and economic dark days of the depression.[6]

Assisted by other black activists, these men called mass meetings in prepartion for the May convention. On April 7, 1879, they addressed a large crowd at the First African church and stressed the necessity of gaining black jurors, a long-standing popular demand that the Republican party never supported. Two weeks later, the anniversary of the Fifteenth Amendment was marked by a grand parade, and "oberved by the colored people as a general holiday." Joseph Brown Johnson, as commander of the First Colored Battalion, led the march, which included "four military companies, thirty benevolent societies, two bands of music, a triumphal car, with 38 girls dressed in white, and a large number of carriages." William Roane delivered the oration of the day, to a crowd far in excess of what had been the usual turnout.[7]

Ward meetings convened across Richmond a week before the convention. Each ward elected five delegates, with five alternates. We can get an idea of the growing popular base in 1879 by examining the Jefferson Ward delegates. All possessed characteristics in common: they lacked previous "political" experience, were workingmen, were literate, had families to provide for, and were well-situated within the black social network.[8]

The expanding movement voiced an increased sense of "race pride." Traditional demands for "equal rights" were recast within a new framework, promoted with a new vigor, and backed by a swelling movement. William Roane, who had led fruitless struggles for a number of legal measures in the 1870s—from the Sumner Civil Rights Bill to the placement of black men in the jury box—now, in his capacity as convention chairman, told the assemblage that "it was useless to look to the president and Congress for relief from their grievances. They must help themselves and maintain their rights." Of the fifty-nine delegates who had assembled "for the purpose of considering matters connected with the welfare, rights, and improvement of the colored race," fifty were from Richmond and Manchester. They eagerly endorsed Roane's reformulation of their problems and prospects. Resolutions tinged with "race pride" were passed, including one that called for the organization of all Virginia blacks along strictly racial lines; another resolution threatened white employers with a massive black migration, "provided our condition is not bettered."[9]

The *Richmond State*, a conservative paper, expressed the white establishment's concern with the growing black militancy:

> We find in the tenor of their action, supplemented by violent speech, no hook to hang a hope upon that any good understanding will be reached in the near future by which the two races may act together in political harmony or unity, save through our surrender of everything that distinguishes our race as the

> superior of theirs in all its moral, intellectual, and physical characteristics, traits, conditions, and traditions. They are not, it seems, willing to accept their logical status, but would violate every principle of the ethics of class established by the immutable laws of nature.[10]

On May 28, Harris, Bowe, Roane, Johnson, and J. Anderson Taylor presented a petition to Judge Christian asking that blacks be allowed to serve on juries in the Hustings Court. It was an issue of major importance to the black community. Between 1870 and 1892, over 500 black men were convicted of felony or petit larceny in this court and were "thereby disfranchised." Judge Christian added insult to injury. In turning down their petition, he claimed that "quality" and not race was his concern in picking juries.[11]

The movement continued to grow and develop. The following month, Bowe, Harris, and Thomas Hewlett began publishing the *Criterion*. Hewlett, a carpenter and active Methodist, had organized a black cooperative building society in 1868 and had been an officer in the Odd Fellows as well as the Friendly Sons of Temperance. In 1871 he had been elected one of the twenty-four vice-presidents of the local branch of the Colored National Labor Union. His participation, like that of other experienced activists, was indicative of the spread of new ideas and of the ability of the reviving popular movement to integrate older perspectives with new ideas. Respected veterans of community activity in the 1860s and early 1870s joined with younger men who had promoted community issues in the depression years to provide the active core of the reawakened black popular movement.[12]

• • •

These activists faced a difficult question—what stance to take in the state political campaign in the fall of 1879. Black Virginians made up almost one third of the electorate and held the balance of power after the Conservative party split in two. Still, a distrust of both factions informed black activism, and finding a comfortable political role was no easy matter.[13]

Blacks knew what the Conservatives stood for—white supremacy. Senatorial candidate Robert Withers, on the stump in the heart of Southside Virginia's "black belt," "raised the flag of the white race in the face of a large crowd of Negroes present" in Petersburg. He publicly spurned black voters, claiming "they neither possessed information or intelligence to enable them to decide matters of statecraft." Another prominent Conservative publicly opposed "the common school education of the Negro, . . . on the grounds that the Negro does not need it to fit him for the right of suffrage, since the Negro will soon be stripped of that right."[14]

But the Readjusters hardly inspired black faith. Though claiming that their role was to "crystallize the sentiments of the people and enforce them" against "the rings and court-house cliques, the brokers, and the broker press," they remained silent on black issues. In the fall the Readjusters, eager for votes, suddenly made a direct appeal for black support. But their offer remained vague, and black suspicions were hardly put to rest.[15]

In Richmond and throughout Virginia, black activists remained aloof from the Readjuster organization: The *Virginia Star* reprinted an editorial from the *Washington People's Advocate*, which urged Virginia black voters to reject the Readjusters. In a letter to the *Star*, John Oliver, former president of the local CNLU, urged blacks to avoid all parties in the fall of 1879. In place of party politics, he suggested concentration on specific issues, such as the right of blacks to serve on juries, and their promotion by tightly organized black voting blocs. "There is no other method within our reach but to nerve ourselves with becoming determined not to be the willing subjects of our political oppressors."[16]

National Republican leaders counselled opposition to the Readjusters. President Hayes announced his personal hostility to Readjustment and urged blacks to spurn all forms of financial "repudiation." Grant, Blaine, Sherman, and even Frederick Douglass lent their voices to the anti-Mahone campaign.[17]

Black activists guarded their independence in the fall campaign, while promoting black political organization. They knew that the state's political climate afforded blacks new opportunities, as they held the potential balance of power between the Conservatives and the Readjusters. They hoped independent racial organization could wrest specific concessions from the political parties that courted the black vote. While some black political organizations termed themselves "Readjuster," and others "Republican," the underlying thrust was an independence from all white control.[18]

• • •

The newly divided white vote did indeed create a political opening for black Virginians. Twelve black men were elected to the House of Delegates and two to the State Senate in the fall of 1879. The Readjusters themselves captured half of the State Senate and forty-one of the one hundred seats in the House of Delegates. Hence, the black legislators held the balance of power in both houses.[19]

Black Virginians looked on with interest when the new legislature convened in December 1879. What would the black lawmakers do? What would the Readjusters do? The white Republican apparatus announced its hostility to Readjustment and had the support of President Hayes. The latter even sent emmissaries to Richmond to urge an alliance between the Virginia Republicans and the "Funders." It was rumored that if the Republicans could throw the balance of power in their direction, the Conservatives would elect a white Republican to the United States Senate. But, to seal the bargain, the Republicans would need to control the black legislators.[20]

White Republican pressure on these fourteen black legislators was countered from two critical sources. William Mahone himself took the initiative in approaching them on behalf of the Readjusters. Behind the scene, "he met with them repeatedly, indicating his willingness to fight for improved Negro schools, the abolition of the whipping post, and a variety of other reforms. What was more, the little general promised the freedmen a voice in patronage matters, a share of the government jobs." He even invited them to join the Readjuster "caucus" as equal members.[21]

Black Richmond itself was the second source of pressure on these lawmakers. Once these men took up residence within the community, they were subject to popular sentiments expressed in mass meetings, political organizations, and the local black press. The black legislators themselves attended local black churches and were called upon to participate in social and political activities. Local black sentiments expressed mounting support for the Readjusters, a message the black legislators could hardly have missed. Black activists were rapidly moving into the Readjuster camp, though they maintained an independent racial organization. They organized meetings in November 1879—as the new legislature was about to convene—to express community sentiment. A Manchester gathering was chaired by Martin Woolridge, secretary of the local organization that had coordinated the black state convention in May. This meeting, like others, unanimously endorsed the Readjusters. Black legislators could hardly miss popular support for acceptance of Mahone's offer. On December 3, all fourteen joined the Readjuster caucus.[22]

Their votes enabled the Readjusters to control the General Assembly and to elect Mahone to the United States Senate. The Readjusters, in turn, appointed blacks to a variety of minor patronage posts and addressed black grievances. They immediately put pressure on judges to admit blacks to juries, for example, and made a concerted effort to revive the school system. These campaigns yielded immediate and tangible results. In late March 1880, Judge Christian placed blacks on a Hustings Court jury for the first time. By the end of 1880, the number of black schools in Virginia had nearly doubled over 1879, as had the number of black pupils attending school. The new alliance appeared to be paying off handsomely.[23]

• • •

Despite these accomplishments, and the growing popular enthusiasm for the Readjuster movement, independent black political organization persisted. The black legislators themselves raised a number of questions—intermarriage, lynching, the integration of restaurants—that the Readjusters did not support. Their independence within the legislature mirrored that of black political organization within society at large. Building from the emergent popular movement, black activists sought to adapt the traditional strengths of community organization to the opportunities presented by the new political alignment. They cultivated racial organization as an independent base from which to promote specific issues within the Readjuster-led "reform" movement.[24]

In late January 1880, new black ward committees were elected in Richmond. The very political identification of each committee was in question, as "straight-out" Republican and pro-Readjuster factions battled for control. In Clay Ward, Lewis Lindsay headed the Readjuster supporters in a successful sweep of the ward committee. Jackson Foster, a deacon at the First African Baptist Church and a leader of a lodge of the Good Samaritans, directed the victorious pro-Readjuster effort to control Jackson Ward. The Madison Ward committee, long the stronghold of the "Customs House ring," splintered. The pro-Readjuster bloc could not wrest control of the committee from the entrenched patronage machine, but would not accept its leadership any more.[25]

The Madison Ward schism merits special scrutiny. Those challenging the dominant faction were respected members of their community, long-time residents of Richmond and officers of secret societies. Robert A. Paul had been born a slave in Nelson County in 1846 and, with his mother, had come to Richmond after the war. He worked as a waiter, learned to read and write, and found time for independent study of mathematics, American, English, and ancient history, and even for Blackstone's Commentaries. He became a member of the Knights Templar, the Knights of Pythias, and the Masons; he was elected captain of a local militia unit; and he served on the Board of Stewards of the Third Street AME Church. Paul first became active politically in 1874, when he spoke, with little success, at mass meetings in opposition to the rule of the "ring" within the Republican party. Disenchanted, he had withdrawn from politics until 1878, when he became a local organizer for the Greenback campaign. Paul had not participated in the fall 1879 Readjuster campaign, but turned to the insurgents on the basis of their legislative record. Thirty-three years old, he now worked as a clerk in a grocery store and with his wife rented an apartment in a black neighborhood in Madison Ward. He would soon become one the the city's most prominent black leaders.[26]

The two men who led the Madison Ward campaign with Paul were not unlike him, although they never achieved his prominence. Collin T. Payne was also an officer in the black militia, in the Attucks Guard. A tailor by trade, he had not found it easy to support his growing family; but by 1870, his wife and two young children enjoyed a comfortable apartment in a good neighborhood in Jefferson Ward. After briefly holding a patronage job at the Customs House, he was removed and returned to tailoring in 1873. This trade was anything but lucrative in the depression years of 1873–1878. By 1880, with four children to support, Payne's wife took in washing and boarders to supplement his meager wages. Their household included three single washerwomen and their children, along with four single tobacco factory workers. Payne had certainly seen hard times in the 1870s, and he had personal as well as political reasons for challenging the Customs House "ring."[27]

Winston H. Bannister, a more experienced community activist than Payne, found much security in Richmond. He and his family were deeply enmeshed in secret society relationships. Bannister himself had been an officer in the Secret Sons of Love and had been president of the True Laboring Class No. 1. He was also a popular singer in the First African Baptist Church choir. A tobacco factory worker, Bannister was unable to support his growing family. With six children he could little afford the four-month layoff in 1879. His wife, still nursing their youngest child, could not contribute to the family income. Like Collin Payne, Winston Bannister had shared little of the renewed "prosperity" of 1879–1880. Like many others, they turned to collective efforts in early 1880 to create social conditions in which black people might thrive.[28]

Independent black political expression and organization flowed back and forth between the community network and political organizations. By early February 1880, over twenty local black Readjuster "clubs" had been organized; they supplemented the formal ward committees and linked them to the broader social network. Political figures were integrated into this matrix and articulated "social" as well as "political" concerns. R. G. L. Paige, a black member of the House of Delegates from Norfolk, and local activist William Roane, recently admitted to the bar, threatened to bring a suit against the Richmond Theater when they were refused admittance because the "colored gallery" was closed. Black state senator C. L. Davis made an unsuccessful attempt to obtain service in a "whites-only" restaurant; then, forced to leave, he raised a public protest. While the promotion of such "social" issues tended to distance black activists from their erstwhile white allies, it tied them to the local popular movement.[29]

On February 9, 1880, Paige joined local militants William Roane, Cornelius Harris, and Martin Woolridge to convene a meeting at the black Odd Fellows Hall. Twenty-five veteran activists mapped out a strategy to unseat the established leadership of the Republican party and deliver its resources and ranks to the Readjuster movement. Their plan entailed the promotion of popular politics and mass organizing. Within six weeks, this core group had organized several mass meetings. Other veteran and respected black working-class activists added their efforts and reputations to the movement: John Oliver, J. Anderson Taylor, and William H. Lester, all CNLU officers in the early 1870s, and Jackson Foster, a prominent neighborhood leader in Jackson Ward. Like a social magnet, the revived popular movement attracted activists from the far corners of black Richmond.[30]

• • •

One group—the young educated professionals of the "new" black middle class that took shape in the 1880s—played a particularly important role. A *New York Times* correspondent characterized them as "young, keen, and intelligent politicians, . . . who have enjoyed educational advantages of which their fathers were deprived, and are now ready to go into political combination which assures to them the rights of citizenship, greater opportunities for material advancement, and a share of the public offices." These young men—R. A. Paul, William C. Roane, O. M. Stewart, and Dr. John C. Ferguson among them—lent their oratorical and literary skills to the movement. They provided much of black Richmond's public voice through the *Criterion* and the *Virginia Star*, their independent newspapers. By means of these vehicles, they articulated popular race-consciousness, which grew throughout black Richmond.[31]

A new generation, raised as free children, led the way to race-consciousness. They were the most vocal and enthusiastic advocates of this perspective. By 1890, more than half the Richmond black population had been born since 1865, and two-thirds of the others had been children or young teen-agers when emancipated. They had been raised within a cohesive network of black mutual assistance, baptized into black-controlled churches, and educated in all-black classrooms. Old enough to have experienced the duplicity and hostility of whites, old enough not to see themselves in terms of the "Republican Ark," they gravitated toward a militant race pride.[32]

Within this generation, the core of a new black middle class developed. It comprised teachers, editors, publishers, lawyers, doctors, professionally trained ministers, and a few businessmen. They were products of the collective efforts of the black community since 1865, and their ability to prosper rested upon the further improvement of that community. Outspoken advocates of collective support for black institutions and businesses, they led the battle for the employment of black teachers and clerks in the public sector. While advocating the improvement of the entire community, they emphasized opportunity for individual upward mobility. George W. Williams, in his widely read *History of the Negro Race in America*, published in 1883, wrote: "Waiters, porters, barbers, boot-blacks, hack-drivers, grooms, and private valets find but little time for the expansion of their intellects. Their places are not dishonourable; but what we say is, there is room at the top." They spoke in terms of "the race," and saw themselves as its "representative men."[33]

These young women and men saw themselves as distinct from other blacks. They organized a number of select secret societies geared to their own improvement, education, or entertainment: the Chautauqua Literary and Scientific Circle, the Acme Literary Association, the Palmetto Club, Knights of King Solomon, and the Grand Fountain United Order of True Redeemers. They also joined established lodges of the Masons and the Knights Templar. Their activity ranged from masquerade balls and social festivities to debates on politics, economics, and the "future of the race." Taken together, these new institutions and activities provided them with a growing sense of class cohesion.[34]

They believed they were fulfilling a special role within the community. As "representative men of the race," they expected their own achievements to inspire others to emulate them and improve themselves. R. A. Paul, referring to his prolonged struggle for education and self-improvement, advised: "By a proper improvement of time, the day laborer and the mechanic, the clerk and the businessman, may so develop the several faculties as to stand by the side of those who have grown up in the full blaze of a collegiate education." Lawyer and community activist E. A. Randolph published a biography of John Jasper, a controversial minister in frequent demand among whites because of his sermon, "The Sun Do Move and the Earth Do Stand Still." For Randolph, the key element of Jasper's life was that he had been a "self-made man," and thus an example for his community. The local black press lauded the economic accomplishments of community members and listed their net worth as a measure of the community's success. The *New York Globe* Richmond correspondent observed: "Much progress is being made by the colored people of this city, and the neat stores that we notice here and there show that our people realize their needs."[35]

Young middle-class militants saw their role as providing leadership and an example to the community. The Acme Literary Association, for instance, claimed to "consider questions of vital importance to our people, so that the masses of them may be drawn out to be entertained, enlightened, and instructed thereby." They invited the public to their lectures and discussions on topics such as "The Trades" and "The Vexed Problem: Labor," held in the city's larger black churches.[36]

This new middle class was critical of many social practices that were popular in the black community. Intemperance caught their attention. Traditional excursions were criticized as encouraging their participants to skip work and become spendthrifts. The hostility of black church leaders to secular dancing was publicly discussed. Robert Chiles, the Richmond *Industrial Herald*'s youthful editor and an active member of this new middle class, spoke for it:

> A great reformation is needed among the large masses of the colored people in the South, who are yet in the wilderness of ignorance, oppression, and helplessness. Few and far between are the educated colored men of our race and among our people who are trying to lead up to higher planes of life, to broaden fields of action, to a nobler race-pride and a unification of purpose, the millions of our benighted people.[37]

The middle class's function, then, was to guide the community in these directions. R. A. Paul told the Acme Literary Association: "The men to lead the Negro should be selected with great care, because the masses of his people are, from circumstances over which they have no control, ignorant, and hence they are easily deceived by dishonest, trading politicians." Men are needed—men with "common sense, courage, and honesty"—to persuade the "African American to lay aside all differences and contend, with pride of race and love of fireside, for the general welfare." Should such leaders be successful, "the future prospects of the Negro for acquiring wealth and education, for receiving due recognition and power, are bright and glorious."[38]

This new black middle-class program was clear: The black community should support black businesses and professional occupations, especially in institutions that directly served them, and they should promote education by the public schools and apprenticeship. As individuals, blacks should be temperate, hard-working, and thrifty. In politics, they should look to the educated, articulate, and honest men in the community, those with "pride of race." Formal politics should be emphasized. R. A. Paul claimed: "When we say that, to our mind, the politician is as of much importance to the political liberties of the people as the minister of the Gospel is to the salvation of the souls of men, we speak in all sincerity."[39]

Though the social distance between them and the black working class loomed large, these militant professionals provided evolving popular attitudes with an articulate voice. Their references to "the race," and their advocacy of independent racial organization touched responsive chords in black Richmond. As the black popular movement reemerged in 1880, it understood itself in these new terms—and it demonstrated its independence of white organizations and control.

• • •

By late spring 1880, the popular movement had already overflowed formal political channels in a flood tide of activism. Changes in popular consciousness shook institutions inside, as well as outside, black Richmond. Even the venerable First African Baptist Church was in turmoil. In April, Henry Buford, a lay preacher, led a challenge to Reverend Holmes and the board of deacons, which involved several hundred male and female parishioners and some outside activists as well. Buford charged Holmes with "unchristianlike conduct" towards several female members of the congregation and called for a vote on removing him. After several disorderly meetings, which went on until 2:00 and 3:00 A.M., the vote was taken. Holmes, supported by the deacons, barely withstood the challenge. But the struggle was far from over.[40]

Holmes and the deacons continued to face a vocal opposition that threatened established authority within the church in unpecedented ways. Henry Buford served as opposition spokesman because of his position as a lay preacher within the church. Born a slave in Rockingham county, he had come to Richmond as a teen-ager in 1865. He went to work in Pace's tobacco factory, joined the First African church, and attended night school, where he learned to read and write. By 1870, he headed a growing family and was elected a trustee of Combination No. 14, one of several loosely affiliated secret societies that grouped men who worked at a variety of jobs in tobacco factories and warehouses. Though granted a license to preach by the First African church in 1878, Buford had remained a tobacco factory worker.[41]

The church's monthly business meeting in May found the congregation deeply divided, with factions on opposite sides of the aisle. The "rebels" refused to allow the deacons to proceed with normal business until the Holmes question was reconsidered. The deacons called in the police, and they cleared the church. A month later, the reconvened meeting again found the congregation divided. Susan Washington, long a church member and secret society officer—and sister of Winston Bannister, a prominent advocate of black cooperation with the Readjusters—presented a petition signed by more than 200 female parishioners asking for the right to vote in church affairs. Disorder reigned, and the deacons again called the police. This time, the rebellious faction left en masse, and the deacons went on with their meeting.[42]

The deacons then considered a list of forty-seven men that Holmes wanted excluded for "rebelliously attempting to overthrow and seize upon the church government." Familiar names of this list alert us to both the social and political character of the "rebel" faction. Two deacons headed the list—F. A. Williams and Clairborne Storrs. Williams, a tobacco factory worker, had been a delegate to the May 1879 black state convention. Storrs, a blacksmith, had been an officer in the United Sons of Adam as well as a church deacon, and his family lived next door to veteran tobacco factory activist Stephen Jones and his family. The list of expelled members also included O. M. Stewart, the editor of the *Virginia Star*, and political militants William Roane and Edinboro Archer.[43]

Thus, the political struggle reached the church in the form of a "rebellion" mounted by a significant portion of the membership and led by race organization and pro-Readjuster militants. These were women and men deeply rooted in black Richmond's social network and attracted to the new ideas that had begun to circulate through it. Tobacco factory workers, skilled craftsmen, and small shopkeepers joined with new middle-class advocates of "race pride" like O. M. Stewart and William Roane. They had found the leadership of the First African Baptist Church unresponsive to their new concerns and perceptions. Unable to supplant them, the militants organized the Fifth Street Baptist Church, were joined by several hundred former First African members, and applied to the Shiloh Baptist Association for recognition and affiliation. Though their petition was opposed by the First African's deacons, the Association granted them recognition.

The deacons of the First African church later complained that, by taking such action, the other congregations had

> . . . recognized the right of expelled and disorderly persons to call a council, and they also set them apart and received them into fellowship as a regular Baptist Church, thus stepping in between us and the proper subjects of our discipline, and forcibly taking out of our hands the jurisdiction which properly belonged to us, bidding defiance to the rights which we, as a Baptist Church, had in the matter.[44]

That Richmond's other black Baptist congregation would "extend their hand of fellowship" to a rebellion against the leadership of Richmond's most prominent black church was an indication of the depth of the growing popular movement.

The involvement of women and the extension of the conflict into the church itself reflected deep-seated changes in popular consciousness. Similar indications bubbled to the surface all over Richmond. Wealthy whites complained about their inability to secure satisfactory black servants. One dissatisfied employer wrote the *Dispatch* of a job applicant who "'longed to siety' and must have every Wednesday and Saturday afternoon off for the purpose of mingling with the Loving Daughters of Ruth." Black children participated in this upswell. During the fall 1883 campaign, black newsboys refused to sell the Democratic paper and pressured their white counterparts to do the same.[45]

There was growing popular support for the construction of a large black hall, for entertainment purposes as well as meetings. "It is one that will protect us from insult. Today we cannot go into the Richmond Theater, no matter how much money we pay, unless we go into the part known as the 'peanut gallery.'" In 1883, the seniors and staff of the Richmond Normal School voted to hold graduation ceremonies in one of the school's small classrooms, rather than to accept the ample, but segregated, facilities at the Richmond Theater.[46]

Race consciousness and race organization, mixed with themes of "class" and "labor," provided the social and ideological framework for emergent black Richmond. An announcement of the Virginia Building and Savings Company suggests the broad applicability of the new perspective:

> To the Officers of Churches, Institutions, and Societies:
>
> It gives us great pleasure to inform you of this company as a convenient and safe depository for your money. We confidently appeal to you to deposit your money with us, believing that you are willing by this method to aid us in promoting industry among our people. By combining our means great good can be accomplished. For "In Union There is Strength." We desire to encourage and support our mechanics, and to supply capital and business for our merchants.[47]

• • •

Black militants capitalized on Richmond's fluid political situation. They promoted independent popular activity and employed it as a means by which to wrest control of the local Republican apparatus from the "ring." In April 1880, they tried to capture Republican party ward meetings that were held to elect delegates to the upcoming GOP state convention. The convention itself was to be held in Staunton, which white party leaders had chosen as a safe distance from the volatile and influential Richmond black community. The militants sought to elect delegates pledged to "coalition" with the Readjusters, to push the party from within. Local ward meetings were organized in early April, as militants worked to build popular support for their strategy. They were successful in Monroe, Marshall, Clay, and Jefferson wards—in bitter contests—but were defeated by the "ring" and its patronage machine in Jackson and Madison wards. But even the defeats had their partial victories. John Oliver was elected an alternate from Jackson Ward; thus he would gain admittance to the convention. Madison Ward insurgents had caucused on their own and decided to send R. A. Paul to challenge that ward's official representative. Thus, a predominantly black Richmond delegation committed to "coalition" left for Staunton in late April.[48]

R. A. Paul fought for his seat on the convention floor. His "scathing speech" against the "illegal meetings" operated by the "ring" won him widespread support among the delegates. Victorious, he then led the struggle for cooperation with the Readjusters. "There is no difference between the Readjusters and the Republicans so far as equal rights before the law are concerned," Paul contended. Many of the delegates, however, were already committed to the "ring," and others feared a Readjuster alliance would hurt the candidacy of their favorite Republican, U. S. Grant, in his quest for a third term as president. Hayes's administration had been disastrous for Virginia blacks, and many hoped that Grant could gain the nomination and return the GOP to its "radical" traditions. But Paul and his supporters were unable to carry the convention, and the Virginia Republican party publicly repudiated the Readjusters.[49]

Local activists continued to promote independent racial organization; the Readjusters accommodated them. They nominated candidates for city council in May 1880. They ran a full slate in every ward except Jackson, which was left unchallenged in the hands of black activists. As a result, four black men were elected to the city council and one, to the board of aldermen. The Readjusters hoped to receive black voting support in the other wards in exchange for this cooperation. While support was forthcoming, it was drastically limited by poll tax and disfranchisement clause restrictions. Though black militants had won in Jackson Ward, their white Readjuster allies were defeated throughout the city.[50]

This defeat, however, did not deter the black popular movement, which drew on extrapolitical as well as political sources. As one "highly intelligent young colored man" told a northern reporter: "Now for the first time colored men begin to feel that they are men." There were many ways to express this. When, for example, veteran political activist Joseph Cox died in April 1880, some 3,000 blacks marched in his funeral procession. Lewis Lindsay, Cornelius Harris, and Jackson Ward city councilor Richard Forrester—all promoters of "coalition" with the Readjusters—led the impressive parade.[51]

Local GOP officials attempted to reign in the popular movement by manipulating black loyalties to their party's national ticket. Though Grant, the black's favorite, had not won the nomination, James Garfield, the party candidate, had a reasonably good reputation among Afro-Americans. In late July, the Republican leadership created a "Central Garfield and Arthur Club," with delegates from recently organized clubs in Richmond and Manchester. They intended to keep this network under their control, and use it to channel the energies bubbling within the black popular movement.[52]

Much to their chagrin, black insurgents seized control of these clubs and turned them against the white party bosses. John W. Johnson, a delegate to the Readjuster state convention, became chair of the Monroe Ward Garfield and Arthur Club. A literate but propertyless shoemaker, he had been an officer in no less than seven secret societies in the 1860s and 1870s. Charles W. Thomspon, a widely respected advocate of independent labor organization, headed the Manchester Club. Black activists ran their own Garfield and Arthur campaign, autonomous from the GOP apparatus.[53]

Meanwhile, Mahone and his Readjusters, fearful of losing the white votes they so tenuously held, gave their support to Winfield S. Hancock, the Democratic candidate for president. Black militants then rejected the Readjusters, despite their falling out with the Republican bosses. None attended the Third District Readjuster convention in Richmond in August. Even Jackson Ward's delegation was all white. Nor did any blacks participate in the organization of a Readjuster City Executive Committee in September. Three white men represented Jackson Ward.[54]

Richmond Afro-Americans spurned both political parties in the November elections. They supported a "split" ticket of their own making—the Republican Garfield for president and Readjuster John S. Wise for Congress. They promoted their candidates through a network of popular organizations: ward committees, Garfield and Arthur clubs, Readjusters clubs, and secret societies. While both candidates ultimately lost, the continued independence of black popular organization was the real winner.[55]

• • •

The presidential campaign had torn the Readjusters apart, and their electoral ticket finished a poor third statewide in November. Mahone and his aides charted a new course in the wake of their defeat. They would make an overt appeal for black support. Party spokesmen throughout the state laid new emphasis on equal rights, criticized discrimination, and offered a larger share of patronage positions to blacks. Mahone initiated discussions with the Garfield administration, and, as a United States Senator, moved toward a Washington-based alliance with the Republican party.[56]

This shift in Readjuster strategy was a mixed blessing for black activists. On the one hand, they welcomed the new interest in "black" issues and new willingness to provide some patronage rewards. On the other hand, the new national alliance between Mahone and the GOP apparatus held out the danger that local party bosses would manipulate it to co-opt the black popular movement. Working-class activists found the maintenance of independent organization difficult, especially when facing such astute politicians as William C. Wickham, John S. Wise, and William Mahone. These men had once been their dangerous enemies, but now, as friends, they could be treacherous. Their thinking is reflected in this letter to Mahone, written by a Richmond associate after the November 1880 elections.

> I would suggest the formation of colored clubs under colored management. . . . All this must seem to emanate from the negro. . . . Unless you can effect this organization you will fail to control the negro. After you get it up, then Col. Brady, . . . and others, together with the local white Republican Readjusters to help, we can utilize the organization with all its power.[57]

Whether the Readjusters would actually be able to co-opt independent black organization remained an open question. The Republicans had certainly never been able to do so. Now, ironically, the GOP leadership itself contributed to the ability of black political groups to continue independent of white control. In mid-January 1881, GOP Chairman Wickham announced plans for a Republican state convention in the spring. Delegates who had participated in Readjuster activities were to be barred from this meeting. In response, black activists called for a state convention of their own to organize support for the Readjusters in the 1881 state elections. They beat the party bosses to the punch, and had an independent organization on solid footing before Wickham could even convene his delegates.[58]

The local black popular movement, its working-class features more pronounced than ever, grew apace the spring and summer of 1881. In May, black brickmakers in Richmond and Manchester struck for an additional fifty cents a day per four-man work group. Experienced with organization and encouraged by the improving local economic climate—a building boom coincided with the beginning of the brickmaking season—more than one hundred men walked off the job at a dozen or more "yards." Their employers gave in a day after the strike began.[59]

The popular movement soon reached the Tredegar Iron Works, where skilled black ironworkers founded a lodge of the Amalgamated Association of Iron and Steel Workers shortly after the National Lodge voted to admit blacks on an equal basis with whites. Although the lodges of the Amalgamated were instructed to avoid political matters, these black workers publicly named their union the "Sumner Lodge," in honor of the recently deceased radical Republican. Once excluded from the union, scorned by the national labor press, and considered a potential source of strikebreakers, these Tredegar ironworkers manifested an impressive commitment to trade unionism. When a northern labor recruiter came to Richmond to find skilled black ironworkers to break a strike at the Pittsburgh Black Diamond Works, he had little success. A black union member explained in a letter to a national labor newspaper:

> A minister from Parke's church [the Black Diamond Work's owner was named Parke] came to this city two weeks ago preaching anti-unionism; but the brother was too late, for he found that the true gospel of the A. A. of I. & S. W. had been preached, and all the darkeys of any account had been converted, baptized, and received the right hand of fellowship in the union.[60]

The multidimensional black popular movement reached new proportions in the summer of 1881. Born in an atmosphere of conflict—with white Republican leaders, conservative black forces, and employers—this movement spoke with an increasingly independent and militant voice. The Richmond *State*'s description of R. A. Paul as a "very impudent and forward negro, who pushed himself everywhere and who by his officiousness and persistent demand for recognition has rendered himself very offensive and annoying . . ." might well have described the popular campaign itself.[61]

In this setting, the Readjuster state convention assembled in Richmond in June 1881. It offered local black activists an opportunity to influence that party's direction and to extend their own plans for statewide black political organization. Of the 756 delegates, more than 100 were black, and most boarded in the local black community during the convention. Led by R. A. Paul, Richmond militants played an active role in the sessions. Both the final platform and the ticket reflected their efforts. The delegates voted to repeal the poll tax, remove disfranchisement as a penalty for conviction of petty larceny, eliminate the disabilities imposed on those already disfranchised, dismantle the whipping post, promote free public education, and build an insane asylum for black mental patients. Mahone urged the convention to excise "all race distinctions from Virginia law." Both of the party's standard bearers enjoyed the respect of black activists. Gubernatorial candidate William Cameron was the popular mayor of Petersburg, Virginia's largest city with a black majority. In his acceptance speech, he told the assemblage: "I don't propose to carry the war to Africa, but to carry Africa into the war." His running mate, John F. Lewis, was a well-known agrarian radical from "the Valley," long respected as an opponent of "rings" and "cliques" in both major parties. Hence, the Readjuster ticket, as well as the party platform, reflected the strength of the black popular movement. Never before had a political party so expressed widely felt black perspectives.[62]

• • •

In mid-1881, black activists and the popular causes they promoted were enjoying their greatest influence since the days of the "black and tan" Constitutional Convention. Their new alliance with the Readjuster party, which was capturing every major elective office in the state, symbolized and institutionalized this new influence. But their "victory," which generated complex repercussions, altered the course of the black popular movement. As the Readjusters publicly adopted one black issue after another, they put themselves forward as the central expression of the popular movement. The black activists' dream of a powerful political body linked to reliable white allies and promoting black issues had become a reality. Suddenly welcomed into the Readjuster fold with apparently open arms, militants muted their emphasis on independent political organization. R. A. Paul, for example, urged the formal dissolution of the Republican party, even though the GOP had been captured by black insurgents and used as an independent base for political expression in many parts of the city and the state.[63]

The Readjusters altered their own local structure. They sought to integrate all local party groups. A black activist from Petersburg later recalled the new rule: "Colored and white Readjusters, in their local assemblies, should meet as one body; if the chairman were white, the secretary should be colored, and if the chairman was colored, the secretary should be white." Black activists welcomed this new recognition, endorsing the integration of local Readjuster units.[64]

In November 1881, following one of the most heated gubernatorial campaigns in Virginia's history, the Readjusters captured the governorship by twelve thousand votes and solidified their control of the legislature. Their black base was undeniable. Of the state's thirty-two counties with black majorities, Cameron carried twenty-eight. Fifteen black state legislators were elected. In Richmond itself, Jackson Ward was the bulwark of Readjuster strength.[65]

The Readjusters put their legislative power to work, and kept most of their promises on the race question. The state debt was slashed, and the state's tax structure was reformed. The revenues made available were devoted to educational and social services. New black schools were opened, along with a new black college and an insane asylum. Enrollment in black schools skyrocketed from 36,000 in 1879 to 91,000 in 1883. The poll tax was repealed and the whipping post was abolished. Readjuster-appointed judges placed blacks on juries throughout the state. Patronage jobs, now in the hands of the Readjusters, were liberally distributed.[66]

The Readjuster appointive practices gave blacks a greater voice in the direction and operation of black schools. In March 1882, for example, Cornelius Harris, Stephen Jones, John Oliver, and black city councilor Nelson Vandervall convened a mass meeting at the Ebenezer Church, to urge the employment of black teachers and principals in black schools. The Readjusters proved willing to meet this demand. The number of black teachers in Virginia tripled to 1,300. In Richmond itself, black principals as well as teachers were placed in black schools. Black East End residents were finally given the school that they had sought for years, and John Oliver's Moore Street Industrial School was integrated into the public school system. Occasioning much political turmoil, R. A. Paul and Richard Forrester were appointed to the Board of Education, the first black men to fill such posts in the city's history. The Readjusters had thus accommodated themselves; by meeting demands to enlarge black control of public institutions, they earned the deeply felt gratitude of the black community. A mass meeting at the First African church hailed the appointment of Paul and Forrester as proof that the Readjusters were "activated by the great principles of equal political and civil rights for all classes, irrespective of race and color."[67]

As the Readjusters delivered their promises, black gratitude toward them grew apace. The *Virginia Star*, a critical voice of local black political expression, described approvingly "What the Readjusters have done for the Colored people":

> The Readjusters have (1) Abolished the whipping post; (2) Re-enfranchised the colored people of Virginia; (3) Made free speech possible; (4) Commenced the obliteration of the color line in politics and in civil intercourse; (5) Put judges on the bench who do not condemn a prisoner because he is black nor acquit him because he is white; (6) Put colored men on our school boards and appointed colored teachers to teach in our colored schools; (7) Nearly doubled the number of our public free schools, and are still increasing them. Besides, they have paid back nearly a million dollars to the school fund which was stolen from it by the Bourbon state government which preceded them; (8) Reduced the rate of taxation 20 percent and forbade the burdensome penalty against delinquent tax-payers in cities; all this reduction, and more (9) They have appropriated $100,000 to found a college, with an annuity of $30,000, for the higher education of our colored youth; (10) They have put colored doctors in our lunatic asylum; colored clerks in our state government departments, and appointed colored persons to other important positions.[68]

• • •

The stunning success of the Readjuster movement proved less than beneficial to the black popular movement. On the one hand, these political victories weakened the drive to maintain independent racial organization, the very drive that had infused the reawakening of popular activity. On the other hand, Readjusterism did not build new bridges between blacks and reform-minded whites in Richmond. Ironically, the "insurgent" movement brought black voters back under the influence of the Republican "ring."

The enjoyment of the fruits of political victory muted the voices of once outspoken black militants. Rewarded with patronage appointments, black political activists drifted into new social and political circles. R. A. Paul was appointed Governor Cameron's personal messenger. Despite the valuable experience it might bring, this patronage position took him out of the black community for most of each day. When serving on the Richmond School Board, he had to function differently from the neighborhood stump speaker of earlier years. His biographer noted approvingly: "His intimate association with men of eminence and worth has taught him to consider with impartiality the views of opponents." Paul, it should be cautioned, did anything but "sell out" the popular movement. While on the school board, for example, he was instrumental in gaining jobs for black teachers and principals. "Had not the bold and gallant Paul uncompromisingly contended for colored principals, it would have been impossible to choose them." Yet his ability to articulate the vision of the popular movement diminished, even as he successfully promoted its concerns among white politicians. In 1885, he told the Acme Literary Association: "We do not mean that white men must be dispensed with as leaders. On the contrary, we must encourage them to act in harmony with our leaders, and in time of political warfare we should be willing to allow them to name the commander-in-chief of the united forces.[69]

Other black activists experienced similar shifts, subtle changes in relationships and outlook. Lewis Lindsay was given a patronage job in the post office, in the hopes that he would "do good service" for the Readjuster party. Mahone himself noted privately several years later: "Lindsay has been a useful and consistent friend of the party." William C. Roane also received a patronage appointment and gave up his legal practice in the community to accept a clerkship in the post office. Dr. John C. Ferguson, the city's only black doctor, was appointed assistant superintendent of the new Central Lunatic Asylum. Because it was located in Petersburg, he had to leave his black Richmond patients to take the job. To refuse these appointments would have been unthinkable, but to accept them was to leave the context of the black social network.[70]

As black activists were increasingly integrated into the Readjuster party, they became free from their earlier dependence on the black popular movement. O. M. Stewart, editor of the *Virginia Star*, assumed the leadership of local Readjuster clubs and turned his paper into an open advocate of the Readjuster party as the answer to black problems. In September 1883, he wrote to Mahone that "we have done what we could in our feeble way to mould public opinion amongst our race in favor of the great liberal movement of which you are the acknowledged leaders." Stewart and other black militants saw far more of each other, socially as well as politically, and of their white Readjuster allies than they did of black workers. Individual advancement became their primary criterion by which to assess the collective self-improvement of "the race"; increasingly, they based their political judgments on their personal successes. Small wonder, then, that—however inadvertently—they grew apart from the popular movement.[71]

Success undermined the black popular campaign in another subtle but important way. As one long-standing demand after another was met, and as political recognition was accorded in unprecedented degree, there seemed to be less need for the preservation of independent organization. Many no longer perceived any need for mass-based activism. The *Washington Bee*, a black newspaper, commented: "In Virginia, before this revolution under General Mahone was made a fact, a black man stood just as much chance to get justice as a cat would to get out of perdition with out claws." Now, they suggested, "justice" was within the reach of black Virginians.[72]

The organizational alliance between the black popular movement and the Readjuster party did not build new bridges between black activists and white labor reformers. Between late 1880 and early 1882, when the insurgent movement had adopted a number of popular black demands, the local white base of the party had undergone a subtle shift. The white labor reformers who had first evinced an interest in Mahone in 1879 and 1880 had dropped away. Their places were quickly taken by former Republicans, many of who had been part of the "ring." A "committee of 100," all active party members, issued a broadside to all Republicans in the state "who love principle more than office to unite with us in support of the Readjuster Liberal party." So many responded that when blacks came to the altar for their marriage to the Readjusters, they found Republican bosses wearing the groom's suit.[73]

• • •

The black popular movement continued to overflow its political channels. Reverberations continued to echo throughout black workplaces. Brickmakers and ironworkers had begun to move forward and were soon joined by coopers. Mostly semiskilled machine operatives, their livelihood was imperiled by both the advance of mechanization and the operation of a large barrel shop in the state penitentiary. Hopeful that the Readjuster-dominated legislature would prove sympathetic to their demand, the interracial Coopers' Protective Union sought to close the penitentiary shop. In January 1882, they sent a petition signed by "300 or more coopers" to the House of Delegates. The convicts, they claimed, were leased at forty cents per day each and could produce twelve barrels each because of the advanced machinery in the penitentiary shop. The results were "crowding the market with barrels and taking from the coopers of Richmond their only means of support."[74]

The coopers' union was enmeshed with the black popular movement, from which it drew encouragement. Union secretary Robert Beecher Taylor's father had been an officer in the old coopers' society a decade earlier and had been president of the Kingdom of Wealth, a beneficial secret society. The son learned to read and write in the freedmen's schools, followed his father into the coopering trade, and shared his commitment to interracial trade unionism. He was also a Sunday school teacher at the First African church. Richard Carter, at fifty, a former officer in the old union, played a prominent role in founding the new one and lent his experience with interracial unionism. With their experienced black leadership, their integrated officers, and their interest in the convict labor issue, the coopers pursued an alliance with white workers outside of political entanglements.[75]

Black ironworkers at Tredegar, undaunted by the mid-1882 recession that had hit their employer fairly hard, followed a similar course. With a separate union lodge, they drew greater sustenance from the black popular movement than from the traditional sources of support available to the white Richmond Lodge, No. 2 at Tredegar. The latter declined with the sudden downturn in the iron industry. By August 1882, this lodge was "not in a condition I would like to see," according to a white union activist. But Sumner Lodge No. 3, on the other hand, was "young, strong, and in a healthy and prosperous condition," its 125 members "all colored, in good standing and working nicely." The momentum of the popular movement was carrying black ironworkers through their industry's temporary difficulties.[76]

Like the coopers, they extended mutual support to their white union brothers. In fall 1882, this offer took a concrete form. Both Tredegar lodges of the Amalgamated resolved to win back the job of a recently fired white roller. On October 8, four hundred blacks and whites—double the number of actual union members—struck in response to a joint call from both lodges. The men remained firm for a week, but then the nonunion strikers began to return to work. Unable to hold the predominantly white ranks, the lodges gave in and called for a return to work.[77]

Through 1882, neither such defeats nor the subtle changes in the orientation of many "representative men of the race" had discouraged the black popular movement. "Race pride" infused this movement and strengthened its dual demands for equal treatment and political recognition as the necessary foundations of any popular interracial alliance. As one student of this period has suggested: "Old habits of subordination were dying; a new, more aggressive spirit had been born."[78]

• • •

Just as the course of events appeared to bring the black popular movement to a critical threshold in which difficult questions about independent organization and individual mobility would have to be answered, the political climate changed drastically. In the course of 1883, the Conservatives organized a powerful machine in their desperate efforts to regain power. Their attempts were bolstered by widespread white disaffection with the racial policies of the Readjusters and fear of the black resurgence. The Conservatives, under the direction of ruthless railroad magnate John S. Barbour, renamed themselves "Democrats." With their eye on the November state elections, they dropped their opposition to the readjustment of the debt, championed free public education, and seized upon "the color line"—race relations—as their rallying cry.[79]

Under Barbour's direction, the Democrats thus launched a racially charged campaign. They claimed that the Readjusters promoted "social equality" and raised the flag of "Negro domination" in Virginia. In Richmond, the Readjusters' appointment of R. A. Paul and Richard Forrester to the school board was seized upon as an example. The State attacked "Captain" Paul as "a very impudent and forward negro, who pushes himself everywhere." Popular white fears were exploited: The black popular movement, linked with the Readjuster party and led by "officious and persistent" men like Paul and O. M. Stewart, would challenge the traditional patterns of social relationships between the races. Bourgeois orators skillfully wove these themes of insecurity and fear together with visions of "savages and despots, lechers, polygamists, cannibal, worshippers of snakes and devils." They depicted the Readjusters as the architects of economic ruin and the exponents of "social equality."[80]

Virginia's political climate became racially charged as the elections approached, swamped by "a wave of politically engineered racial hysteria." The climax came in Danville, not Richmond. Black Readjusters had captured Danville's city government, appointed black policemen, and contributed to an atmosphere in which ordinary social relationships, from markets to sidewalks, were under attack. Democratic spokesmen across the state pointed to Danville as an example of the "social equality" and "Negro domination" that Readjusterism had promoted. A few days before the November election, a shoving incident on a Danville sidewalk turned into a race riot. One white and four Blacks died. Within hours, Democratic newspapers and campaign sheets were exploiting the episode, and party orators hailed it as the opening battle of a racial war in Virginia.[81]

Election day dawned in an atmosphere of potential armed battle. Memories of the 1870 mayoralty conflict, with its street wars, resurfaced. "Aristocratic Richmonders carried their guns into the streets on the way to and from the polls." Black turnout was low. The Democrats swept the city and the state. "The defeat of the Readjusters has been silently received by the people," reported Richmond's correspondent to the *New York Globe*. Few drew consolation from the Reverend Holmes's assessment that, "if they had not beaten, they had scared the other side badly." Though the other side had been scared badly, they were now back in control of Virginia's potential apparatus.[82]

This sudden shift in the balance of political power did not bode well for the black movement. It would bring long months of indecision and fear. But these postelection developments had compensatory features as well: the restored ties between the popular base of the black movement and the articulate new activists and the reestablished need for independent organization. Most important, the spirit of the movement was kept alive. R. A. Paul presented a paper on "The Danville Massacre" to a "mock congress" organized at the Second African church by the Chautauqua Scientific and Literary Circle. Read before the large working-class assemblage, it concluded:

> Though the present prospect of the Negro seems a little dark, yet we look with hope to a just God and a generous people for that guidance and support which will enable us to steer with safety the bark of equal rights amidst the raging elements of an adverse world. For it is
>
> "Better to dwell in Freedom's hall,
> With a cold, damp floor and mouldering wall,
> Than bow the head and bend the knee,
> In the proudest palace of Slaverie."[83]

CHAPTER 7

Black Richmond Adopts the Knights of Labor, 1884–1885

IN THE aftermath of the defeat of Readjusterism and the rise of virulent white racism, black Richmond found itself in the throes of a counterrevolution. At first, popular activism fractured along dual poles. Ideologically, the notions of racially based political organization and black labor organization competed for the minds of black workers. Socially, the "new" middle-class advocates of the first tactic and the factory-based advocates of the second pulled back from each another.[1]

The Readjuster and Republican organizations formally merged early in 1884, under the direction of the white political chieftains of each machine. Former Readjuster leaders retreated from their advocacy of black issues. One accomplishment after another was rolled back. A black activist later recalled these events: "When they lived, they lived in clover; but when they died, they died all over." Widespread anger greeted John S. Wise's testimony in the spring of 1884 before the congressional committee investigating the electoral violence of the previous fall.

> The social problem is as distinct from the political problem as two things possibly can be. I have never had a negro to presume socially upon my political affiliation with him. I have always treated the negroes as they expect me to treat them. The fact that I agree with them politically does not mean that I invite them to my house socially. I could not do such a thing in Virginia and maintain my social standing. Black members of the Legislature have come to consult me as to politics; they go to the kitchen and send up their message and I went to the back yard to see them.[2]

At work, the counterrevolution took the form of new machinery that threatened the jobs and conditions of black workers. This was especially true of tobacco factory workers (see Table 1) and coopers, both an integral part of the resurgent popular movement. The lump rooms had long been the center of workplace organization in the tobacco factories. For decades, the skilled lumpers and twisters and their young helpers had set the pace, communicated through songs, for the entire workforce. Hand flavoring and shaping the twists and plugs of chewing tobacco, these workers were pivotal to the production process. Their importance was often recognized in the community, for they often served as the officers of nonworkplace political, beneficial, religious, and charitable secret societies.[3]

Recent years had seen an attack on those skilled lumpers and twisters in one tobacco factory after another. Employers wanted to break their hold over the pace of work. The only other powerful work group, the pressmen, had been regimented ever since the hydraulic press was introduced. The Jones Lump Machine of the late 1870s had started manufacturers thinking, and the appearance of the Scales Automatic Lump Machine in 1881 was hailed as their solution. The local manufacturer of this machine eagerly promoted it. They claimed in local advertisements:

> This machine will turn out from 2,000 to 4,000 pounds per diem, according to size and thickness of lump. It flavors, equalizes and presses the leaf; divides the sheet into lumps of equal size and weight, all in one single movement. It is suitable for any kind of lump tobacco, and is said to save 33 percent in the operation.[4]

To be sure, the overall pace of change was uneven, and the economic recession of 1882–1885 slowed the introduction of expensive machinery. When the automatic lump machine appeared, it prompted the mechanization of production processes on both sides of the lump room (see Table 2). The larger factories added machines to strip the leaf and package the final product. The skilled lumpers and twisters were not the only ones to suffer. Unskilled women and children also found a decreased demand for their labor. Those working in the factories that remained open but had not

TABLE 1 Job and Wage Breakdown in a Plug Factory Before the Introduction of the Automatic Lump Machine

Occupation	*Employees*	*Wages per day*
Foremen	6 men	$2.00–$3.00
Laborers	20 men	1.00
	10 youths	.50
Lump Makers	58 men	1.00
Pressmen	20 men	1.00
Pressmen's Helpers	10 youths	.50
Stemmers	25 women	.50
	25 youths	.25
Wrappers	125 youths	.50

Source: Carrol Wright, *First Annual Report of the Commissioner of Labor* (Washington, D.C.: GPO, 1886), 398.

introduced the new machines knew that they were next. And for those whose jobs were not directly threatened by machines, their work pace was nonetheless regimented by the overall process of production, itself now geared to the speed of the new machines. Collective singing began to disappear. A northern visitor to a "modern" plug factory noted of the unmechanized stemming department: "It is only in this room that one is likely to hear the old-time spirituals and shouts, and not always here."[5]

These changes had a far-reaching impact on the black community. Lumpers and twisters often had roles in community organizations that paralleled their central place in the factory. Other displaced workers faced similar crises. Widows and single mothers had long depended on the tobacco factories for income, often for their children as well as themselves. This had been a respectable way to earn a living, with better pay and more independence than domestic service. Moreover, it offered an opportunity to keep much of the family unit together all day. Like the skilled lumpers and twisters, these women were active participants in community social organization. Finally, wages earned in tobacco factories had encouraged the growth of small businesses, contractors, and professionals. The crisis faced by tobacco factory workers constituted a crisis for Richmond's entire black community.

Coopers, like tobacco factory workers, had traditionally stood at the

TABLE 2 Mechanization of Tobacco Production

	1880	*1885*	*1890*
Chewing and Smoking Tobacco			
Firms	39	37	23
Capital	$1,683,000	$1,788,500	$2,450,375
Workforce	5,656	4,941	3,339
Men	2,843		2,060
Women	1,644		1,005
Children	1,169		234
Average Capital	$ 43,154	$ 48,338	$ 106,538
Average Workforce	142	134	145
Capital per Worker	$ 298	$ 362	$ 734
Stemming and Reprizing			
Firms	27	26	12
Capital	$ 435,084	$ 690,000	$ 606,889
Workforce	1,068	1,090	794
Men	382		386
Women	470		365
Children	216		43
Average Capital	$ 16,114	$ 26,538	$ 50,574
Average Workforce	39	42	66
Capital per Worker	$ 407	$ 633	$ 764

Sources: Manuscript Census of Manufactures, 1870 and 1890; John D. Imboden, "Virginia," *Report on the Internal Commerce of the U.S.: The Commercial, Industrial, Transportation, and Other Interests of the Southern States* (Washington, D.C.: GPO, 1886), 80; *Report on the Manufacturing Industries of the U.S. at the Eleventh Census: 1890, Part III, Selected Industries* (Washington, D.C.: GPO, 1895), 486–89.

head of black working-class organization and expression. They, too, faced mounting pressures at work. Technological change and work reorganization appeared in barrel making in the 1880s and threatened the jobs and status of the machine coopers. Having mastered earlier innovations like the stave bucker and wheel stave jointer, coopers now found themselves at the mercy of the cylindrical stave saw. The latter, perfected in the early 1880s, permitted manufacturers to shift production from their urban factories to new shops at timber sites. These new saws cut staves "mechanically from the bolt," and eliminated the labor-intensive "bucking" work done by black machine coopers.[6]

The "sawn"—as opposed to "bucked"—staves were then sent to urban barrel shops, where they were mechanically assembled by the wheel stave jointer and finished with a mechanical heading planer. The traditional shops, in short, were being turned into mere assembly operations. "All that remained to be done by hand was to insert the heads, spoke shave the barrel, rivet and drive down the thin hoops which were also supplied punched and flared and all ready for use." The expression "cooper shop" gave way to that of "barrel factory." Symbolic of black cooper frustrations and fears was the barrel factory in the state penitentiary where, with the newest machines, unskilled convicts were paid twenty-five cents a day to produce barrels for the local market.[7]

The resurgence of the popular movement had encouraged coopers to revive their organization and challenge the convict labor system. But even three hundred coopers speaking with one voice were unable to dislodge that symbol of their degradation, the penitentiary shop. Wages remained abysmally low, and unemployment grew with the introduction of new machines and the expansion of prison labor. Trade organization alone, even on a biracial basis, could not provide black coopers with the protection they sought. By 1884, their hopes seemed slim indeed.

Just when all seemed bleak for black Richmond, with tobacco factory workers, coopers, ironworkers, brickmakers, and the like in retreat, "new" middle-class activists came forward once again. In the dark days following the November 1883 Democratic victory, John Mitchell, Jr., R. T. Hill, and Edward A. Randolph began to publish the *Richmond Planet*. They defined their purpose explicitly: "We speak for our people when we declare that we intend to agitate the political equality of all men before the law."[8]

These middle-class activists kept the discussion of ideas alive. Mitchell, Hill, and Randolph were all members of the Acme Literary Association. It had been established as a middle-class society both to provide a channel for discussion among local race leaders, intellectuals, activists, and professionals and to present a vehicle through which "the masses of our people may be drawn out to be entertained, enlightened, and instructed thereby." Their success exceeded their expectations and spurred unanticipated developments.[9]

Working-class activists and rank-and-file workers attended one Acme

Literary Association event after another. They heard lectures and engaged in debates on such subjects as "The Relative Condition of the Colored Man, North and South," "The Trades," "The Political Outlook of the Negro," "The Physical Effects of Intemperance," "Our Religious Status," and "The Colored Mechanic." Older, established working-class activists like Stephen D. Jones and J. Anderson Taylor were invited to join the association, and they helped focus its attention on the problems and prospects of black workers. New societies with similar functions ad composition—the Chautauqua Scientific and Literary Circle, for example—were spun off, often led by some of the same men. Events were scheduled for traditional public meeting places like the Ebenezer Baptist Church, the Third Street AME Church, and the Second Baptist Church, where large crowds discussed "The Danville Massacre" and "What is the Future Destiny of the Negro Race in America." Consonant with established traditions, these meetings issued resolutions and circulated petitions. With formal political channels closed off to them, black militants had found other ways to express community sentiment.[10]

An embryonic movement and the notion of independent racial organization were nourished during the dismal months of 1884. In January 1885, young Daniel Webster Davis (later known nationally for his poetry expressing race pride) addressed the Acme Literary Association on "The Best Course to Pursue under the Present Administration." He "advised the race to think well before voting for any party, to judge it by its fruits rather than by its professions; not to be frightened into the Democratic Party or to be duped or fooled by the Republican Party, as they had in days past."[11]

While middle-class activists kept the possibilities for independent organization alive, they were unable to realize them. In particular, they could not meld the two most vibrant forces in black Richmond—the working-class quest for labor organization and the interclass pursuit of racially based political expression. The emergence and growth of a cultural and political gap between the black working class and the new middle class undercut the latter's claim to the mantle of community leadership.

Increasingly challenged by the developing class awareness among black working women and men, middle-class activists could not build a broad-based organization. Even as they courted black workers in the fall of 1884, indications of tension in their relationship surfaced. In October, for instance, a "Colored Industrial Fair," organized by middle-class activists and businessmen, generated little enthusiasm in black Richmond. Two months later, controversy surfaced around the decision of a local black militia unit to participate in Grover Cleveland's inaugural ceremonies in Washington. Robert J. Chiles, Richmond correspondent for the New York Freeman and a well-known middle-class activist, reported that the subject was "the theme of animated discussion in social, religious, and business circles. Speculation was rife and astonishment knew no bounds," he added. While "our intellectual circle differed as to its expediency and propriety, the majority of our illiterates heartily damned it."[12]

The wider the gap grew between them and black workers, the more strident their criticisms became. In March 1884, Dr. R. F. Tancil, speaking on "The Vexed Problem: Labor," had told an Acme Literary Association audience that he "deplored the fact that there was so much poverty among the mass of the people, and ascribed it to ignorance." A *Planet* reporter highlighted one example of this "ignorance" when he toured Richmond's saloons on a Saturday night. He noted that the black patrons "are not loafers and tramps; they are men and women who have worked hard from Monday morning until Saturday night; men and women who earned from four dollars to twelve dollars as their week's wages, and are having what they call 'a good time.' " Not only was this "good time" a waste of money, the reporter suggested, but it had become "a lucrative trade" for the "mostly German and Irish and Italian" saloon keepers. Another middle-class journalist complained openly to the *New York Freeman*: "A great reformation is needed among the large masses of the colored people in the South, who are yet in the wilderness of ignorance, oppression, and helplessness."[13]

These "large masses" were neither "ignorant" nor "helpless." These observations reveal more about middle-class perceptions than about working-class reality. The extent of these misperceptions is surprising, but the reaction of black workers is not. In February 1885, the *Richmond Planet*, besieged by criticism, defended itself:

> Many persons seem to think that because a person happens to dress respectably, and draws a reasonable salary, that they look with contempt upon those in the lower walks of life. This is a mistake, and the sooner the idea is gotten rid of the better it will be for all concerned. There may be cases in which some persons do look with contempt upon others, but the many should not be judged by the few.[14]

By winter 1884–1885, the chasm between the new middle-class militants and the local black working class appeared insurmountable. At precisely this moment, a new vehicle appeared, one which offered an opportunity to supplant middle-class "spokesmen" with popularly chosen working-class leaders and to provide an organizational framework for a mass-based movement. Moreover, it held new promise of an alliance with reform-minded white workers on both local and national levels.

The "Noble and Holy Order of the Knights of Labor" gave new hope to working-class activists of both races. Some of this was kindled by the Order's unusual institutional structure. Its basic building block, the "mixed" local assembly, grouped like-minded men or women regardless of trade. Workers and non-working-class reformers and sympathizers could be brought into the Knights of Labor through fraternal, ethnic, neighborhood, familial, or religious channels and relationships, in addition to trade and workplace contacts. The Order's structure accorded maximum autonomy to local organization, which seemed to guarantee that there would be no challenges to local practices and mores, leaving whites to organize with whites, and blacks with blacks. The overall structure, meanwhile, held the promise of an alliance above this level, so that unity of action might be pursued in spite of separate organizations. The Knights' structure was as amenable to political action as it was to trade and workplace action. The network of local assemblies, tied together on a regional base through district assemblies, appeared an ideal organizational vehicle.[15]

The Knights offered a language and vision that contributed to their appeal. They incorporated moral and religious concepts that made both white and black workers comfortable in expressing their concerns. Notions of justice and dignity, from the Bible to the workplace, informed black and white working-class activism. This language provided a sharp cutting edge to popular concerns about mechanization, especially in the context of the economic slump of 1882–1883, and the layoffs and cutbacks it occasioned. The Knights' attack on "the wage system" expressed deeply felt concerns in a new, aggressive, optimistic way.[16]

• • •

In April 1884, eleven white workers organized themselves as "Eureka Assembly"—Local Assembly No. (LA) 3157 of the Knights of Labor. They were convened by William E. Cree, a German-born labor reformer who had been active in Richmond for more than two decades. Over the years, he had been an officer in the Knights of Pythias, the Gesangverein, the Red Men, and the Druids, as well as the short-lived machinists and blacksmiths' union in the early 1870s. He had joined the Knights of Labor in New York City while on the tramp during the economic slump of 1882–1883. He had returned to Richmond in 1884, eager to build a local Knights of Labor movement.[17]

Although never formally commissioned an "organizer" by the national office, Cree initiated ten white labor militants into the "mysteries" of the Order. Only twenty-three more joined the initial group over the spring and summer of 1884. "It seemed to be an uphill business," commented one activist to the *Journal of United Labor*. The greatest stumbling block came in a wave of paternalistic gestures toward white workers by the local bourgeoisie. Democratic leaders appealed to white workers on the basis of "racial unity." They pointed to the unification of the Republican and Readjuster parties as vindicating their dire predictions about defections from the white consensus. "The salt and pepper were well-mixed," crowed the Democratic-controlled *Dispatch* in its account of the GOP convention held in the spring of 1884. Local Democratic leaders added the phrase, "friends of the workingman" to their rhetoric. They even proposed protective tariffs contrary to national party policy. Party demagogues blasted the Republicans as "the rich man's party," even as they continued to insinuate that behind it lurked the threat of "Negro domination."[18]

Democratic party leaders tried to use Grover Cleveland's presidential campaign to reassert their leadership over white workers. Cleveland was portrayed in the local press as the protector of white labor from the "pro-black, big business" candidate, James G. Blaine. Tredegar owner Joseph R. Anderson and veteran Congressman George D. Wise spearheaded the local campaign, stressing how much Cleveland's election would do for the local economy. Wise cast himself as a proven "friend of the workingman" and took the stump in white working-class neighborhoods across Richmond. Revitalized ward committees opened up to include white workers, and the party gave the appearance of solid "racial unity" as the election approached.[19]

Political and business strategists dusted off another vehicle, the corporate-organized parade, in the quest to strengthen their hegemony. They organized three massive parades between late October and mid-November, each meant to symbolize the unification of the white race with them at its helm. On October 24, Democratic party leaders and ward chairmen organized a torchlight Cleveland parade. Following the election victory, Anderson led an "impromptu" rally through Richmond's streets. Ten days later, beginning with the firing of 219 guns at sunrise (one for each electoral vote), he was joined by merchants, manufacturers, and businessmen in a grand "trades parade," celebrating the election of the first Democratic president since the Civil War. White workers were invited to participate by workshop (not by trade union, fraternal society, or Knights of Labor local assembly) under the direction of their foremen and supervisors. These parades were clearly meant to symbolize the power of the local bourgeoisie.[20]

In this atmosphere, LA 3157 had floundered. William Cree, swept up in the resurgent political paternalism, had assumed a seat on the Jefferson Ward Democratic committee. By fall, his fellow activists were thoroughly frustrated with him; William H. Mullen, another charter member of the local, stepped forward to wrest control. Mullen had been prominent in the city's white labor movement since 1874 when, at age twenty-four, he had been elected recording secretary of the Printers' Union. As a union officer over the next decade, he had stood by helplessly as conditions in his trade deteriorated and wages stagnated. In the Knights of Labor, he thought he had found an organization capable of promoting his interwoven interests in temperance, trade unionism, and social reform.[21]

In September of 1884, Mullen raised his own funds to attend the General Assembly of the Order in Philadelphia. He returned to Richmond and set about building the Knights into a strong organization. He lectured his own assembly on the purposes of the Order, elaborating a popular language drenched with religious images. One member of LA 3157 urged the *Journal of United Labor* to publish the text of Mullen's "brilliant effort," which "portrayed the trials and ordeals through which labor's cause has been called to pass from the time labor was first introduced to the human family in the Garden of Eden."[22]

Under Mullen's direction, Richmond's Knights of Labor began to grow.

By the end of November, five new local assemblies had been organized by white workers. While experienced trade unionists played an important role, all the local assemblies were "mixed" in character; fraternal and benefit societies, with their elaborate rituals, mutualistic values, and mixed occupational compositions, provided more serviceable models than did the handful of small, struggling craft unions.[23]

Mullen and his fellow activists promoted the Knights among veteran white trade unionists as the answer to the problems posed by the limitations of their craft organizations. They promised an expansive network of support for the cigarmakers' union's faltering label campaign. Similar promises were made to Mullen's own union, International Typographical Union No. 90, thirty-nine of whose members had recently drawn travelling cards. Appeals were also launched among white iron molders, granite cutters, and builders. Three more "mixed" local assemblies emerged in December 1884. By Christmas, eight white local assemblies were meeting and growing, initiating new members, still largely from the ranks of veteran trade unionists and labor reformers.[24]

In the late summer and fall of 1884, black workers organized several local assemblies of their own. They were soon compelled to seek out white supporters, since their assemblies could only become actual Knights of Labor local assemblies by receiving a charter and instructions from the local organizer; He was white and was subject to the formal and informal pressures of his fellow Knights of Labor members. Though both blacks and whites knew that the Order was nominally open to all, regardless of race, the actual details could prove quite sticky. Charles Miller, the white organizer, informed General Master Workman Powderly on December 20:

> At the last meeting of my local (3380) the subject of organizing the colored men was discussed with much interest by members. Some in favor of organizing them, and others opposed to it. It is believed by many of our Order here that if the colored men are organized it will break up our whole assembly. . . . You are well aware that there is yet in a large section of our country a strong objection on the part of whites to mix with the colored race. This objection may lessen as time goes on, but it cannot be gotten over all at once. As this is the only reason given by those opposed to organizing the colored men, I do hope that you will suggest some way to overcome this trouble and so arrange it that all matters of interest to both white and colored assemblies can be done through committees and that no visiting be allowed except by special invitation. As to helping the colored man in any attempt to benefit himself or to advance the cause of labor or to call on him to assist us in time of trouble, we do not object. . . . I as organizer have no objection to organizing the colored men and if the matter in regards to visiting can be arranged I can organize several assemblies here in a few weeks.[25]

• • •

In a two-day visit in late January 1885, Terence V. Powderly pushed the local organization beyond its traditional bounds, in the direction of a mass-based biracial popular movement. Powderly, the country's best-known labor activist, used his reputation to attract large audiences to his public appearances. Possibly fifteen hundred people attended an open meeting at the Old Market Hall; Powderly and his local allies made the most of the opportunity by presenting the Knights in such a way as to appeal to the broadest potential audience.[26]

William Mullen and a small group of white activists had met Powderly on his arrival and briefed him on what they saw as the most important local issues. They all wanted to demonstrate that the Knights could successfully address popular concerns in ways that eluded traditional labor organizations. Only two weeks earlier, the local activists had circulated a petition calling for the use of local granite and local builders in the construction of a proposed new city hall. The city council had seemed willing to use outside materials and contractors as an "economy" measure. "You, the lawyers, merchants, and doctors," the petition pointed out, "promised us protection if we would elect Grover Cleveland. . . . and now you propose to protect us by having the city hall built of Ohio sandstone or Maine granite, and built by Ohio mechanics or Maine mechanics." Some six hundred white "mechanics and property holders" had signed the petition, but it appeared to have had no effect.[27]

Powderly understood the unity that could be forged through such a campaign. He committed the Knights to it at his initial local meeting—open only to the white activists who had already joined the Order. He explained how its structure was ideal for exerting the sort of political pressure needed to bring results. At the huge, open, racially-mixed Old Market Hall meeting, Powderly opened with reference to the city hall issue and promised the Order's full support in the local campaign.[28]

The General Master Workman also raised national issues that had local resonances, such as the demand for the shorter workday, soon to reach a crescendo across the nation. He linked the length of the working day to both the current economic recession and the introduction of new machinery: "We should demand that it be used for the good of the many. I advance this argument: cut down the hours of labor. Take two hours from the day's labor of each man and it will go far toward supplying with work the many whose places have been supplanted by "labor-saving machinery."[29]

Powderly tried to do more than merely show how the Order could obtain practical results; he sought to expand traditional sensibilities without jarring them too much. Such was the case with his major innovation: the creation of a biracial labor organization through the extension of the Knights to the black community. Powderly had not replied to a letter on this subject from Charles Miller, a white organizer. Nor had he announced his position when he arrived in Richmond. Rather, he paid local white members the courtesy of first discussing the topic in a closed meeting with them. Still, he was as firm as he was courteous, telling them:

> We organize the colored workers into separate assemblies, working under the same laws and enjoying the same privileges as their white brethren, and in such matters as we can agree upon we work unitedly to the same end. In every place where the Order has been established, the colored men are advocating the holding of free night schools for the children of black and white. . . . The politicians have kept the white and black men of the South apart, while crushing both. Our aim shall be to educate both and elevate them by bringing them together.[30]

Powderly's formulation won the approval of those present. The following night, before the overflowing Old Market Hall audience, which included several hundred blacks, his message was much the same:

> Mr. Powderly said that he recognized the fact that there are two kinds of laboring men in the South. He did not expect the black men to be received into the homes of white men, but when their labor is exactly alike—when their productions are such that no man can tell the difference in the work—then they ought to have equal wages. He asked the two races to stand side by side, "to the end that wages shall not drop."[31]

The audience seemed satisfied, if not aroused. Even the hostile local middle-class press could neither distort his closing remarks nor the reception that greeted them:

> North and South, we stand as one today, and I hope and pray forever will. (applause) We have made many sacrifices. Blood has been shed, tears have flowed, hearts have been broken, and after all of that, shall American labor be put down to the level of the serfs of the earth? No! (cheers)[32]

Black workers in the audience were as enthusiastic as their white counterparts. Powderly later told a northern reporter:

> A large part of the audience was of the colored persuasion. They were evidently impressed with what I said, for at their request I organized an assembly of colored men at the conclusion of the meeting. At the close of my lecture I was subjected to a course of hand-shaking such as I have seldom experienced except during a political campaign at home.[33]

Powderly returned their enthusiasm. Before the large, mixed crowd that had not left the hall, he initiated twenty-four tobacco factory workers into the Order and organized them as LA 3564. His Solomon-like formula of separate, equal, and structurally parallel assemblies, meeting "under the same laws," formally tied together only at the national level, appeared, for the moment, to be the right tactic. By the time Powderly left Richmond after his two-and-a-half-day visit, the Knights had exploded. There were now eleven white assemblies—Nos. 3157, 3380, 3471, 3488, 3505, 3519, 3545, 3563, 3568, 3569, and 3579. The total white membership of the Order swelled from little more than two hundred to nearly one thousand. More than numbers was involved—the Order had clearly burst the limits of the formal trade union movement. LA 3568 was composed of young white female cigarette makers—the first women's labor organization in the city's history. LA 3569, with seventy-five charter members, was the first Manchester Assembly, drawing together for the first time the labor movement on both banks of the James River. Meanwhile, another black assembly, LA 3572, with seventy-nine charter members, was also formed. With Powderly opening the door to independent racial organizing, local popular activity spurted.[34]

• • •

The white activists threw themselves into an organizing campaign. "Organizing is going on here unparalleled in the history of the labor movement," was the report in an early February edition of *John Swinton's Paper*. Activists promoted issues that cut across trade and even racial lines. In addition to the city hall construction issue, the Knights took up the convict labor question. Though white workers had traditionally been more concerned with this problem than blacks, the Knights called special attention to the plight of black coopers and its basis in the convict labor system. "The cooper business of this city has practically been killed, as the two largest flour mills take all the barrels made in the prison. The wages paid to coopers here is shameful—barely enough to prolong life." Tactics (such as the boycott) that would make maximum use of the increasingly popular character of the movement were discussed.[35]

For the time being, the movement's rapid growth tended to gloss over potentially divisive issues. However, the very style of the Knights' organizing kept divisions alive; they integrated people into the Order on the basis of their existing associations, while they forged new relationships. Local assemblies reflected common residence in a neighborhood; shared membership in a fraternal or beneficial society; collective commitment to a common goal, such as Ireland's independence; or another set of existing social relationships. These local assemblies organized themselves by their own internal logic, with the "organizer" doing no more than officially sanctioning their action. Such an organizing style promoted the stunningly rapid growth of the Order; yet existing social divisions also tended to be incorporated into the Knights and were reproduced in a salient form. Thus, the most serious division remained the one between black and white workers. The Knights had barely constructed a footbridge over the chasm between the workers of both races.[36]

The Knights' growth among both black and white workers was fueled by thrusts toward social and cultural independence on the part of each. Among whites, the paternalism and corporatism offered by the bourgeoisie were losing their hold. In early February, for example, white workers and labor reformers from a variety of backgrounds, veterans of the Union and Confederate armies, indicated their willingness to bury the "bloody shirt." Led by two Knights of Labor activists, they established the "Organization of United Veterans." In this way, they demonstrated their distance from the North-South sectionalism promoted by local politicians. White working women demonstrated their growing social independence. Allen and Ginter Tobacco Company put on a ball for their employees in February 1885, but few of the young cigarette makers chose to attend. Perhaps they preferred to spend the evening within the sisterhood of their LA 3568.[37]

The Knights' star had risen among blacks while that of the new middle class had declined. The latter's articulation of race pride and stimulus to community organization in 1884 had been invaluable; but as their tone grew more condescending, they had begun to speak *to* black workers rather than *for* them. Their ability to command collective respect faltered, and their organizational ventures remained isolated from the mass of Richmond blacks. Built on an independent base, grounded in the black working class, the Knights stood ready to assume the mantle of race leadership.

The Knights of Labor thus emerged on solid, if separate, foundations. Though no new white local assemblies were organized between February and May 1885, existing assemblies grew steadily. According to observers, 100 to 150 new members, distributed among the assemblies, were added each week. Popular movements gathered steam among both blacks and whites.[38]

Experienced activists linked the Knights to resurgent trade unionism among white workers. The Knights offered the granite cutters' union a broader network to influence such issues as the new city hall construction. The Knights strengthened the cigarmakers' and printers' unions in their continuing battle against "rat" shops. With the Knights' assistance, a bricklayers' union was organized in April, and iron molders, machinists, and boilermakers joined the Order as their own unions collapsed.[39]

Activists linked the Knights of Labor to other white working-class organizations and concerns. Mutual reinforcement blossomed between the Order and Irish nationalism, for instance. By the mid-1880s, workers had challenged the "lace curtain" Irish and taken control of Richmond's organized Irish nationalist movement. Questions like Irish landlordism and the roots of Irish poverty as well as national independence were discussed. Parallels were drawn between the American colonies in 1776 and Ireland in 1885. The problems of Irish workers in America were considered. In Richmond, by early 1885, a core group of working-class militants—among them John Ryall, Frank Reilly, Joseph Devine, John Molloy, James Healey, and C. W. Burr—had assumed major roles in both the Knights of Labor and local Irish nationalist organizations. These two broad movements expressed mounting support for each other's goals, and they spoke a shared language of "independence."[40]

After two months of phenomenal growth, the eleven white local assemblies came together in late March to discuss the creation of another structural level, a District Assembly. William Mullen was elected District Master Workman, and Charles Miller, the organizer who had met with black local assemblies, was chosen District Recording Secretary. This was obviously to be an active organization. One of its first acts was to order a boycott of the products of the Haxall-Crenshaw Flour Company, which packaged these products in convict-made barrels.[41]

Under Mullen's leadership, District Assembly No. (DA) 84 had carefully picked its target: Haxall-Crenshaw, the city's most prominent user of convict-made products. Not coincidentally, the aggrieved coopers were predominantly black, though there were many white coopers as well. For many blacks, the DA's boycott of Haxall-Crenshaw vindicated the claim that the Knights could—and would—address black concerns. Ten new black local assemblies had been organized by May—Nos. 3572, 3619, 3620, 3626, 3637, 3732, 3783, 3808, 3821, and 3822.[42]

Powderly himself had organized LA 3564, Richmond's first black local assembly. Shortly thereafter, Mullen had sanctioned the organization of LA 3572, with seventy-nine charter members. The absence of a black organizer hindered the chartering of new local assemblies. Mullen and Charles Miller, the two local men with "organizer" papers, were occupied in February and March with the activities of the white local assemblies. The demand soon became too loud to ignore. On March 7, Mullen wrote to Powderly: "We have several Colored Assemblies in good working order. I organized a fine one Saturday night in Manchester (LA 3619)—a city across the river from here. Your visit done us much good."[43]

In a month's time, six more black local assemblies had been chartered in Richmond. LA 3619, the first black local assembly in Manchester, had been founded by twenty-nine men, but it had rapidly become the largest single local assembly in the area. Over the next three weeks, with Mullen's eventual sanction, twenty-seven black men established LA 3626; nineteen formed LA 3637; and forty set up LA 3675. In the first week of April, Mullen sanctioned the organization of LA 3732 by 101 tobacco factory workers and LA 3783 by another thirty tobacco factory workers. By mid-April 1885, despite the absence of official black "organizers," more than five hundred black men belonged to nine functioning local assemblies of the Knights of Labor.[44]

On April 12, 1885, DA 84's Corresponding Secretary DeVoto wrote to *John Swinton's Paper*: "The negroes are with us heart and soul, and have organized seven assemblies." Four new black local assemblies—Nos. 3808, 3821 (Manchester), 3822, and 3895—were established by the end of May. Encouraged by DA 84's espousal of the cause of black coopers, black workers joined their revived popular movement to the Knights of Labor. Even as new assemblies were being organized, existing ones expanded rapidly. The black social network, that web of relationships woven between family, secret society, church, and workplace, provided the institutional channels for the Knights. Familiar with secret organization, comfortable with elaborate ritual and evangelical expression, and increasingly conscious of themselves as part of the working class, black workers took readily to the Knights as information about how to organize black assemblies spread throughout the black community.[45]

Delegates of the twelve black local assemblies—ten from Richmond, two from Manchester—met in late May to establish a district assembly. They organized DA 92, the first black district assembly in the nation. Now, as the black members of the Knights sought to expand their organization and employ its strength, they would have their own leaders, organizers, judges; in short, they would have an autonomous structure, equal in stature to DA 84. From this point on, the black Knights of Labor and the black popular movement in Richmond became virtually indistinguishable.[46]

By the late spring of 1885, the Knights of Labor had fully articulated structures in place among both black and white workers, a total membership of approximately fifteen hundred, and a dynamic, respected leadership. Under their direction, black and white households throughout Richmond and Manchester had banded together in the much-publicized boycott of the Haxall-Crenshaw Company. Over the next year, the Knights would attempt to improve the social, economic, and political status of Richmond's workers, both black and white. In so doing, they would shake the status quo across the South.

CHAPTER 8

Popular Activity, the Knights of Labor, and the Movement Culture

BY THE late spring of 1885, the Knights of Labor had emerged at the heart, and the head, of black and white popular movements. Over the next six months, working-class activists of both races forged a movement culture that centered on the Knights; they promoted a biracial popular struggle that threatened to turn southern society upside down. In cities across America, the Knights of Labor, engaged in a similar process, were generating "a new way of looking at society, a way of thinking that represented a shaking-off of inherited forms of deference."[1]

Working-class activists built the Knights through a well-crafted campaign over the summer of 1885. They chose as their focal issue one that had frustrated the local labor movement for more than a decade: "convict labor." They took up the cause for the coopers, Richmond's best-integrated trade with a history of interracial organization. These activists chose a tactic that depended on mass participation and personal responsibility: a consumer boycott. Even their choice of an opponent was strategic. The Haxall-Crenshaw Flour Company was one of the city's biggest and oldest enterprises, and its profits had nourished many other local industries. At the moment, Haxall-Crenshaw also happened to be the biggest purchaser of convict-made products in the entire state.[2]

Skilled activists turned the coopers' struggle into an organizing drive for the Knights among working men and women of both races. They refused to leave the matter in the hands of the legislature, where it had lain dormant, since "recent events leave great doubts in our mind as to the sincerity of politicians in this matter." A mass consumer boycott now made sense, in the words of District Assembly (DA) 84's Master Workman William H. Mullen, because "it is only in the past twelve months that the working men of this city have become sufficiently organized to use this weapon." In a *Labor Herald* editorial, Mullen explained:

> They knew all the time that coopering, shokemaking, and other trades in this city had been paralyzed by this unjust competition, but they were powerless and could make no move against their oppressors. The working classes of Richmond are generally speaking very conservative people, and even when they were organized to the extent of five to six thousand, notwithstanding the fact that they were fully aware of the abject poverty to which the coopers of this city had been reduced, they did not rush into this boycott in a manner that might be expected of people who had long been oppressed; but, on the contrary, they did all in their power to settle this matter in a peaceful and quiet way.[3]

The boycott facilitated the expansion of the popular movement, because it reached beyond the adult male activists of each family. Women and children did much of the family's shopping; therefore, most of the responsibility for the boycott rested on their shoulders. Entire households were drawn in first to the boycott and then to the Knights' formal organizational structure. Trade unions also became involved. The granite cutters' union informed DA 84 in early May 1885: "We will not buy or allow to be used in our families, any flour, meal, or mill-offal manufactured by the said Company." The Knights justified the boycott with a language, rich in religious and political symbolism, shared by both black and white workers. This very language promoted not only the popular involvement among both races, but also a common outlook and set of beliefs. Mullen told readers of the *Labor Herald*:

> The divine right to boycott is accorded us by the Holy Bible, and it has been practiced in one form or another in all parts of the world from time immemorial. We might name instance after instance in the good book where boycotting under a different name has been used as a means of ridding the people of both evils and obnoxious individuals. Was there ever a more severe boycott issued than that of our Lord against Pharaoh in behalf of the oppressed children of Israel? First he sent the plague of frogs, then lice, then flies, then murrain among the cattle, then hail, then disease, then locusts, then darkness, then the first-born were slain, and finally the hard-hearted oppressor was forced to yield and release the children of Israel from the bondage of slavery. It is thus by degrees that the oppressed and downtrodden working classes of this country will eventually bring their oppressors to terms and obtain their rights, and we believe the same just God that aided Moses in bringing the children of Israel out of the bonds of slavery will aid us in our struggles for justice.
>
> Why, the right to boycott is handed down to us by our forefathers. The Revolutionary War, which resulted in throwing off the yoke of British tyranny and oppression and giving us our freedom, commenced with one of the greatest boycotts ever inaugurated in this country. . . . These old patriots, who battled so nobly for our rights, were not satisfied with refusing to buy tea and withdrawing their patronage from those who sold it, but they absolutely refused to allow it to be landed on our territory, and went so far as

> to board the vessels of their oppressors and willfully destroy their property. Such action would not be countenanced by the Knights of Labor, yet there are some people in this city who applaud the boycott of our forefathers and at the same time hold up their hands in horror because we have quietly withdrawn our patronage from the Haxall-Crenshaw Company and those who sell their products, because they are using convict made barrels in preference to those made by free labor. These people are the Tories of the present day.
>
> It must be plain to every fair-minded man that it is not only the right, but the duty of the workingmen to use this weapon whenever occasion requires it. It is patriotism in us. . . . We are performing a Christian duty and we have the law of both God and man on our side.[4]

The boycott campaign not only brought workers together under the Knights' sponsorship, it also widened the wedge between them and local businessmen, manufacturers, and politicians, who closed ranks behind the Haxall-Crenshaw Company. The Richmond Chamber of Commerce condemned the boycott and endorsed Haxall-Crenshaw's contention that "the avowed object of this is to injure our business as much as possible." The boycott similarly distanced white workers from the Democratic party. The state legislature, which the party dominated, failed to restrict the employment of convicts, much to the anger of its once-loyal constituents. Further hostility toward local party officials was engendered by the city council's inaction on the proposed construction of a new city hall. Rumors that the contract was awarded to an outside firm, with its own workers, rather than to a local firm, using local granite and local labor, infuriated white builders. The Democratic party's hold over white workers grew more tenuous daily. Mullen voiced their skepticism: "We have many promises now for the future from both parties, but it remains to be seen what will be the outcome of promises made by skilled politicians upon the eve of a hot and escalating canvass."[5]

Black disaffection with both the Republican and Readjuster apparatus mounted. The white party leaders had made a costly mistake in taking the black electorate for granted. Militant black self-expression grew in the vacuum left by the party's silence on racial issues. The failure of national party leaders to secure the passage of the Blair Education Bill further alienated black Richmonders. In September the "State Executive Committee of the Colored People of Virginia," a core group that had met irregularly since the black "labor convention" of August 1875, issued a call to blacks "desirous of establishing their political independence" to send delegates to a state convention to be held in Lynchburg on October 3, 1885. W. J. S. Bowe, the Richmond printer and veteran spokesman for independent racial organization, chaired the convention. Thirty delegates, many of them veteran activists, represented Richmond. Under Bowe's chairmanship, the convention issued a declaration articulating black popular dissatisfaction:

> We, the colored people of Virginia, believing as we do that the time has come for us to call a halt in the unqualified support that we have given to the Republican party here. In convention assembled, we do solemnly declare ourselves politically independent in all matters which pertain to us as citizens and voters of the Commonwealth.
>
> . . . Now the time has come for us to think, act, vote, and speak for ourselves, and especially so since the Republicans have practically abandoned us in former campaigns, and in all matters where the Negro ought to have recognition in proportion to his voting strength and experience.
>
> . . . We therefore appeal to the colored people . . . to in the future make such political alliances as will most advance our interests, educationally, financially, and politically.[6]

Black Richmond employed the Knights of Labor as the primary vehicle through which to express racial pride and build community organization. Through the Knights of Labor, traditional forms of popular activity were revived. For instance, veteran leaders breathed new life into the traditional "Emancipation Day" celebration. The April 20, 1885 procession, several thousand strong, was headed by Joseph Brown Johnson, the Manchester barber who had been a spokesman for independent racial organization since the 1875 black labor convention. Now Virginia's highest-ranking black militia officer, he was soon to become DA 92's official organizer. Johnson's role in community parades reflected the growing power and influence of the Knights of Labor.[7]

Black working-class activists adapted funeral processions to their purpose. The death of black city councillor Nelson P. Vandervall occasioned a tremendous outpouring of community sentiment. The funeral procession was barely distinguishable from a political parade. Joseph Brown Johnson and the black militia led the way, followed by the members of more than fifty black secret societies. In years past, the positions of honor at the head of such a procession would have been filled by white and black Republican officials. Now, however, they had been displaced by black Knights of Labor stalwarts.[8]

• • •

The Knights' organizing strategy followed several clear steps. Under the shared direction of DA's 84 and 92, the Haxall-Crenshaw boycott attracted thousands of black and white men, women, and young adults to the order. They were recruited into local assemblies, initiated into the Knights' visions and practices, and tied into the district assemblies. The traditional multiplicity of working-class organizations began to give way to an emerging universal organization. Working-class militants struggled against the power of the received culture to draw the recalcitrant members of their communities into the new movement. The Knights' "constructive" projects were integral elements of this new strategy.[9]

Most important was the establishment of the Richmond *Labor Herald* in September 1885. The Knights' *Journal of United Labor* noted approvingly, "It is in good hands, has a bright editor, one who will make the paper rich in its editorials; a splendid field where it will be appreciated . . ." Founded as a cooperative by William Mullen and three other printers and members of Typographical Union No. 90, the *Labor Herald* was the first "labor" newspaper in Richmond's history. In Mullen's inimitable style, the paper wove together moral, social, economic, and political issues and elaborated a new language and a comprehensive vision of "reform." In its first issue, Mullen described the glorious victory of the Knights over Jay Gould in the Wabash Railroad conflict. In character sketches of the chief protagonists, he framed the struggle in moral terms. He wrote of General Master Workman Powderly:

> He has sacrificed his time, his money, his health, the associations of home and family, all in behalf of the poor working people. . . . He seeks not wealth nor place, but is happy always when he can accomplish something for his people. He lies down at night and sleeps quietly, with no thought of stock, bonds, or percentage to harass his sleeping hours. Picture to yourself a representation of all that is good, lofty, intelligent, honest, kind-hearted, and true, and you then have T. V. Powderly before you.

As for Gould: "He is a man whose check is his altar; whose exchange is his church; whose banker is his minister; whose gold is his god."[10]

The *Labor Herald* filled a number of functions in the popular movement led by the Knights. Mullen's ability to present a complex vision of social conflict and change was absolutely critical to the Knights' success among both blacks and whites. His language helped cement discrete aspects of the movement. The *Labor Herald* informed Richmond workers of the struggles of the labor movement nationally, which helped to broaden their perspectives and identification. Boycott lists of both local and national concerns were given front page space. Local campaigns were highlighted; popular support urged.[11]

Shortly after its organization, DA 84 established a "reading room," which assisted the Order in its "educational" work and functioned as a meeting place. It was also intended to serve as a "labor bureau," a hiring hall and job information center controlled by the Order. Militants from both district assemblies adapted a popular form of working-class recreation by sponsoring excursions for members and their families to such cities as Washington, where they visited with members of the Order. Richmond, in turn, played host to Knights and their families from other urban centers. These projects widened the horizons and social bonding of local workers of both races.[12]

Working-class activists further developed the movement culture through the organization of producers' cooperatives. Rather than focus on the establishment of small shops with highly skilled workers, the Knights opened several large shops, where semiskilled and unskilled workers—mostly white women—made consumer products for the local market. Knights of Labor militants tried to meet local women's needs for safe decent jobs and, especially, to imbue their undertakings with the cooperative values of the Order. They thus provided an indirect critique of the dominant political economy by creating jobs in a time of high unemployment, paying decent wages, providing humane working conditions, and demonstrating that production itself need not be ruled by the pursuit of profit or managed in an autocratic fashion. Such undertakings became critical elements of the emerging movement culture for both those participating directly and those who made it a point to purchase their products.[13]

In June 1885, DA 84 opened a cooperative soap factory. Women, who had always made soap as part of their nonwaged household work, were the natural employees for this cooperative; only white women were included. John M. Ryall, a veteran of labor reform and Irish nationalist activity since the late 1870s, was put in charge. He had worked his way through the metal trades, from a machinist's position to that of engineer (largely machine repair) in a tobacco factory. Despite his youth, Ryall was a well-respected figure in local working-class circles. Since he had no apparent knowledge of soap making, he was largely dependent on the women when it came to organizing production. His role was to ensure that the concern's cooperative character remained uppermost.[14]

Though these and other cooperative ventures apparently employed only white workers organizationally bound to DA 84, they did not ignore black labor. The soap factory, for instance, actively sought black patronage. The pages of the *Labor Herald* and personal appearances before black church congregations by the likes of Mullen and Ryall reflected as much. They couched their appeals in noneconomic terms, since commercial producers were underselling them with much publicity. From all accounts, though, black consumers heeded these appeals with a fervor comparable to their boycott of Haxall-Crenshaw products.[15]

DA 84 also organized a cooperative building association that, after some discussion, opened to black participation. The association's elaborate rules were devised to insure fairness and impress members with the value of cooperation. Each member paid fifty cents a week in dues; when five hundred dollars accumulated in the treasury, a lottery was held among the paid-up membership, and a house and lot were awarded to the winner. The "drawer" had a choice of several potential lots and "the right to state the style that he desires the house to be built"; upon moving into the residence, the "drawer" was to refund the association at a rate of ten dollars per month. When the full five hundred dollars was paid, the winner received the title to the property.

Whatever had been paid in dues would be credited to the winner's account. No one was entitled to more than one entry.[16]

Here was a practical solution to the continuing housing problems faced by Richmond's black and white working-class families. In 1890, while half of all local families included six members or less, half of the local residents lived in dwellings with eight or more people. Home ownership had eluded them over the past decades, as the ups and downs of the economy obliterated savings accounts and promoted mortgage foreclosures. By collectively creating a pool of capital in which all were eventually to share, they could reasonably expect to attain this long-sought dream. Here was to be a practical example of the ability of workers to "manage their own affairs."[17]

The building association promoted the movement culture fashioned by the Knights. The principle of equality—in dues, shares, and opportunity—was itself a critique of standard banking and financial operations. The association's founders pushed beyond traditional capitalistic practices. Well aware of the ravages of an unpredictable economy, they made special provisions in case a winner could not keep up monthly payments. Their by-laws stipulated that all such cases be brought before the elected board of directors, who would weigh each one on its merits. "But in all such cases we would recommend that the Board of Directors be as lenient as possible according to the financial standing of the Association and the merits of the case." Individuals who admitted to a continuing inability to make payments would not lose their investment. Rather, the total investment to that point, "less four per cent which shall be deducted for the running expenses of the Association," was returned in cash. The individual was to be bought out, not foreclosed upon because at this time the individual's family would be in its greatest need.[18]

Other social and moral restraints were imposed on commercial real estate practices. The property could be resold only to "a Brother or Sister Knight of Labor in good standing." While a winner could rent the house, the tenant "must be a Knight of Labor until the house is paid for," and "the tenant must be acceptable to the Board of Directors." Governance of the association was strikingly different from mainstream financial institutions. The board of directors would consist of one representative from each participating local assembly. It would elect the normal range of officers (president, secretary, and so forth), and a "managing Director of Building . . . who shall be a competent builder and a judge of material who shall have charge of the purchasing of materials and direction of the work in general." The "managing Director of Building" was also given specific directions in the bylaws: "We recommend that in all of our work that we adopt the eight hour system and a fair day's pay for a fair day's work."[19]

Working-class militants used the building association as a vehicle to promote their analysis of society and their vision of the cooperative solution. The *Labor Herald* printed and distributed one thousand copies of the association's "Preamble." This document placed the blame for "the ills to which laboring people are subject," at the door of those who "monopolize the land . . . , contrary to natural laws that should regulate these matters." Land, air, water, light—"natural elements essential to existence on this earth"—must be equally available to all, the activists argued. In their "Preamble," they claimed this was the intent of "the Great Architect," and they called for:

> Returning to first principles and securing the land (our natural inheritance) to the masses. As this can only be accomplished by placing the means within reach of those who are forced to rent, to purchase a home for themselves, at a cost no greater than the paying of rent to a landlord, we have formulated a plan to this end; and call on all working people, old and young, male and female, who are members of the Knights of Labor in good standing and living in rented houses, to come forward and give us a helping hand to accomplish this great work, that only needs your co-operation to make it a success.[20]

The Knights expanded this movement culture through projects aimed directly at those workers new to the cause of reform. They were provided with educational activities within local assemblies and were encouraged to make use of the reading room. Nothing was more effective than the project undertaken in the fall of 1885 by the "Richmond Knights of Labor Dramatic Society," a group of whites led by Joseph Devine. They performed "The Long Strike," a play written twenty years earlier by Irish maverick dramatist Dion Boucicault. Tickets for the performances ranged from fifteen to fifty cents, and the house was packed each night. Blacks and whites attended, but the conventions of racial separation were observed. Set in Manchester, England, this drama portrayed for its working-class audience the conflict between their moral values and those of the bourgeoisie. Interweaving a militant strike with a love story, making its major points through the latter, the play highlighted the moral contrast between a young workman and a mill-owner.[21]

"The Long Strike" opens with a confrontation between the strike committee and the employers' association. In response to the strikers' demands for improved wages and working conditions, the employers announce a general lockout. The scene then shifts to a romantic rendezvous between Richard Readley, the leader of the employers' association, and one of his female operatives, Jane Learoyd. She is the daughter of one of the strike committee members and the beloved of Jem Starkee, a young striker. Jem enters and, confronting Readley, demands that he not take advantage of Jane.

> *Jem*: I'll tell you in plain words what I've got to say. Jane Learoyd loves ye. I ha' known her long enough to feel sure she'll make a noble wife for any man, be he who he may. Do you mean to marry the girl?
>
> *Readley*: Are you her brother?
>
> *Jem*: I mean to stand by her like one. If you mean rightly, you won't think the worse of me for what I'm saying, but if not, for your sake as well as for hers, let her alone and never speak to her more.

Readley: Has she authorized you to take this step?
Jem: I want no authority to do what's right.
Readley: You are neither her father nor her brother, and you have no right to interfere.
Jem: Neither father nor brother could love her as I ha' done. Aye, as I love her still. If love gives any claims, then no one can come up to my right. Do you mean fair by Jane or not?
Readley: Confound you, man, stand back.

Following a brief shoving match, broken up by a passing policeman, Jem adds: "Heaven shall judge between us two." Boucicault has set the stage for the moral conflict.

The scene then shifts altogether, to give a picture of mutual support among the strikers as they share their meager strike benefits, doled out by a London-based trade union official.

Noah (Jane's father): You mean it [the union] will enable us to starve by inches, and by so doing, it will continue to support us in the strike. Go tell Lunnin' that we looked death in the face long enough—long enough not to be affeared of it now, and if it's got to come, we may as well fetch it in striking for our rights.

Appalled by the strident talk of violence around him, the union official takes back the much-needed strike benefits. But he still faces a dilemma. When Noah shows him the door, he responds: "Go! It's all very well to say go, but look at this money. How shall I carry it through the famishing crowd outside?" Boucicault then demonstrates the moral superiority of the strikers vis-à-vis the callous union official, as well as the employers:

Noah: (looking round) Come here, Maggie. Go wi' this man, and, as you walk along, tell them ye meet that he's carrying the poor men's money. Go wi' that lass, man, and ye'll meet wi' no harm.

None of the strikers, no matter how hungry, would consider stealing the funds, and so Maggie was all the protection the official needed.

The action picks up as a crowd attacks Readley's mill and heads for his residence. He seeks refuge, desperately, at Jane and Noah's house. He is discovered by Jem, who volunteers to save Readley from the crowd, even at the risk of his life, and to save Noah and Jane's reputations should the hated employer be found there. While waiting for the opportunity to flee after Jem has decoyed the mob away, Readley overhears Noah and the strike committee make plans to "burn a mill to the ground each night" until the lockout has ended. With this knowledge, Readley makes his escape.

Boucicault provides the audience with another idealization of working-class values and social relationships. He introduces Johnny Reilly, a young merchant seaman and lifelong friend of Jem's. While in port, he has been sharing Jem's lodgings. He appears at Jane's the next morning. Johnny, too, the audience learns, loves Jane, and this shared devotion has brought him even closer to Jem. Preparing to ship out, Johnny had come to discuss Jem with Jane.

> *Johnny*: It's Jem I want to talk to ye about. Jem and me have been sweet on you this many a while—bout of us was bad about you—one worse than the other—but especially Jem! Ah! A pair of honester hearts a girl never had to her back. Many a night we've spent the night talking over you and swapping minds about ye.

He told her that Jem had come home the night before distraught and silent, and that he had set his pistol on the table. Johnny, having taken the gun, gave it to Jane as he told her the story.

> *Johnny*: Put them things away and never let on I told you this, and begged you to be kind to him. His love is as proud as that gunpowder, and would take fire more easy. But, oh Jane, do let your heart soften to him—do, dear, and then if—if—you marry him some day when I'm gone, and you are happy together—you can give him back them things and tell him what I've done for his sake and yours. Good-by.

This was the stuff of working-class friendship.

The audience is then returned to the strike action. Readley, it learns, has informed the police of the strike committee's plans, and all except Noah and Jem have been arrested. A policeman is sent to help Noah escape. He explains that Noah and Jem have been singled out for special treatment because his daughter had hidden Readley in the house the previous night, which had enabled the mill-owner to overhear the strikers' plans. Noah is crushed by this revelation, which he misinterprets.

> *Noah (sinks into chair)*: My child—my flesh and blood—his paramour? It was for this, then, she locked him in. Twas for this that she betrayed the cause that we have starved for—we have prayed for. They are in prison asking one another where is Noah Learoyd? There—don't you see him—skulking behind his daughter? Livin' on her shame? She is to meet Readley tonight! (Rises—sees pistol on table.) Ah! What's this? (Takes up pistol.) Their fate hangs on Readley's breath. No breath of his shall ever testify against them.

Out of his senses, he takes Jem's gun and seeks out Jane and Readley. Hiding in the bush along the path, he—and the audience—overhears Jane try to break off her relationship with Readley. We then see the manufacturer for the scoundrel he is. When Jane apologizes that she cannot marry him, he laughs: "Ha! Ha! My wife! My dear girl, I never contemplated imposing matrimony upon you." Neither is he prepared to let her go. Readley offers her a "bargain": If she will become his mistress, he will not testify against her father. Appalled, Jane begs for mercy: "I had rather die. I would—I would—I saved your life. Spare mine! Oh! Hear me!" But Readley is deaf to her pleas.

The melodramatic action that follows is rather predictable. Noah emerges from the bushes and kills Readley with Jem's gun. Jem, who has walked all night to the Merseyside with Johnny in order to see him off, returns the following morning to be charged with murder. The only man who can support his alibi is on board ship, possibly under sail already. Jane desperately wants to save Jem but cannot bring herself to reveal her father as the murderer. The old man has by now lost all grip on reality and could not clear Jem even if he were asked. Meanwhile, taken aback by Readley's murder, the strikers decide to return to work. Maggie speaks for them: "I don't mind throwin' a brick through a pane o' glass or destroyin' a man's jacket in a nob stock, but, when it comes to shootin' or stabbin', I don't hand wi' thee. For my part, I be going back, whether I get paid or not."

The strike over, the remainder of the play centers on Jane's efforts to clear Jem. With the reluctant assistance of a lawyer, she reaches Johnny, on ship about to sail, with a telegram. When his profit-hungry captain refuses to let him debark, Johnny jumps ship, swims to shore, and runs to Manchester, arriving just in time to save Jem. The curtain falls.

"The Long Strike," performed by the Richmond Knights of Labor Dramatic Society, allowed activists to dramatize the clash of values inherent in their struggle. The self-serving, tight-fisted, antiunion employer appeared immoral, callous, and lecherous. The hero, a young striker, was self-sacrificing, a devoted friend, and an honorable man. The values of working-class mutuality and collectivity were contrasted to the selfish, heartless values of a mill-owner. Though the strike was lost, love triumphed in the end, and so did self-respect and hope. Hardly one of the better known plays of the nineteenth-century American theater, "The Long Strike" gave the movement culture a powerful emotional charge. Thousands of workers absorbed the play's message, viewed themselves through the mirror it held up, cheered its performances, and discussed its implications.[22]

The rituals, symbols, and rules of every local assembly also influenced the emergent movement culture. Workers of both races were familiar with "secret" organizations that involved complicated rituals and complex symbols. Most had already participated in one or more religious, social, or beneficial society. In this sense, the Order's emphasis on ritual suggests its foundation in traditional working-class culture. Yet the specific rituals, symbols, structures, and rules employed by the militants also pointed to the new culture that was possible. General Master Workman Powderly pointed out: "When a man stood before the altar in an assembly of the Knights of Labor and drank in the lessons running through the lines spoken by the officers, he realized that something more was expected of him than to allow others to do his future thinking for him."[23]

The process began with initiation. Every new member, regardless of race or gender, was told by the Worthy Foreman of the Assembly:

> In the beginning, God ordained that man should labor, not as a curse, but as a blessing; not as punishment, but as means of development, physically, mentally, morally, and has set thereunto his seal of approval in the rich increase and reward. By labor is brought forward the kindly fruits of the earth in rich abundance for our sustenance and comfort; by labor (not exhaustive) is promoted health of the body and strength of mind, labor garners the priceless stores of wisdom and knowledge. It is the "Philosopher's Stone," everything it touches turns to wealth. "Labor is noble and holy." To glorify God in its exercise, to defend it from degradation, to divest it of the evils to body, mind, and estate, which ignorance and greed have imposed; to rescue the toiler from the grasp of the selfish is a work worthy of the noblest and best of our race.
>
> You have been selected from among your associates for that exalted purpose. Are you willing to accept the responsibility, and, trusting in the support of pledged true Knights, labor, with what ability you possess, for the triumph of these principles among men?

A firm, positive answer had to be given before the initiation ceremony could continue.[24]

In the local assembly meeting room, the new member encountered one symbol of knighthood after another. The first entrance, or "outer veil," was marked by a globe, "symbolizing the field of our operation, and signifies 'Universal Organization.' " A lance, signifying "defence," was emblem of the "inner veil." Passing through the "inner veil," one entered the assembly room proper, where a book, signifying "Knowledge" was located prominently in the center. In order to pass through the "veils," in addition to giving the password ("Discourage Discord," for the latter half of 1886), each member had to write her or his full name and local assembly number on a card. Powderly later explained the purpose of this part of the Order's ritual:

> The lesson taught the entering member is EDUCATION. The first step on the road to progress is intelligence. That this intelligence may have full play, it is necessary that education be made an auxiliary to the natural attainments of man. That every member should know how to write his name in full and read the same when written is a necessity. That every member should be forcibly reminded of the duty he owes to himself in acquiring a knowledge sufficient to prevent the evil-disposed from imposing on him, this stimulus is given to the entering member.

Education itself was but a means to another, higher end.

> It is to be hoped that the day will come when men of all the nations of the earth shall govern themselves; that he who governs shall do so by and with

the consent of the governed. That the government of all nations may be properly administered, it is necessary that the governed be educated; therefore, the first step taken in the Knights of Labor is toward that end.[25]

The internal organization of a local assembly meeting was indicative of the Order's principles and goals, and intended to instruct the initiates and remind the veterans of why they were there.

That which strikes the newly initiated most forcibly on entering the sanctuary is that all members, whether they hold positions or not, occupy the same level. This is to indicate that there are no degrees or rank, no upper or lower class—all men are admitted on an equal footing. . . . On entering he becomes the equal of all other members, and no power save his own will can destroy that equality.

Another lesson taught by the placing of all members on the one level is that all branches of toil are regarded in the same light by the order of the Knights of Labor. The laborer, the artisan, the craftsman, and the professional man each has equal share in the inheritance left to the Order.[26]

Thus all members and officers sat at the same level. Each local assembly had a "master workman," a "worthy foreman," a "worthy inspector," an "almoner," a "statistician," an "Unknown Knight" (who greeted candidates for membership), a "venerable sage" (the librarian of the assembly), an "inside esquire" and an "outside esquire" (who guarded the two "veils"), and local court officers, including three judges and a clerk. Each of these elected officials (at least sixteen served every local assembly) had a specific symbol as well. The master workman's symbol, for example, was a column three feet in height. Its base was made in imitation of coral, "as coral was at one time supposed to be the product of the combined efforts of the coral animals. It is from this theory that the idea of adopting the base of coral, as being emblematic of the labor of many hands, was conceived. To perfect the union of crafts, the work of many hands is necessary." The shaft of the column was "reeded" in imitation of "closely-bound rods," that is, a bundle of sticks bound closely together, which symbolized that men of all trades needed each other's support. The top of the column imitated fruit and leaves, "surmounted by a human bust. The whole column was a sign of the Order, and signified 'Co-operation based on labor creates capital when directed by intelligence.' "[27]

Virtually every aspect of a Knights of Labor assembly was richly symbolic. New elements of the movement culture emerged around the Knights of Labor: experiences in self-government, lessons in popular political economy and political power, and implications for labor organization. All were expressed in a language that reached back through generations of working-class experiences and was deeply embedded in allegory.

• • •

This movement culture pushed against, but rarely penetrated, one rigid barrier: the color line. Though both blacks and whites had been drawn to the Order through the Haxall-Crenshaw boycott, new members were organized into racially distinct assemblies. While these assemblies could participate in joint campaigns, they were affiliated with separate districts; thus, their personnel and identities remained distinct. Two essentially autonomous structures contained the popular movements that were growing within them. The Knights, then, were composed of two distinct currents that flowed in the same direction, but rarely intermingled.[28]

This biracial character allowed black workers to retain control over their organization and activities. Well-versed in secrecy and ritual, they were attuned to symbolism and to the "inner workings" of the Order. They expanded their experience with self-organization, self-education, and self-government and integrated these new experiences into their own social and intellectual frame of reference. DA 92 and its network of local assemblies provided black Richmond with its first comprehensive, unitary body. While black workers had been actively organized for two decades, and an independent central organization had been a goal of militants since the days of the Colored National Labor Union, the black social network had never been so successfully focused and cohesive. The very racial separation of the Richmond order gave Afro-Americans the space they needed to create this for themselves.

Although some bridges had been built between black and white Knights, continued separation remained the reality for most. "The Long Strike" was performed by an all-white cast for mixed—but segregated—audiences. The Co-operative Soap Factory and Co-operative Underwear Factory (which would open later in 1886) employed only white women. Blacks were reached out to, but only as prospective customers. White activists organized the Co-operative Building Association, which they opened to black members only after prolonged debate. There were few opportunities for rank-and-file Knights of different races to develop any personal experiences with one another. Traditional prejudices and preconceptions were hard to combat.

The resolution of a complex internal issue in fall 1885 suggests the difficulty encountered by any thrust toward interracial organization. The court of DA 84 was to hear an important case, but only two of its judges were available. According to the Order's bylaws, however, three judges were required to serve together at every DA court session. In the absence of a judge, bylaws provided that a judge be borrowed from the nearest district assembly. District Master Workman William Mullen argued that DA 84 must do so, that two judges could not hear the case, and that a third has to be drawn from DA 92. But the white delegates of DA 84—five from each local assembly in its jurisdiction—out-voted Mullen, and the case was heard by their two judges. Mullen appealed to Powderly:

> The result of the whole thing is that District Assembly 92 is a colored District and the court of District Assembly 84 would have had to apply to it for a

judge to fill the vacancy, and they did not want a colored judge in the court. They may sugar-coat the matter as they please, but this is the true pinch.[29]

In the latter half of 1885, DA 92's activists were too preoccupied with community problems to worry about sending one of their judges to DA 84's court. In June, two new black local assemblies, Nos. 3912 and 3929, were founded. The latter, with forty-nine charter members, was the first black women's assembly organized in Richmond. Two months later, black women's Local Assembly No. (LA) 4096 was established. Militants and organizers spread the Order's influence throughout black Richmond and beyond; they generated local assemblies in Manchester and rural parts of Henrico and Chesterfield counties. The entire black social network, including its connections in the countryside, was encompassed by DA 92.[30]

The Knights of Labor General Assembly of October 1885, held in Hamilton, Ontario, assured DA 92 the indisputable leadership of the black community. The treatment accorded Joseph Brown Johnson, as DA 92's official delegate to this meeting, put to rest any remaining doubts of black Richmond about the Knights. As the only black delegate present, Johnson was invited to join General Master Workman Powderly on the platform for the convention's opening ceremonies. A prominent labor reformer reported to *John Swinton's Paper* that Powderly, in the midst of his address, "turned to the brother from Virginia, and taking him by the hand, pledged him the services of the Order for his race to fulfill for them their complete enfranchisement in common with those whose faces were white." Later, Johnson was appointed to the important committee on the State of the Order. This sort of recognition cemented black Richmond's allegiance to the Knights.[31]

William Mullen's role at the General Assembly further encouraged black identification with the Order. Given the honor of convening the first session, Mullen presented Powderly with a gavel specially made by members of DA 84. "It is as plain a gavel as I have ever seen," he declared; "it is not decked with silver or gold or precious stones; in this, it is in fitful keeping with the plain but beautiful workings of our honored Order." It was for Mullen symbolic of the nation's history, seen from the new perspective of the Knights' movement culture. The Order, it was understood, was ready to assume the mantle of responsibility first worn by the revolutionaries of the 1770s, and then by the liberating forces of the Civil War. The handle of the gavel was made from "a piece of the sounding board that stood in old St. John's Church at the time that Patrick Henry made his famous speech in that church, and therefore is a piece of the instrument that echoed and re-echoed the patriotic words, 'Give me liberty or give me death!' " It was "topped" with a piece of wood cut from a tree "at Yorktown, Virginia, as near as possible to the scene of the surrender of Cornwallis to Washington, and therefore represents the close of the first revolution." The ball of the gavel was made from "one of the pillars of the old Libby prison" where "were confined true and patriotic sons of our common country as prisoners of war for being engaged in a struggle to liberate a race of people from the galling yoke of slavery." Mullen, a native southerner, paid eloquent tribute to Union soldiers:

> These men were firm in their opinion that all men should be free, and enjoy the sunlight of heaven provided by a kind Providence, as men free and independent. In order to support their convictions, they brought all they possessed and at the altar of their country offered it as a willing sacrifice to liberty. Home, wives, children, mothers, fathers, sisters, brothers, friends, and all the associations and comforts that had surrounded them from the cradle were counted as naught, if they could but wipe out foreover the blot and blight of slavery from the future history of America.[32]

Mullen then offered an effusive vision of the future remaking of American society to be accomplished by the Knights:

> There still remains a battle to be fought for the establishment of universal freedom. Can those who are now the slaves of monopoly and oppression be liberated as easily as was the African race in America? Yea, even more easily! To accomplish the first required men to bare their breasts to the rage of battle, second only in its terrors to the furies of hell. It required that thousands of widows and orphans should be made; that acres of land should be so saturated with previous blood drawn from the veins of some of the purest and best of our country; and that tears should flow like living streams. To accomplish the second requires only organization, education, and co-operation. It must and shall be done, and to you, sir, as the representative of that grand army that is to work the third revolution, in which no single race is to be set free, but in which all the nations of the earth are to be liberated, I present you with this gavel, clothed with so much of our past history. I know that I but utter the sentiments of District Assembly 84 when I say, God grant that this gavel may, in your hands, preside over, in the future, many happy gatherings of the noble hearted sons of toil to celebrate the holiday of the establishment of these grand principles—a fair day's pay for a fair day's work, and an injury to one is the concern of all.[33]

Mullen's oration touched responsive chords. The *Journal of United Labor* reprinted the complete text, insuring that it would be reread by virtually every local assembly in the country. At the General Assembly itself, Mullen was accorded considerable recognition. He was nominated for the executive board by none other than Joseph Brown Johnson. While Mullen lost this contest, he received an indirect honor when the delegates voted overwhelmingly to hold the 1886 General Assembly in Richmond. Here was a reward that could be shared with the entire community, white and black.[34]

The role played at the General Assembly by DA 84's other delegate, Frank Reilly, also encouraged black support for the Order. Already a leader in Richmond's "Order of United Veterans," Reilly promoted the organization of a "Gray and Blue of the Knights of Labor" at the convention. Former soldiers from Arkansas, New York, Missouri, Illinois, Louisiana, Pennsylvania, Connecticut, Indiana, Virginia, West Virginia, and Maryland joined him. They adopted a motto: "Capital divided, Labor unites us," and they issued a declaration that contended: "wars have been injurious to those who toil, and that the workers of the world have been the instrument where by governments have been set up and overthrown." The "Gray and Blue of the Knights of Labor" saw the organization as the first step in building "the great army of peace, whose mission is to abolish poverty and establish the universal brotherhood of man."[35]

When reports of these proceedings reached black Richmond—carried in person by Joseph Brown Johnson as well as by the national labor press—local enthusiasm for the Order reached new heights. In November, black quarrymen and stonecutters in Granite, the company town established north of the city by the Richmond Granite Company, were ready to organize themselves as a local assembly of the Knights of Labor. They sent for Johnson, and he hurried to them and gave them official sanction and a charter. Existing black local assemblies swelled.[36]

There were new organizational advances among whites as well. Charles M. Miller, an organizer for DA 84, chartered new women's local assemblies 4474 and 4684 in Richmond and extended the DA's field of operation into Berkeley and surrounding rural towns. Mullen gave lectures to interested groups in Drewry's Bluff, Newport News, Portsmouth, and Petersburg. There appeared to be no limit to the fields being sown by the Knights.[37]

• • •

This sort of rapid growth created problems of its own. New members joined at a pace that outstripped the ability of veteran activists to "educate" them and integrate them into the Order's "constructive" projects. New recruits brought significant vestiges of the received culture of both races into the Order. And the strongest vestige, the one hardest to root out, remained the racial frameworks and commitments adhered to by both black and white workers.

When he attempted to analyze Virginia politics for Powderly, the master workman of a rural-based local assembly affiliated with DA 84 commented: "Taking everything into consideration, the political differences between the whites and blacks and the general opinions held by them. . . . The colored man in this state feels that the white man is his enemy." Democratic and Republican politicians alike were determined to keep black and white workers apart and under their control. The fall 1885 elections gave them an opportunity to spin their intrigues.[38]

The Democrats were particularly skillful at such tactics. Their ticket carefully blended traditional "cavalier" visions with the party's newer planks, which would promote "New South" economic development. Democratic orators claimed to be the true "friend of the workingman." Their platform included protectionism and public works jobs for local residents, as well as innuendos about "Negro domination" and about economic disaster that would follow a Republican victory. Robert E. Lee's nephew Fitzhugh Lee headed the ticket, and he stumped the state on Traveller, the General's aging but well-known horse. Congressman George D. Wise took to the hustings in white working-class neighborhoods to advocate high tariffs and expanded public works projects. Local Democratic newspapers played up State Senator J. Taylor Ellyson's public letter to the *Journal of United Labor* in which he asked Powderly to present a model convict-labor statute. The *Dispatch*, printed a letter from "A Workingman," which charged that "the Republican tickets for this congressional district were printed in a rat office in Washington, an office which is being boycotted by all the labor organizations of that city." The Democratic slate carried every Richmond ward but one—Jackson Ward, the ghetto.[39]

While electoral politics generated divisions within the movement, the boycott continued to provide a powerful unifying influence. Before the end of the year, the Knights won a clear-cut morale-boosting victory over the Haxall-Crenshaw Company. They had forced the management to give a "writren promise that they will not buy any more convict-made barrels, and will not discriminate against Knights of Labor in their establishment." The boycott had held firm for nine months and had pushed Richmond's most powerful firm "to the wall." It had also provided the Knights with their major vehicle for growth as it spread through both black and white communities and drew thousands of men and women into the Order. Their victory demonstrated to workers how much could be accomplished by united action and gave them new confidence in their own abilities. At the same time, it demonstrated the Knights' potential to those thousands, both black and white, who had stayed on the sidelines to this point.[40]

In the wake of this victory, Knights of Labor activists looked to the city hall issue as a new rallying point. The city council appeared no closer to beginning construction than it had two years earlier, when the issue was first raised. In the interim, rumors of letting contracts to outside firms using Ohio sandstone or New Hampshire granite, rather than local materials, and outside laborers had angered Richmond workers. Shortly before Christmas 1885, DA 84's executive board sent a petition to the city council, "in the name of the 8,000 Knights of Labor of this city." Their demands were simple and straightforward: "the City Hall be built by day-labor, with Virginia granite, and the work performed by Richmond workmen." They supported these demands with a vision and language shared by Knights of both races.

> You have God-given material within your reach; you likewise have the workmen, your own citizens, your tax-payers, whom you represent, artisans skilled in every line of work; men able, efficient, anxious to secure it and needing the work.

> Your own citizens will take a local pride in performing their tasks in a workmanlike manner and rearing a building that will not only be an ornament to the city, but will reflect credit on the workmen.[41]

The Knights' local legitimacy took a quantum leap with the Haxall-Crenshaw victory. By mid-January 1886, the local correspondent wrote *John Swinton's Paper* of the "new revival of the Knights of Labor" sweeping Richmond and of the "many new members flocking in." Four new white local assemblies were organized in January and February. Two were women's assemblies 5069 and 5607, a third was "trade" assembly 5192, organized by tinners, plumbers, and gas-fitters, and a fourth was "mixed" assembly 5001. Moreover, plasterers and painters announced plans to form "trade" assemblies affiliated to DA 84. Both district assemblies were granted formal permission to expand their jurisdiction within a radius of twenty-five miles from Richmond. Mullen even organized a local assembly of black town officials and patronage job-holders in Petersburg over the objections of white Knights of that city. Early 1886 saw a veritable explosion in Knights' membership across the state of Virginia with Richmond as the radial center.[42]

By midwinter, Richmond's Knights of Labor had reached a new peak of influence. Ten thousand blacks and whites had joined and been exposed to the Order's movement culture. Still, despite the phenomenal growth of the movement among both races, the color line held as tenaciously in February 1886 as it had in 1885. It remained the great divide of daily organizing and activity, and few workers crossed it to build a new interracial culture.

CHAPTER 9

Spring 1886: The Apex of the Knights of Labor

By early 1886, the Knights of Labor stood at a critical threshold. After months of mass boycotts, constructive projects, cultural undertakings, and internal education, its militants had undermined the traditional balance of power in Richmond. Over the next months, they would push the Knights to the height of their popularity and power. But this entailed, on the one hand, the sharpening of class lines between the bourgeoisie and white workers. On the other hand, militants narrowed the division between the two district assemblies toward the end of a biracial Order. By late spring, they provided a political expression for these trends with their Workingmen's Reform party.

Within District Assembly (DA) 92, in these critical months, black tobacco factory workers rose to leadership positions. They blended race and class consciousness, their own industrial experience, and the acumen of the veteran activists who moved over to share the mantle of leadership with them. This new leadership alliance guided DA 84. Every step toward racial cooperation provided an experiential base for further cooperation: The orders' progress in this direction opened new possibilities for black and white workers alike.

Militants also directed the popular movement in a significantly new direction altogether—toward independent political organization on a biracial, working-class basis. The Workingmen's Reform ticket would ride the crest of an electoral tidal wave in May and seemingly take majority control of both the city council and the board of aldermen. White and black activists alike would enter new arenas and confront new problems.

• • •

Tobacco factory workers were the nucleus of the first black local assemblies. But when DA 92 was organized some months after Powderly's January

1885 visit, the mantle of leadership had been assumed by veteran activists from nonindustrial backgrounds: a dairyman, a porter, a shoemaker, a barber. These men had the combination of experience and popular legitimacy necessary to promote the Knights of Labor in its first months. Industrial workers, however, rapidly gained the experience and built the following necessary to take the reins of power within DA 92.

By March 1886, fully two-thirds of Richmond's five thousand tobacco factory workers were members of the Order. They pushed forward one of their own, Richard Thompson, for District Master Workman, supplanting dairy farmer John T. Mitchell, who had completed a six-month term. Thirty-eight years old, Thompson was well situated within the black social network, even though he had made little public name for himself before the emergence of the Knights. His father, a carpenter, and his mother were active participants in the collective life of black Richmond after the war. In 1869 his father had been a founding member of the interracial "Richmond Radical Association," whose major goal had been a "reading room" in the city's impoverished East End. Five years later, he was elected an officer of the United Sons and Daughters of Love, a beneficial secret society. Thompson's mother was president of the Young Sons and Daughters of the Valley, a religious society. He and his brother worked in tobacco factories to support the household, and they were integrated into the black social network by their parents. In 1872, still single and living at home, twenty-four-year-old Richard had served his mother's secret society as secretary. He married soon after and began his own family. They joined the First African Baptist Church, but left amidst the Readjuster controversy of 1879–1880. By 1880, Richard and Adelaide Thompson were the parents of four children. They lived in a three-family tenement near his parents' home in an almost entirely black section dominated by tobacco factory workers. While his brother William had followed their father into carpentry, Richard remained a tobacco factory worker, a skilled lump-maker.[1]

Other new officers joined Thompson at the helm of DA 92. Joseph J. Burwell, a literate barber in his early forties, became the district recording secretary. A long-time resident of Jackson Ward, he also came from a family well established within the black social network. His late father had been a slave and had belonged to the First African Baptist Church from its inception in 1842. He also had been a trustee of the Baptist Helping Society as well as president of Lincoln Lodge, No. 20, a political secret society, in the early 1870s. Like Richard Thompson, Joseph Burwell had not emerged from the black social network until the Knights appeared. Much the same could be said of the newly elected district financial secretary, William W. Fields. His mother, like Burwell's father, had been baptized into the First African Baptist Church in 1842. After her husband's premature death, Sarah Fields supported her son and five daughters as a washerwoman. Her efforts enabled him to attend school during the difficult years of the late 1860s. By the early 1870s, still only a teenager, "Willie" became the "man" of the house. He got a job moving hogsheads in tobacco warehouses. In 1874, he was elected secretary of the Independent National Blues, a militia unit composed largely of tobacco factory workers, and he served as secretary for its female affiliate, the Loving Daughters of the Independent National Blues. Thompson, Burwell, and Fields, the new leadership of DA 92 in the frantic days of 1886, were deeply involved in the black social network and tied in a variety of ways to the tobacco factory workforce.[2]

James H. Washington was appointed to the vital position of district organizer. Born a slave in Alexandria, he had been hired out to work in the tobacco factories of Richmond in the 1850s. After Emancipation, he settled in Richmond with his wife, his children, and his parents. Articulate despite illiteracy, Washington soon emerged as a respected activist in tobacco factory worker circles. In 1870, he was elected an officer in the Star Union Sons, a secret political society organized by tobacco factory workers and its female affiliate, the Star Union Daughters. By fall 1875, caught up in the trend toward independent black labor organization, he became an officer in the State Assembly of the Industrial Brotherhood. In the early 1880s, Washington had emerged as a pro-Readjuster activist in Richmond's East End. A neighbor of Richard Thompson's, he had the experience and prominence to serve as DA 92's organizer, a post he assumed with enthusiasm.[3]

Assembly 92's new leaders had no public identification with the political thought once dominant in the black community. They were thus able to express the new ideas and forces bubbling up in the black wards; they wove together the rhetoric of "equal rights" and "race pride" to present a militant racial perspective cautiously open to cooperation with white workers. They were echoed by Thomas Fortune's widely read *New York Freeman*, which noted in spring 1886: "The revolution is upon us, and since we are largely of the laboring population it is very natural that we should take sides with the labor forces in their fight for a juster distribution of the results of labor."[4]

Black workers had been drawn to the Knights by the Haxall-Crenshaw boycott and the special recognition accorded Joseph Brown Johnson at the October 1885 General Assembly. Their integration into the Order was facilitated by its dual organizational structure, which proved adaptable to independent racial organization and to the local black social network. Their integration had been enhanced by the evangelical fervor and language of the Order, its ritualized and symbolic procedures, and its acceptance of the "equality" of "all men." DA 84's leaders, in taking up the cause of both black and white coopers in the Haxall-Crenshaw boycott, in encouraging the founding of black local assemblies across the state, and in contributing to the Ontario General Assembly, had encouraged black identification with the Knights. Despite its impressive growth, DA 92—and the black popular movement it represented—did not adopt an aggressive stance during the next year. The local economic and political climates remained grim for black workers, and caution continued to accompany black identification with the Knights.[5]

DA 92 entered a new phase in early 1886—as had DA 84 and the growing trade union movement around it. The victory over Haxall-Crenshaw in December 1885 had much to do with this shift in mood. The tobacco factory workers' assumption of the central role in the movement signaled a new boldness. Tobacco factory workers had traditionally been the core of black popular activity. Now, imperiled by the introduction of new machinery and the growth of the cigarette industry, they brought an added urgency to the Order early in 1886. With DA 92 as their spokesmen, they began to push the black popular movement forward. They also tried to reach over to DA 84. In February, a group of tobacco factory workers joined with William W. Childress, a white engineer employed at F. B. Pace's factory and an active member of Union Assembly No. 3545, to develop plans to "steady employment for about two or three thousand men and bring about a million dollars into circulation for the benefit of the brothers of our Order." They planned to open a series of cooperatively managed tobacco factories, using labels such as "Master Workman" and "Unknown Knight," which would readily attract working-class consumers across the country. Though this project was never realized—due to lack of capital—its very consideration reflected the spread of new ideas within DA 92.[6]

The black members of DA 92 were inspired by the victories gained by the white members of DA 84. With the support of the black social network, organized through No. 92, black workers pushed forward.

On April 1, 1886, forty-seven black coopers, the employees of two medium-sized barrel shops, struck for a wage increase. Acting through DA 92, they were able to close both shops for two full months. They returned to work on June 1; they had won the moral victory of a slight increase from ninety cents to one dollar a day, although their sixty-hour work week remained unchanged. The strike was a triumph for all of DA 92 as well. As the first offensive strike launched by Richmond's black labor in almost two decades, the coopers' walkout received widespread popular backing. The strikers were given material assistance through No. 92, and strikebreaking was kept to a minimum by the Knights' presence in the black community.[7]

Another group of black workingmen also struck on April 1. One hundred twenty black hod-carriers, organized as Hod-Carriers' Union No. 1, struck sixteen contractors for an increase of twenty-five cents a day, to bring their daily wages up to $1.50. White bricklayers that very day had been granted a wage increase, to $4.00. DA 92 helped the hod-carriers prevent strikebreaking by black workingmen, while No. 84 policed the ranks of possible white strikebreakers. A Manchester employer reported that his foreman boasted, "I can get plenty of men at what you have been paying." But only four strikebreakers appeared the following day, and they were driven off by a large crowd of black women and men. Other contractors found their attempts to employ scabs, whether white or black, similarly frustrated. By the end of the month, the contractors had yielded.[8]

In late April and early May 1886, the black popular movement was building rapidly; its progress was parallel to and consonant with the momentum of the white popular movement. When Powderly's March ban on further expansion was lifted, three new local assemblies were organized: two mixed locals of workingmen, 6099 and 6545, and one mixed assembly of white women, 7283. Established assemblies, black and white, continued to grow, with an estimated two hundred new members joining each week.[9]

• • •

A vivid illustration of the new possibilities opened up by the Knights' progress is found in the developing relationship between the two district assemblies, the granite cutters' union, and black and white quarry workers. Traditionally, hierarchy and hostility had characterized race relations in this industry, to the benefit of quarry owners and managers.

Granite quarrying and stonecutting had been of minor importance in Richmond until 1872, when the Old Dominion Granite Quarry secured a major federal contract to supply granite for the new State Department building in Washington, D.C. Colonel Albert Ordway, a Union army veteran, was put in charge of the project, and he recruited two hundred skilled white granite cutters from the North. Ordway also needed a large workforce of unskilled quarrymen. In a labor-intensive industry like this, a profit depended on low labor costs. Since the skilled stone cutters were unionized, politically astute, and absolutely essential to the quarrying operation, they could not be alienated. The manager turned instead to the unskilled quarrymen.[10]

Ordway solved his unskilled labor needs when he negotiated a contract with the Virginia State Penitentiary to lease 277 black convicts at twenty-five cents apiece per day. While also responsible for providing them with food, clothing, and shelter, he cut corners on these expenses whenever possible. Consequently, the harsh living and working conditions took their toll; in the first year of Ordway's contract, thirteen black convicts died.[11]

Quarry managers, who copied and modified Ordway's formula, superimposed racial distinctions on the division of labor and adopted different tactics toward each group of employees. Highly skilled and motivated granite cutters were attracted to each quarry; their employers met with their union and satisfied many of their requests. Each quarrying operation also depended greatly on unskilled labor. Since more convicts were not available, quarry managers hired black workingmen, paid them seventy to ninety cents a day and pushed them relentlessly. In this manner, labor costs could be kept down and added profits could be realized. Divided among themselves, the workforce of each quarry could be better controlled and manipulated.[12]

But white union members were not entirely immune to ill usage. Witness, for instance, employer response to the depression which began in late 1873, when contracts began to dry up. Even Ordway was forced to temporarily shut down the Old Dominion Quarry in the winter of 1874 when the federal government withheld its appropriations for the State Department project. Competition among contractors increased, with each desperate to submit the lowest bids for the few projects available. Quarry managers, in turn, were pressed to further reduce labor costs and production time. They could no longer afford to favor their skilled white workers, and their resistance to union demands increased. Ordway continued to set the pace for local quarry employers and managers. In 1874, when work resumed because federal funds were forthcoming, he tried to reduce the traditional lunch break from forty-five minutes to a half hour. He also introduced new punitive features into his piecework wage system; he docked skilled granite cutters for work done on stones that became damaged. In 1877, he reduced piece-rates, and the wages of the skilled men were cut from an average of $3.50 per day to $2.50. Ordway also experimented with training black convicts in the art of granite cutting. The city's other quarry managers watched Ordway carefully and mimicked his innovations whenever they could.[13]

The skilled white granite cutters had never recovered from the losses they had suffered in the depression of the 1870s. The operation of one major "scab" quarry, run by the Philadelphia-based Richmond Granite Company, epitomized their plight. Work was scarce in the winter of 1885–1886; their hopes revolved around plans for the construction of a new city hall and an addition to the Customs House. The persistent work shortage weakened the union's bargaining power. "We hear it too often to our displeasure," noted the union's secretary, "from contractors who tell us how cheap other contractors can have their work done, and how can we expect them to compete for work against such odds, which is a fact we can't deny." There were rumors that the Richmond Granite Company would receive the contract for the stone for the new city hall. White unionists had seen reduced earnings and a diminished demand for skilled labor while they worked under a hated piece-rate system with fines and increased work hours. Black quarrymen found their wages held down, although their hours lengthened.[14]

Encouraged by the new possibilities engendered by DA's 84 and 92, the Richmond granite cutters' union launched a campaign for a shorter work day in January 1886. Quarry managers consented immediately to union demands "to work nine hours after April 1st, one hour for dinner, and quit on Saturdays at 4 o'clock." Fearing the strength that the Knights had recently demonstrated in their victory over Haxall-Crenshaw, the quarry managers readily granted the union's demand for a shorter workday.[15]

The union enjoyed a close relationship with the Knights. The union's leaders and the leaders of DA 84 had worked together on shared concerns—the eight-hour day, the restriction of convict labor—for almost ten years. Their current concern with the construction of the new city hall cemented their ties all the more. Above all, it was the problem of cooperation with their local black counterparts that turned white granite cutters to the Knights. White unionists had traditionally shown little respect for the nearly three hundred black granite cutters and quarrymen who worked for the Richmond Granite Company. They had written off the "scab" yard and made no attempt to organize its black work force. They scorned these black workers by continually referring to them as "convicts" (though none were after 1879) and to their product as "striped" granite. The conclusion of the massive State Department job in late 1885, in the context of the economic recession after 1882, had pushed white unionists to look closely at the Richmond Granite Company's ability to underbid unionized contractors for new projects and the potential strikebreaking role that its black workers might assume.[16]

Black quarrymen had their own history of self-organization, which dated back to the "Grand Lodge of Quarrymen." This secret society initially intended to provide insurance to members, especially in the case of injury or death. In spring 1874, amid extensive layoffs and increased work pressures, they withdrew $50 from their treasury to send a delegate to the Rochester convention of the Industrial Congress. The late 1870s and early 1880s brought new opportunities and new problems. Offers to black quarrymen to operate new machines or to learn the art of granite cutting were eagerly accepted. By the early 1880s, the Richmond Granite Company sought blacks for skilled as well as semiskilled jobs. Labeled a "scab" quarry by the white union, it employed an overwhelmingly black workforce. Its employees, like black quarry workers generally, continued to receive low wages, to experience lengthy bouts of unemployment, and to work under iron-clad discipline. With the revival of the black popular movement in 1885 and the establishment of DA 92, they sought to improve their conditions. In December 1885, a group of Richmond Granite Company workers contacted No. 92's organizer and applied for recognition as a local assembly.[17]

The involvement of both black and white quarry workers with the Knights of Labor offered a new and creative approach to the problems posed by the Richmond Granite Company. Though no social interaction existed among rank-and-file members of the two granite cutters' organizations, the two district assemblies provided a structure of support. It was founded on the recognition that mutual support must flow in two directions and that conditions for stone cutters and quarry workers of both races must improve. This new structure of support would soon be put to a practical test.

In January 1886, the white granite cutters' union had won the promise of employers to reduce the workday from ten hours to nine, as of April 1. Employers also agreed to increase piece rates by twenty cents per hundred blocks, so that the shorter workday would not cause smaller paychecks. Two weeks after the new arrangement had gone into effect, the union asked for another fifteen-cent increase from the Westham Company. Though "business continues dull" with "quite a surplus yet," according to that month's report of union secretary Burwell Eaves, 210 union members struck the city's largest unionized quarry on April 14. Several hundred black men could well have applied for the strikers' jobs, but none did, as the district assemblies discouraged cross-racial strikebreaking.[18]

The black quarry workers showed no interest in scabbing at the Westham Quarry. Instead, they demanded a comparable wage increase. When turned down, all 285 black workers employed by the Richmond Granite Company walked out and requested the assistance of DA 92. The executive boards of the two district assemblies directed both strikes simultaneously. The Westham quarry workers soon got what they wanted, but the Richmond Granite Company stubbornly held out. The joint efforts of assemblies 84 and 92 helped the black workers shut them down for a month. However, this powerful, shrewd antiunion company had substantial resources. Gradually, a scab workforce was recruited and operations were resumed. Because the worksite was several miles from the black community, crowds could not mobilize to discourage strikebreakers. DA 92 assessed its local affiliates for financial support for the strikers and, together with 84, called for a boycott on the quarry's products. The black strikers stood firm for 234 days, until December 21. Their wage increase was eventually granted, but to only 65 of the 285 strikers. However, the persistence of this strike, a center of public attention and popular support from mid-April through fall 1886, contributed to the militance of the black popular movement and its labor representative, 92. It also stood as evidence of the potential for interracial cooperation organized by the district assemblies.[19]

The Order facilitated a coordinated struggle among both black and white quarry workers and allowed each to maintain its own organization. The two district assemblies exercised controls over cross-racial strikebreaking, provided strike benefits through assessments of uninvolved local assemblies, and organized boycotts of the products of quarries that refused to cooperate. On one level, this support significantly improved wages and working conditions for both black and white quarry workers. On an even greater level, it provided a foundation for future biracial cooperation. Where institutional separation had left black and white workers pawns of management, interracial unity brought new strength and hope to working-class activity.

• • •

Across North America, the movement culture reached a peak in spring 1886. Estimated numbers of women and men riding the Knights of Labor bandwagon ranged from 700,000 to 2 million. The wave of popular self-consciousness and self-confidence crested. In city after city, militant Knights sought to channel the movement culture into political expression. "Beginning with the early spring municipal elections and symbolically sanctioned by the special General Assembly session in late May, the Knights sought political power virtually everywhere they were established."[20]

"Organized labor in this city numbers about 12,000, organized on the grand principle that an injury to one is the concern of all," wrote a member of Local Assembly (LA) 3157 to the *Richmond Dispatch*. "Organization is going on in every section of the state in a way unknown before in Virginia," William Mullen reported to *John Swinton's Paper*. "There is a splendid feeling among all classes of toilers, and a brighter time seems coming." Richmond had prominent activists among both races who had extensive experience in "independent" and "reform" politics. Their natural target was the May municipal election, which provided opportunities to contest the local bourgeoisie's power and to unify the movement's biracial base. Because the two dominant sectional parties of the 1880s both reflected and served to maintain racial divisions, "the Knights had to extend bi-racial co-operation into politics; or, sooner or later, abandon it altogether."[21]

On the evening of May 5, 1886, eighty-four delegates from twelve of the local assemblies affiliated with No. 84 assembled at Laube's Hall. Seven representatives from each local assembly freely debated the proposed course of action. They overwhelmingly agreed not to participate in the forthcoming Democratic primary for the selection of municipal candidates. The alternative, however, generated hours of debate. Some felt that the mainstream candidates should be selected and then pressured for commitments on specific issues such as employment of local labor on the new city hall. Others urged boycotting the elections altogether, then lobbying the city council, regardless of its composition, to accept their demands. The dominant mood was expressed by an unnamed delegate who "advocated putting out a Workingmen's ticket for Council and Board of Aldermen after the primary and supporting such a ticket." Following the convention, the *Labor Herald* advised its readers: "DON'T VOTE IN THE PRIMARY ELECTION." It editorialized: "The best of policy demands that the city government be cleansed with a washing out, and practical men selected to do practical work."[22]

The delegates reassembled at Laube's Hall the night of May 17, after the Democratic primary, to hear the report of the committee appointed to draft a statement of principles. They clearly expressed popular militancy, its deep-seated traditions and emerging vision:

> Your committee submits the following preamble and platform of principles for adoption by the Convention, that it may be unfurled to the breeze by the workingmen of this city upon the dawn of tomorrow, and kept steadfast to the mast by men of strong arms and of an iron will, determined to know no such word as surrender, but firm in the belief that the setting sun of the evening of the election will sweep away all obstacles to the true advancement of the interests of the workingmen of this city, and establish a feeling of good will and peace on earth to all men in its triumphant march onward and upward to the pinnacle of fame.
>
> Platform
>
> In thus presenting ourselves to the public in what may be by some considered a new departure, we desire a careful reading of the following:

In exercising the right of suffrage all should be left free in their efforts to secure "the greatest good to the greatest number," and on all such we call most earnestly to assist us in attaining the ends hereafter set forth.

It should be borne in mind by all, when exercising the right of franchise, that most of the objects herein set forth can only be obtained through legislation, and that it is the duty of all to assist and support by their vote such candidates only as will pledge their support to the following measures regardless of party:

1. We desire that industrial and moral worth, not wealth, be considered the true standard of individual and national greatness.
2. We desire to secure to the industrial classes the full enjoyment of the wealth they create, sufficient leisure in which to develop their intellectual, moral, and social faculties, to enable them, to share in the gains and honors of advancing civilization.

3. We desire that all wage-workers be paid weekly by the city in lawful money.

4. We desire the abolition of the contract system of municipal works.

5. We desire absolute discontinuance of imported foreign labor under contract.

6. And particularly do we demand that all efforts at contracting for the erection of our future city hall be at once, if at all practicable, discontinued, and that its construction be performed by day labor and of Virginia material as far as practical in the strictest sense of the word.

7. We desire that the most rigid economy in all municipal affairs be exercised, so as no longer to overburden the power of industry. To this end, we submit for your suffrage the nominees of this Convention to represent our desires in the two branches of our city government.[23]

Endorsing this platform, the delegates then nominated a slate of candidates under the banner of the "Workingmen's Reform Party." Tickets for council and aldermen from every ward except Jackson were selected. The candidates included veteran trade unionists, labor reformers, social and fraternal society leaders; skilled workers, shopkeepers, and small manufacturers; native-born Virginians, northerners, and first- and second-generation Irishmen and Germans. All were white.[24]

Although black Richmond revolved around Jackson Ward, significant pockets of black population existed outside the ghetto. Some 30 percent of Marshall Ward's eleven thousand residents were black, as were 28 percent of Jefferson Ward's. While Madison and Monroe wards, the twin sites of the city's commercial and governmental districts, had fewer blacks, Clay Ward, dominated by iron and quarry workers, was 25 percent black. Many of these black residents had been organized into Knights of Labor local assemblies, but the structure of the "Workingmen's Reform Party" left them voiceless in their own wards.[25]

The Workingmen's Reform party refrained from challenging for power in two important areas. They chose not to contest for the city-wide offices, like mayor, and thus left that field open to the Democratic nominees. No arrangements had been struck with the Democratic party, but the reformers chose to endorse Mayor William C. Carrington. Whether they freely supported Carrington and his running mates or whether they simply felt themselves unable to win on a city-wide level, their hesitancy to challenge for political power at this level is surprising. Clearly, they could expect to win in the Marshall, Jefferson, and Clay wards—two of which were the city's largest—and to lose in the Madison and Monroe wards. Jackson Ward, whose black electorate represented a third force, could swing the balance in a close contest.[26]

Jackson Ward represented the second area that the reformers had refrained from entering. Some among their white candidates in the city's five other wards were known to openly sympathize with the Republicans. These sympathizers were not close to the power centers in the party machine, but they had been attracted to the GOP fringes through old allegiances, labor reform, the Readjuster movement, Irish nationalism, and antitemperance campaigns. There they had remained, equally distant from the Republican "ring" and the Republican party's black base.[27]

Richmond's black political expression had come to focus on Jackson Ward, where black workingmen made up the overwhelming majority of the electorate. Under the influence of the Readjuster movement, informed with the race consciousness that emerged with it, black working-class activists had wrested control of the ward organization from the Republican machine. "Republican" affairs in Jackson Ward were controlled by an independent black political organization with a popular base. This political organization, wearing a nominally "Republican" label, nominated its own slate for council and aldermen from the ward. The Knights' white reformers did not embrace the Jackson Ward organization; nor did they challenge it. They did, however, publicly endorse the organization's slate, an indirect but significant step.[28]

The black Jackson Ward officials made rather traditional choices. Despite their autonomy they continued to rely on the Republican party for support. The party "ring" controlled the channels of communication, patronage, and power between Washington and Jackson Ward. James Bahen, a white grocer and influential machine boss, was nominated for reelection as alderman. He had proven, while in office, more successful than the ward's black representatives in obtaining public improvements for his constituents. More important, he remained the primary connection between the ward and the "ring," the man everyone had to see about their requests. Nevertheless, the source of his power was precisely what the white reformers were committed to eradicating. The willingness of Jackson Ward's politicians to nominate him reveals the political limitations of the black popular movement, even as it embraced race pride and the Knights of Labor.[29]

Despite these limitations, there were important new breakthroughs. For the first time since the creation of Jackson Ward in 1871, all five candidates for city council were black. Surely it was an indication of the influence of race pride. Yet most of the candidates were members of the black middle class and not affiliated with the Knights of Labor. Dr. Robert E. Jones, at age twenty-six, and attorney James H. Hayes, at twenty-eight, were two outstanding young members of the youthful new black middle class. They were educated professionals, committed activists, and advocates of race pride. Though a Richmond native, Hayes, like Jones, had begun his local practice in the early 1880s, after an extended education in the North. The political involvement of both men had grown slowly, and their nomination for city council in 1886 was their first public recognition by the Jackson Ward black community.[30]

The three other council candidates were older men with long-established local roots. Though active politically in the past, they were not tainted by connections with the "ring." Jeremiah B. Griffin was the free-born son of a black tobacco factory worker. He learned to read and write, struggled to support his family, and became a pillar of the First African Baptist Church. While his older brothers had worked in the tobacco factories, Jeremiah had finished school. By the early 1880s, he had become a Richmond teacher. Joseph E. Farrar and Edinboro Archer represented an earlier generation of black activists, men who worked with their hands. Farrar, in his mid-fifties, had been a successful carpenter and contractor, a respected church and society officer, but had not shown much interest in politics until the rise of the Readjuster movement in the early 1880s. Archer, a wheelwright, had also entered the political arena in the early 1880s. Although Griffin, Farrar, and Archer were experienced in political matters, they kept their distance from the "ring."[31]

The efforts of these five candidates did not go unopposed. On May 24, a "number of leading Republicans" assembled, and the meeting was chaired by black associates of the "ring." They suggested overturning the party nominations and replacing them with "ring" allies, including several white grocers and liquor dealers. But black workingmen packed the meeting and voted down the proposals. When the white reformers announced their support for the officially nominated Jackson Ward slate, black workingmen in Clay Ward organized the "Clay Ward Colored Independents" to support the Workingmen's ticket in this district. Similar actions were reported in Marshall and Jefferson wards. The black and white popular movements, strongest in the wards dominated by working-class families of both races threatened to become a single political movement in late May.[32]

Allied yet independent, militant black and white workingmen pressed for political power by linking with the popular movements in their respective communities. Though the two structures and their mass bases were not fused, their shared focus and mutual support represented a marked departure from local political traditions. The political sphere now offered the opportunity to establish connections between them. A single Workingmen's ticket included black candidates nominated by black men (restricted to Jackson Ward), and its proponents sought biracial working-class support across the city. The *Labor Herald* asked voters to support candidates "regardless of all former party associations who will carry out our wishes and legislate for the public good."[33]

The campaign took on an intensely popular character. In the final week before election day, William Mullen, the architect of the independent political movement, left for the special General Assembly of the Knights of Labor in Cleveland. In his absence, some two hundred white delegates assembled to map out last-minute campaign plans. They extended their movement to Manchester, where they endorsed a workingmen's ticket headed by M. R. Loyd. He was an officer of Manchester Assembly No. 3619 and the Knights of Labor Building Association. Election day itself took on a popular cast, as many militants stayed away from their jobs in order to watch the polls and get out the vote. They were well aware of the Democrats' capacity for pressure tactics, used so effectively against black voters in the past, and they were determined not to fall victims themselves.[34]

When the ballots were counted, the Workingmen's ticket, which had carried every ward except Madison, scored a resounding victory. "We had a slight volcanic eruption here on Thursday last," one Republican leader wrote Mahone, "at which time all nature seemed convulsed. And all indications point to further upheavals during the year." Enthusiasm and confidence swept the white and black popular movements. The *Labor Herald* reflected this new confidence:

> The cause of the workingmen has triumphed. . . . It is the proud boast of the workingmen of Richmond that no man or clique—whether it be Mahone or the Democratic City Central Committee—can lead them around by the nose. The elements that composed the Reform Party will now drift like regular channels until reform is needed again, when all may rest assured they will speak with a still louder voice.[35]

With their impressive sweep of the council and aldermanic election at the end of May 1886, the Knights of Labor had reached the peak of their popular power. The ranks of both district assemblies had pulled together on behalf of the Workingmen's ticket. Thus did two traditionally separate, racially based popular movements begin to flow together. Burwell Eaves, secretary of the granite cutter's union, understandably exulted: "We have just had our city elections and the workingmen succeeded by an overwhelming majority in electing the Reform Ticket. This election is unparalleled in the history of this city, from the simple fact that the workingmen were never known to stick so closely together before."[36]

At the same time, both the political organization and the election campaign had called new attention to the wide divisions within the ranks of the Knights. If anything, the unity that existed in the campaign bore testimony to the result-minded willingness of labor to set aside immediate differences and to leave competing demands to a day of reckoning in the future. Nor could the electoral victory gloss over the deep racial divisions made obvious by the all-white character of the Reform party and its formal negotiations with Jackson Ward's black political organization. Here was the Achilles' heel of the Knights of Labor.

CHAPTER 10

Politics, Race, and the Decomposition of the Movement Culture

THE KNIGHTS of Labor's impressive success in Richmond in 1885 and early 1886 had established numerous links between local black and white labor. It was accomplished by a combination of developments and activities: the Haxall-Crenshaw boycott in support of coopers, a racially mixed trade; the *Labor Herald*, which gave voice to a language drenched in the Old Testament and the political tradition of equal rights; cooperative projects, which involved militants of both races; ritual and symbolism, which applied equally to white and black local assemblies; and the espousal of biracial solidarity at local, district, and national levels of the Knights of Labor. Considering the centuries of racial separation and discrimination, we appreciate all the more the accomplishments represented by this interracial collaboration and recognize its terribly fragile quality.

While black and white popular movements joined increasingly in a formal sense, both remained deeply rooted within their traditional communities. Indeed, this was both the Knights' strength and weakness. On the one hand, local organization grew easily from preexisting institutions that were formal (trade unions, fraternal societies, and church congregations) and informal (neighborhoods, ethnic groups, friendship networks). On the other hand, traditional habits and perceptions remained within these institutional channels. Such was the case in late 1885 and early 1886 when so many new members joined that existing structures were nearly swamped. Indeed, it was at this point that General Master Workman Powderly called for a nationwide, forty-day moratorium on new organizing.

The movement culture, nurtured by activists of both races, pushed gently against these structural limits. Recruits to the Order were integrated into constructive projects and educated in its goals. Although these projects promoted a sense of biracial solidarity and allowed some cooperation among militants, they fostered little face-to-face contact among the rank and file.

Without such contact, mutual understanding was difficult, and traditional misperceptions and prejudices endured.

The stunning victory of the Workingmen's Reform ticket of May 1886 did not push the Knights to greater heights in Richmond. To the contrary, the electoral triumph generated the disintegration of the biracial popular movement that it represented. This victory suddenly posed a host of problems for which the biracial movement and its culture were unprepared. Issues were pushed to the top of the agenda long before there was a foundation for their resolution. Meanwhile, political vultures of all stripes descended on the movement; exacerbated tensions; revived traditional mistrust, hostilities, and loyalties; and wove a web of intrigue and co-optation. Committed militants from both races, struggling against these influences, tried to resolve complex issues as they arose and build a foundation for biracial cooperation. Despite their creativity and commitment, the Knights would disintegrate as rapidly as they arose.

• • •

Awareness of their central role in the election victory heightened the assertiveness of black workers. "Without their solid support, the ring would have again triumphed," a local associate wrote William Mahone. "These people know this well." Under the headline "What Will Be Done for Our People?" the postelection *Richmond Planet* warned:

> All hands in this city are gazing on the newly elected members of the City Council. What will be done for our people? To a great extent that will determine their actions in future campaigns. Now will be demonstrated whether liberal Democrats are willing to recognize the colored brother. Can they cast aside race prejudice long enough to heed not the whispers of partisan Bourbons flaunting in the faces of weak-kneed constituents the ghost of Negro supremacy?[1]

The black popular movement around District Assembly No. 92 became particularly assertive in late spring and early summer 1886. The possibility of economic revival, combined with the new scope and power of workplace and community organization represented by the Knights of Labor, encouraged groups of black workers to raise demands and be ready to act on them. Before the May elections, black coopers, hod carriers, and quarry workers launched strikes under the auspices of No. 92. Though their demands had been influenced by those gains of their white counterparts, each strike contributed to the black dynamism. Black workers influenced, encouraged, and assisted each other, and the collective activism that emerged bespoke a racial pride and militancy comparable to the explosion of 1882–1883, but with a much more explicit labor foundation than ever before.[2]

Workplace militancy spread in early June from coopers and quarry workers to the Manchester and Richmond brickyards. Brickmaking was a traditionally "black" occupation. For meager wages, black men spent seventy-two hours a week in the hot sun at the peak of the season and struggled to survive for the four-to-five-month seasonal shutdown.

> We are required to be on the brickyard at daybreak, to make 3,000 bricks in the space of four or five hours, remaining there until four o'clock in the afternoon before we can get the bricks up that we made the day before. This makes us have to be fourteen hours in their employment for the small trifle of $1.50 to the moulder, $1.25 to the wheeler, $1.00 to the bearer, and 25 cents to the mould-washer.[3]

These brickmakers were proud of their trade: "Every paving brick and every brick of any description that you see in your beautiful buildings in Richmond is made by colored mechanics." Their craft pride and their long, harsh days together had laid the foundation for self-organization. So did the organization of brickmaking processes. Each yard's workforce was divided into regular groups of three men and one boy, who labored together every day around their "table." The "moulder" was the unquestioned head of each team. They worked in relative quiet, able to speak freely and to get to know one another. The performance of each worker depended on the performance of the others, down to the young boy who washed the moulds and kept the table supplied with clean ones. Since Emancipation, the moulders in many yards had organized on several occasions. While a number of secret societies and a strong social network were established, black brickmakers had wrested no concessions from their employers over the past twenty years.[4]

By early 1886, however, the brickmakers had built a complex, solid organization, enmeshed within the support network connected to DA 92. Based on their four-person work groups, they had organized a "Consolidated Moulders' Union," which took in all brickyard workers on both sides of the James River. On June 7, emphasizing that they "belonged to the Knights of Labor," some 250 black workers struck all seven Manchester yards and demanded a twenty-five-cent raise.[5]

By mid-June, several of the smaller Manchester companies had capitulated. The ranks of the strikers were joined by Richmond brickmakers who were also members of the Knights. Through the Consolidated Moulders' Union, they raised the same demands. They also threatened that "unless they grant us the demand asked for we will positively make no more bricks this year." Lest employers doubt their seriousness, they warned:

> We would have each and every one of you thoroughly comprehend that we did not appeal to any passions to get our just demands, but the matter was considered mainly with that deliberation that could have no other purpose in its aim but a manly acceptance, knowing the value of our labor in this work, at the same time viewing our almost poor-house homes, with the understanding—that you are fully able to do what is right and should unhesitatingly grant to us our just demands.[6]

At the peak of their season, in the best year in the past five, the strike was particularly threatening to the brick manufacturers. Because they were eager for a speedy conclusion, they tried to exploit its racial aspects. They recruited white strikebreakers at $2.25 a day, fifty cents more than the black strikers were demanding. DA 84 again sought to discourage cross-racial strikebreaking. The Consolidated Moulders' Union noted "only two white strikebreakers at work" in the seven Manchester yards, and "only three" in the Rocketts yards. The black strikers threatened to mobilize crowds to drive even these few away.[7]

The brick manufacturers, seeing that they could not secure enough white strikebreakers, tried a more subtle maneuver. They organized themselves into a formal association and gave J.J. Blanton, the operator of a small yard and a member of a Knights' local assembly, the authority to bargain on their behalf. The black strikers immediately punctured this deception: "They [the manufacturers] then thought very probably we would agree to anything he said, as he was a Knight." The brickmakers weighed Blanton's proposal: They were to increase their daily output from 3,000 bricks to 3,500, in order to receive the raise. They flatly rejected it as "something that was never known in this locality or any other" and renewed their commitment to "shut down for $5 a day per table." Shortly afterward, the employers surrendered.[8]

• • •

The militancy and unity displayed in this strike—and by the coopers and the quarry workers as well—were also evident in relation to the new "reform" city council. Black activists were alarmed by reports in the local press that suggested to them the "ad hoc" character of the Workingmen's ticket. *Richmond Dispatch* reporters interviewed successful white candidates to highlight their individual political loyalties: "I am a good Democrat. . . . I was elected without giving any pledges" (Millo F. Hudnall); "I was born a Democrat and I am one now" (Richard T. Davis); "Democratic square through, and don't you forget it" (A. L. Owen).[9]

Fearful of being given short shrift by the newly elected white councilors and aldermen, black militants issued a call for a "Colored City Convention." They informed the leaders of the Workingmen's party "that in view of the valuable support given the Reform Ticket by the colored people of the city, their race should be recognized in the distribution of minor offices and in employing the workmen on the new city hall."[10]

The newly elected members of the common council met on the night of June 4, 1886. Lack of unity was apparent from the start. Much debate preceded the agreement to hold a formal meeting; then, with veteran reformer John S. Bethel in the chair, nothing was accomplished—other than a decision to reconvene in ten days. Thus opened a brief period in which militants of every kind consolidated their forces and developed new strategies. Through the Reform party ward committees, white Knights tried to exert popular pressure on the newly elected city council to hold it to the party platform. These militants took the party's name seriously: It was committed to "reform" of both the personnel and the practices of traditional municipal government. It was a permanent addition to the network of institutions that provided working-class organization and expression; those individuals who campaigned under its auspices were sworn to adhere to the party program. Because Democratic party leaders sensed that not all Reform party candidates and voters shared these perceptions, they sought to divide them by fanning the flames of racial mistrust and by reducing all social conflicts to a question of race. They depicted the Reform party as a vehicle of "social equality" and "Negro domination."[11]

Black working-class militants refused to back off in the face of these new pressures. Their position toward the white leadership of the Workingmen's Reform party paralleled that toward Republican and Readjuster leaders: Such men would address black concerns only if pushed by a unified black movement. DA 92 leaders began with a traditional tactic—the public mass meeting. In early June, they called a "Colored City Convention" to convey black collective sentiments to the white leaders of the Reform party. Preparations for the convention generated a series of ward meetings; issues were debated and delegates were elected. Formal ward committees were organized and connected in a network. Once again, workplace, neighborhood, political, and social activists were woven into a cohesive force.[12]

They sent a clear message to white reformers, and it went beyond specific positions like the police, the Colored Almshouse, and Lunatic Asylum, and markets in black neighborhoods. They demanded full "recognition" and the share of political power this implied. Such demands were as unsettling to white working-class reformers as they were to businessmen and professional politicians.

The Workingmen's Reform party had no structural mechanisms through which its leadership (still basically a core group of No. 84 militants) could answer such demands. Experienced Republican politicans moved to penetrate this vacuum both to "advise" their former black constituents and to "mediate" between them and the white reformers. John S. Wise, a veteran of political intrigue and Mahone's local right-hand man, held a series of "friendly and informal conversations" with the black city council members. Wise "wanted them to become thoroughly confused," he explained in a letter to Mahone, "knowing that when that occurred, they would be grateful to anyone who could pilot them." At the same time, he waited for "the seceding element of the Democracy to become thoroughly out of the fold before showing my hand, lest they be frightened back." Wise then planned to interject himself, and the Republican organization, between the black and white reformers.[13]

On June 15, the newly elected city officials met once more to iron out their differences. Again, nothing was accomplished. Wise happily reported to Mahone:

> One faction of the Reformers insisted on keeping this officer, another that. The darkies demanded thus and so. The whites of Democratic antecedents this and that. And altogether it was a beautiful mixtry, out of which the Democrats hoped for success. The meeting Monday night, in which they nearly broke up in a row, gave me my cue and I went right to work, seeing man by man, devoting all day to it.[14]

Wise's efforts to insinuate himself into the leadership of the new government, and thereby integrate both the black and white components of the reform movement into the Republican party, ultimately failed. But he did contribute to the air of mistrust and mutual recrimination that settled over the city government. When the new council formally organized itself on June 23, its proceedings were dominated by factionalism as well as growing tension between the new officials and their constituents. After John S. Bethel was elected common council president, Jackson Ward presented a mass petition demanding that black men be appointed superintendent of the Colored Almshouse, weighmaster of the First Market, bailiff of the police court, and janitor of the city hall, and that black workingmen be hired for skilled and unskilled jobs in the construction of the new city hall. The petition had vociferous supporters and opponents in the public gallery, and, amid an uproar, Bethel adjourned the meeting.[15]

When the council reconvened, acrimony continued to plague its discussions. It tabled the Jackson Ward petition and proceeded to consider other patronage posts. Black council members demonstrated their power by voting with the incumbent Democratic bloc, thus thwarting the Reformers' proposals. Neither side could attain the two-thirds majority needed to make an appointment. Instead of seeing the new council controlled by a tightly knit "Reform Caucus" as they had hoped, the militant Knights found their representatives at each other's throats. Several of the white councilors and aldermen announced their intention to withdraw from the "Reform Caucus" altogether, alarmed by the willingness of its members to accept the black councilors and aldermen. The local Democratic press publicized these defections as well as the complaints of the disgruntled officials. Their accounts played up the racial aspects of the disagreement.[16]

By the time the dust had settled, eleven men had withdrawn from the caucus. All publicly embraced the Democratic party. Only two of the eleven were trade unionists, and only one had any previous experience in "independent" politics. The other eight had been nominated and elected despite their lack of involvement with the Knights of Labor. Twelve white reformers held their ground. All had been trade unionists, labor "reformers," Greenbackers, or Readjusters, and were now associated with the leadership of DA 84. They admitted the six black councilors and aldermen—Jones, Hayes, Archer, Farrar, Adams, and Robinson—into the "Reform Caucus." But the eighteen of them no longer constituted a majority of the forty-two-member Common Council.[17]

The reform-minded council members found themselves unable to fulfill their patronage commitments to either their white reform or black constituencies. Most positions were left in the hands of incumbents. Popular black demands were given particularly short shrift. Chairman Bethel tried to appease the distraught blacks, telling them "that square justice demanded that the colored men should have this place, but that policy would forbid, and that policy would have to rule in this, as the reform movement is young and must be surrounded by every safeguard."[18]

• • •

Political controversy had harmed Richmond's Knights where they were most vulnerable—along the color line. For all its limitations, the biracial coalition that had promoted the Workingmen's ticket had been a path-breaking development. Suddenly, the white reformers had been thrust on the defensive, and black militants had come once again to question the viability of interracial class organization. Political vultures, eager to hasten its death throes and feast on its carrion, had descended on the movement. But there was still considerable life left. White working-class activists tried to unite community opinion against the "bolters." In June and early July, they organized ward-based "indignation meetings" to "denounce the traitors to the cause of labor and reform." They also voiced an outpouring of "wrath and disgust" against "the Bourbons." It appeared that the movement might well weather the storm.[19]

Knights of Labor activists, however, could not devote their full energies and resources to resorting their movement to an even keel. Other equally pressing issues arose to occupy them. In the aftermath of the early May Haymarket Square riot, a wave of hysteria, repression, and reaction rippled outward from Chicago and reached Richmond during this postelection turmoil. Through rumor and innuendo, William Mullen, the leading white proponent of biracial unity, was linked to the Haymarket events. A significant chunk of his energy—and space in the *Labor Herald*—had to be devoted to refuting these charges.[20]

Simultaneously, local employers launched a counteroffensive against the Knights. In mid-June, the Old Dominion Iron and Nail Works announced a ten percent wage cut and their intention to introduce the Bessemer Process, thereby eliminating hundreds of skilled jobs. The Baughman Brothers, a nonunion print shop, secured an injunction against the Knights of Labor and the Typographical Union, prepared a civil suit to recover damages, and promoted city-wide organization among businessmen who were hostile to the Knights.[21]

Fissures opened and widened within the Knights of Labor at an ever more alarming rate. Two prominent members of the printers' union's boycott committee publicly renounced the Knights of Labor and, with great fanfare, rejoined the Democratic party. The city council permanently tabled all black demands, failed to enact the eight-hour workday for municipal employees, and resolved only to "employ day labor [on the new city hall] as far as the same is practicable."[22]

Democratic party leaders played on the reticence of many white workers to break cleanly with their traditional allegiances and patterns of behavior. They decried the spread of class conflict and called for a return to the "harmony" of earlier days. When they reorganized their party ward committees, they welcomed "bolters" from the Reform camp with open arms. By late summer they were followed by hundreds of white workers, many of whom had joined the Knights during their revivalistic burst in membership at the beginning of the year. These workers had, in John S. Wise's words, "no doubt been swept along with it [the popular movement] further than [they] originally intended going." Their limited participation in the order's "constructive" projects, the quick "education" they were given by their frenetically busy local assemblies, and the very hesitancy with which they had approached the order before its massive boom of January and February 1886 left them on the fringe of movement culture woven by the Knights of Labor. Consequently, they proved susceptible to the Democratic party's skillful machinations.[23]

• • •

Black militants witnessed this turn of events with an acute sense of irony. "The laboring white men," the *Planet* noted, "who are now being so vigorously ostracized and assaulted on every hand can now slightly realize the position of the colored man for the last twenty years." Some white labor activists, led by Mullen, became even more ardent advocates of independent politics. Over the next several months, they drew closer to black activists than ever before.

Since early summer, black and white militants had increased their contact and cooperation. They had joined forces in spreading the Order's influence among black workers across the state in both urban and rural areas. The executive boards of DA's 84 and 92 jointly managed the black quarrymen's strike against the Richmond Granite Company, which continued through the summer and the fall. No. 84 even pressured the granite cutters' union to admit the black strikers as union members. Though their effort proved futile—the union rejected the "ex-convict scabs"—it was appreciated by black activists.[24]

White Knights of Labor activists made other gestures to black militants. Prodded by Reform City Councilor John J. Unlauf, of Washington Assembly No. 4104, and Alderman John T. Chappell, of Union Assembly No. 3545, the Knights of Labor Building Association reached out to black workers. They sent a committee to District Assembly 92 to explain the principles and practices of the building association and to invite black membership.[25]

In the hope of regaining momentum and restoring harmony to the movement culture, leaders of both district assemblies concentrated on two critical events, which would occur in early fall 1886: the Third District congressional election and the General Assembly of the Knights of Labor. They planned to run an independent, biracial electoral campaign against the prominent Democratic incumbent, George D. Wise. They saw the General Assembly, scheduled to convene in October and bring some one thousand delegates and reporters into Richmond, as a unique opportunity to reaffirm the principles of the Order and restore unity to local ranks. Thus, committed working-class activists would make the Knights' password "Discourage Discord" their own slogan. However, their efforts in both events were to backfire.

In June, with first discussions of the fall congressional election, John S. Wise had promised the Reform party leaders that the Republicans would support their choice in the fall congressional election. But he confided to Republican party boss Mahone that he personally felt that "they will have no man. I think it every way probable they will ultimately ask me to run." In the meantime, he recommended:

> I am sincere in wishing them to select the candidate for if they do it will land about 1500 to 2000 white voters here in the Rep. party before the thing is over. If the Reps. put in a candidate of our own motion we will drive many of them back. . . . Do nothing whatever as to the Third Congressional District but leave it to us. . . . A condition of things exists here now such as I never hoped to see. We have a glorious opportunity, and if left absolutely alone and allowed to work it up in our own way we will astound you.[26]

The political intrigue was just beginning. In August, George D. Wise, in a carefully conceived strategic gesture, announced that he would not seek another term as the Third District's congressman. The Reformers were thus lured into believing that there was a clear field, without either a Republican candidate or the well-known Democratic incumbent. They confidently laid plans for an independent labor campaign that would rejoin and revive the black and white popular movements.[27]

These activists were unprepared for what the veteran politicans of both parties had in store for them. George D. Wise did not intend to retire. To the contrary, his withdrawal was feigned and calculated to force the Third District Democratic convention to draft him by popular acclaim. Hence, he appeared in a very different guise from a three-term incumbent again laying claim to his position. Moreover, wrapping himself in the mantle of "friend of the workingman," he jumped on the anti-convict-labor bandwagon and called for protective tariffs. "The capitalist should grant the reasonable demands of the workingman," he told the convention, and in return, "if they did this kindly and freely, the workingmen would rush to the support of the Democratic Party."[28]

The Republican machinations were no less carefully devised. Mahone and the local party faithful first sought to win the Reform nomination for John S. Wise. Failing that, they prepared to renege on their June promises of support and scuttle the independent campaign altogether. "It may be that towards the close of the canvass we can run Johnny in anyhow," one local official suggested.[29]

Amidst these maneuvers, a District Labor convention assembled on September 10. Its basis of representation reflected the black-white alliance. Instead of separate organizations, with the black one centered in Jackson Ward, every local assembly was entitled to five delegates. At the same time, however, the complexion of the convention reflected the declining popular white support for biracial independent politics. Of the 200 delegates representing forty local assemblies, 140 (seven-tenths) were black. Indeed, blacks now had an equal footing with whites in the Reform organization, and their numerical superiority gave them added power.[30]

John S. Bethel, the veteran Oregon Hill activist who had assumed the chairmanship of the common council, was elected president of the labor convention, and Charles DeVoto, No. 84's recording secretary, was chosen secretary. From that point on, controversy and turbulence befell the convention. The first issue that was raised promptly divided the delegates. It was moved from the floor that all delegates support whatever candidate was selected. The motion carried over heated objections. Some thirty delegates from seven prominent white local assemblies—Tuckahoe Assembly No. 4099, Advance Assembly No. 3519, Mullen's own Eureka Assembly No. 3157, Washington Assembly No. 4104, Old Dominion Assembly No. 3380, Marshall Assembly No. 3479, and Tinners' Assembly No. 5192—immediately walked out; those remaining were mostly black.[31]

After the dissenting delegates left, the convention turned its attention to the selection of a candidate; Mullen, Bethel, John Conner, Henry L. Carter, John Ryall, and John S. Wise were nominated. The predominantly black assembly, defying both major parties, elected Mullen on the first ballot. Thunderous applause, both from the delegates and the largely black crowd that had gathered outside the hall, greeted the announcement. Mullen's acceptance speech provided another high note, and the convention adjourned amid optimism. "The small faction of George D. Wise men who bolted the convention is of no special big influence as their following is small and their action not generally approved of in their respective assemblies," observed one participant. The Reformers "are confident of success," he continued, "provided the Republicans make no nomination (as is rumored they will do) and support Mullen."[32]

These hopes proved wrong on both scores: The Democrats skillfully used "the bolters," and the Republicans directly challenged Mullen. In less than a week, Mullen's campaign had begun to dissolve. On September 14, John S. Wise issued a public appeal for all Republicans to reject Mullen and hold a nominating convention of their own. He rubbed salt in the open wound by stirring up black dissatisfaction with the Reform council's failure to deliver on the promises made in May. He told of one "witty fellow" who had said "he would not mind being made a fool of by Mullen but he did not want to be made a fool of twice in one year, spring and fall." Mullen, he charged, was "at heart a thorough-paced Democrat with no inclination whatever to the Republican Party and only bent on securing their votes if possible." Wise urged Republicans to nominate a candidate of their own. "It is better to lose on a square fight upon principle than to abandon our principles and elect Mr. Mullen."[33]

Addressing an ad hoc convention at the Galillean Fishermen's Hall, Wise focused on the behavior of the "reform" city government, the many broken promises made to black workers, and the insults suffered by black councilors and aldermen. Several white reformers also attended, hoping desperately to maintain the ties that had been initiated at the labor convention. Joseph Devine was one. He had been a Republican in recent years, he admitted, but now the clear national trend was toward the election of "Labor congressmen." Several blacks took the floor to speak in favor of a Republican candidate. One declared that "he was too good a Knight of Labor to vote for Mullen." As the debate wound down, William Fields, the secretary of DA 92, offered the following: "Resolved, That it is the sense of this meeting that a Republican candidate be nominated for Congress by the Republican Party in this district." His resolution was adopted by a vote of sixty-three to twenty-three.[34]

Attacks on both flanks of Mullen's campaign began in earnest. John S. Wise took charge of the local Republican campaign and challenged the GOP's ranks to stop "whoring around after a lot of tramps." The "bolters" and their Democratic allies put their new strategies into motion. They constituted a new organization, the "Democratic Knights of Labor," and elected several former labor reformers as its officers. They laid claim to the legitimate "Knighthood" and suggested it was Mullen and the Reformers who had departed from the consensus. "We deny the right of any man to stand before the people as the Knight of Labor candidate," they charged. "Such action stigmatizes and blurs the Order, which is not a political organization."[35]

The proper political home for every white worker, according to the consensus of the meeting, was the Democratic party. George D. Wise himself delivered the finishing touches. He suddenly entered the hall, came to the podium, and gave a brief but emotional speech attacking the "largely colored" convention that had nominated Mullen. "That's all we know about it." For many at this meeting, that was all they needed to know.[36]

The Republicans found it harder to place their anti-Mullen movement on a solid foundation. In early October, under John S. Wise's prompting, they held a series of ward meetings to elect delegates to their Third District convention. Black and white activists packed these assemblies and turned them into popular expressions for Mullen's candidacy. In Marshall Ward, a stronghold of the Reform movement, a meeting of twenty-five whites and six blacks elected No. 92's District Master Workman Richard Thompson as their chairman and placed a black carpenter in the secretary's seat. They were addressed by alderman Rowland Hill, the former Republican and Readjuster who converted to the Reform movement and brought a commitment to black equal rights with him. In 1883, as a Readjuster appointee to the school board, Hill had supported black popular demands for the hiring of black principals and teachers in black schools. Hill was joined on the platform by veteran labor militant Daniel Alley, president of the carpenters' union in the late 1860s, president of the Mechanics' Trades Union in 1871, a consistent spokesman for the "lower part" of Marshall Ward, and an advocate of "independent" politics since 1877. Together, Hill, Alley, and Thompson urged the Marshall Ward assembly to elect delegates pledged to Mullen. Four delegates and four alternates were selected; half were black, and all were committed to Mullen. They were led by Alley and James H. Washington, the No. 92 organizer. Except for Washington, all of these black delegates were tobacco factory workers. Black and white labor activists, working together, had captured the Marshall Ward meeting.[37]

The story was similar in other wards. Veteran black activist and coopers' union officer Richard Carter chaired the Jefferson Ward gathering. Under his direction, an all-black delegate slate was elected; most of them were tobacco factory workers and all were pledged to Mullen. In Monroe Ward, popular race pride orator R. A. Paul assumed the chair. He joined printers' union activist Julian Wright and Irish working-class organizer Joseph Devine in winning the meeting for Mullen. Veteran black militants William Custalo of the coopers' union and Collin T. Payne, prominent in independent political organization, steered the interracial Madison Ward assembly for Mullen.[38]

The struggles were more intense and complex in Clay Ward, the center of white working-class reformism, and Jackson Ward, the center of black militancy. John S. Wise, desperate to retain his control, personally attended both ward meetings. An impressive contingent challenged Wise in Clay Ward race pride author and orator Joseph T. Wilson, veteran militants Ben Scott and Lewis Lindsay, and respected quarryman and Knights of Labor activist George Woodson. Though this quartet could not prevent Wise from manipulating the meeting in such a way as to elect an "uncommitted" slate, four of the five men chosen were personally sympathetic to Mullen. In Jackson Ward, Wise skillfully "lost control" of the meeting so that no delegates were elected. This ensured that the city's major black neighborhood would be unrepresented at the district convention, a result far more beneficial to Wise and GOP leaders and the Reformers.[39]

Wise had fully expected to lose most of Richmond in the selection of delegates to the district Republican convention. His strategy for the October 2 convention was based on GOP strength among the rural delegates and behind-the-scenes arm twisting by key members of the party machine. Mullen's "whole strength," he realized, "was with the Knights of Labor and they were confined to Richmond and divided there." In the rural districts, "the feeling against delivering our party over 'horse, foot, and dragoon' to such a scheme was more strong. . . . In Richmond we were in the minority and there was little we were sacrificing when we agreed to let the organization go to pieces, but four of six counties in the district are Republican." Wise's tactics proved effective, as his rural and machine bases, aided by rulings from the convention chair and the credentials committee, defeated Richmond's black labor activists. The delegates nominated Judge Edmund Waddill, Wise's choice. Wise, Waddill, and convention chairman J. W. Southward, a rural county sheriff, laid plans "to counteract the insidious work that Mullen was doing in the Knights of Labor assemblies" and to make him feel "the effects of our organization." They assembled a campaign treasury and began their canvass, confident that "with a united party, and the Democrats divided between George D. Wise and Mullen, we can win."[40]

The nomination of a GOP candidate was calculated to tug at black workers' traditional loyalties and hurt Mullen's chances. But his supporters, black and white, were determined to prevail. Black militants tried to challenge Waddill"s selection after the convention had adjourned. Street politics, not parliamentary procedure, was their forte. Ben Scott and Joseph Wilson addressed a Jackson Ward mass meeting, "charging that the Republican managers in this district had been paid money by the Democrats to conduct the present campaign." The *Labor Herald* repeated these charges, and many whites as well as blacks appeared ready to believe them. The *Petersburg Index-Appeal* warned: "The labor element will dominate both parties henceforth, and gentlemen who rashly incur the animosity of those elements may as well get out of politics as soon as possible."[41]

• • •

Black and white militants committed to Mullen's candidacy turned their attention to the Knights of Labor General Assembly, scheduled to open in Richmond on October 4. Preparations for the convention, which was expected to bring about one thousand delegates to Richmond from across the nation, had begun months earlier. Committees had been appointed to plan a reception for visiting delegates, to arrange various entertainments during the General Assembly's two-week session, and to obtain the necessary local financing. With the mounting attack on the Knights, in Richmond as well as nationally, broader concerns also occupied the convention's planners. National and local leaders together made an interesting tactical decision—to invite Governor Fitzhugh Lee to address the opening session. The press was also invited, so that Powderly's opening report might "become a public document" and "go to the world."[42]

Knights of Labor activists hoped that the General Assembly would provide them with an opportunity to halt the process of attrition within the Order. After the mid-September district labor convention had nominated Mullen for Congress, hopes for his candidacy had become inseparable from those for reunification of the Order. For the militants, the General Assembly represented a new and powerful development, one that might well galvanize the sputtering local popular movements behind the independent political campaign. With men like Richard Trevellick, Ralph Beaumont, Joseph Buchanan, and Terence Powderly in town, local Reformers took heart. For their part, Republican and Democratic politicans also eyed the General Assembly to find ways to thwart the Reformers. Sent to cover the proceedings for the *Baltimore Sun*, a reported described some preconvention thinking:

> Mr. Beaumont is the chairman of the committee charged with looking after labor legislation before Congress. His report will be one of the most interesting, especially to congressional aspirants in close districts . . . it is asserted that chairman Beaumont's report will be unfriendly to the re-election of Mr. George D. Wise, the Democratic nominee in this district. All of the members of the Virginia delegation, with possibly one exception, are unfriendly to Wise. So if his friends desire to antagonize this report, they will have to get representatives from other states to fight his battle for them.[43]

Much to the chagrin of local Knights of Labor activists, party politicians were able to find "representatives from other states to fight" their "battle for them." Despite vociferous disclaimers to the contrary, William Mullen had been identified in the national labor press with the "anti-trades union" faction led by the "Home Club" of DA 49. Many delegates to the October General Assembly, concerned about conflict within the Order and suspicious of the "Home Club," were hesitant to lend their support to him. Others, in the aftermath of the Haymarket events and various political fiascos around the country, had rejected all possibilities for independent politics. This turn away from politics received encouragement in important quarters. Governor Lee's welcoming address concentrated on the pitfalls of independent politics. Richmond Bishop John J. Keane, an outspoken supporter of the Knights' cause within the Catholic hierarchy, led the Assembly in prayer, then cautioned:

> She [the United States] feared lately that the methods of some of your associates [Haymarket] were oblivious of this patriotic unselfishness, that they sought their own advantage with great risk to her industrial interests and to that business-confidence which is the very life-energy of her prosperity. I am certain that you mean no such result, and that you will never countenance any methods that would lead to it.[44]

The results began to show. In the elections for General Executive Board, Mullen lost his seat, garnering an embarrassing sixteen votes out of the 613 cast. Individual delegates, some as prominent as Frank Foster, the veteran Massachusetts labor activist, addressed Richmond groups in open opposition to Mullen's congressional candidacy. Hence, the General Assembly undermined, rather than promoted, his independent campaign for Congress.[45]

The manner in which the General Assembly was engulfed by the "race issue" proved even more disastrous to Mullen's campaign. Celebrated by Powderly as "the largest convention representing the interest of labor that has ever been called together in any part of the civilized world," the meeting would not reunite the Order as activists had hoped. Rather, it would further the decline of Richmond's biracial popular movement.[46]

Black popular identification with the Knights of Labor had continued to grow—nationally as well as in Richmond—over the summer and early fall. In August 1886, the National Negro Press convention resolved: "That the establishment of amicable relations between the two races can best be reached through the medium of such organizations as the Knights of Labor." By early September, the cause of independent politics in Richmond rested on a predominantly black foundation. More specifically, it involved black perception of the Knights as the vehicle that would bring equality and social recognition. The local Democratic organ, the *Richmond Dispatch*, quite accurately assessed the situation: "The declaration of the order, that all its members, regardless of race or creed, are on the same footing, is likely to be put to the test during this session."[47]

Hundreds of arriving delegates and outsiders, drawn to Richmond by the General Assembly, were thus suddenly thrust to center stage of the local movement as the city itself became a focus of national attention. Racial controversy began to swirl around the convention even before it had officially opened, as northern visitors challenged Richmond's social and racial codes of behavior. Pushed by the militancy of the local black popular movement and moved by their own conscience and beliefs, black and white delegates expressed their distaste for racial discrimination.[48]

Public attention concentrated on the sixty delegates of New York's radical District Assembly No. 49—especially the leaders of the controversial "Home Club." Its radicals apparently had planned to challenge racial segregation even before they had left New York. Brooklyn's Frank Ferrell was an articulate, militant black delegate. If he were not allowed to stay with the delegation, it would seek accommodations in black establishments and households. Their intentions on record in the *New York Sun*, the delegates boarded a steamer for Richmond.[49]

The delegation had booked rooms at Murphy's Hotel, but when they arrived they were informed that Ferrell could not stay there. In protest, they all left the hotel and found rooms at black boardinghouses. Many more black and white delegates did the same for their two-week stay in Richmond. "Genuine social equality can be witnessed at Harris Hall," the *New York Tribune* observed of No. 49's new center, a black boardinghouse. Delegates and local black workers exchanged ideas and compared experiences over meals, in parlors and kitchens, walking to church, and on the streets of black neighborhoods. Understandably, a wealthy white woman complained that since the general assembly had opened, "her colored cook and servant have been trifling and impudent."[50]

Ferrell himself had won a special place in the hearts of the Richmond black community. The apparent support given him by the leaders of the Order strengthened the bonds between them and the local black community. When the General Assembly opened on October 4, the Armory floor was packed with delegates, and the gallery was filled with spectators, as the public had been invited to attend. *John Swinton's Paper*, writing of General Master Workman Powderly, captured the scene:

> He stood alone upon a small platform at the further end of the hall and looked out upon the faces of a thousand delegates assembled from every part of the country, representatives of a million of our workers. White and black faces, the faces of men and women bound together by a common bond, met his view.[51]

Powderly was joined on stage by Governor Lee, the opening day speaker, and, a surprise addition to the announced agenda, Frank Ferrell himself. While Governor Lee had been given the honor of welcoming the delegates to Virginia, Ferrell had the distinction of introducing Powderly to the general assembly. The black man from Brooklyn spoke of the Knights' "efforts to improve the condition of humanity." He continued:

> One of the objects of our Order is the abolition of those distinctions which are maintained by creed or color. . . . My experience with the noble Order of the Knights of Labor and my training in my district have taught me that we have worked so far successfully toward the extinction of these regrettable distinctions.[52]

Nor did Powderly ignore the issue of discrimination. He called attention to No. 49's stand against it in his opening remarks. With Lee and Ferrell seated behind him, he turned directly to the black man and said:

> When it became necessary to seek quarters for a delegation in this city, and when it became known that there was a man among them of a darker hue than the rest, it became evident that some of these men could not find a place in the hotels of this city, which is in accordance with long and established customs, and customs are not readily vanquished. Therefore, when one that happened to be of a dark skin, of a delegation of some sixty or seventy men, could not gain admission to the hotel where accommodations for the delegation had been arranged, rather than separate from that brother, they stood by the principles of our organization which recognizes no color or creed in the division of men. The majority of these men went with their colored brother. I made the selection of that man from that delegation to introduce me during the address of his Excellency, Governor Lee, so that it may go forth from here to the entire world that "we practice what we preach."[53]

The repercussions of Powderly's effort to "practice what we preach" swept throughout the armory, the city, and the nation. Leaders of the local black popular movement, black delegates from other cities, and Ferrell and his white allies all read his speech as giving the official seal of approval for an assault on Richmond's racial discrimination. The next night, in the company of some eighty white delegates, Ferrell attended a performance of "Hamlet" at the city's Academy of Music. The delegates had been given orchestra tickets by the cast, whom they met on the steamer trip to Richmond. Seating arrangements at the Academy traditionally called for racial separation, with all blacks relegated to the "colored gallery" on the second floor. Afraid to challenge the Knights' delegation, management allowed Ferrell, a rather light-skinned black man, to sit in his orchestra seat. The act was overlooked by most of the theater-goers, but word of it spread rapidly—endorsed by the black community, and arraigned in the local press.[54]

Richmond newspapers headlined the "race question" and gave it extensive coverage. They exploited it in such a way as to drive white workers back into the Democratic party. The condemned delegates' protests against Richmond's segregated accommodations, reducing them, with heavy-handed sexual innuendo, to examples of "race mixing." On October 5, a page one *Dispatch* article "revealed" that four white delegates from District Assembly No. 49 had taken up lodging in a black boardinghouse where four young, single black women also resided. The following day, the same paper reported that a white delegate from Maine was sharing a bed with a black man in another boardinghouse. The ball and banquet that was scheduled to close the first week of the General Assembly raised questions about whether there would be two racially separate gatherings or one mixed social affair. Ferrell's behavior at the Academy of Music was given feature space in the press. Reporters interviewed white members of the Order and encouraged them to voice anonymously their reactions to the seeming trend toward "social equality" occasioned by the convention.

Q. What do you think of the attitude taken by Assembly 49, of New York, regarding social equality?

A. I regard the action of those persons who took Ferrell to the Mozart Academy as an outrage upon the people of this city, and an insult to the Knights of Labor. I feel confident that they do not represent anyone but themselves.

Q. How do the Knights of Labor of this city regard the action of their visiting brethren in this respect?

A. The Knights of this city are justly indignant, and their position of host only restrains them from an outburst of righteous contempt. Most of them earnestly hope that General Master Workman Powderly will avail himself of the first opportunity to administer to 49 the rebuke they merit and justly deserve. The action of 49 will cause a great many to leave the Order, and will in a large measure detract from the parade next Monday. I have yet to meet

> the first man, white or colored, Knights of Labor or otherwise, who had expressed anything but the severest condemnation of Assembly 49.
>
> Personally, I have nothing but kindly feelings for the colored people. I wish them prosperity and success, and I will befriend them in any just claims they may have; but when the plea is put in for social equality, the line of demarcation is clearly and distinctly drawn, so far as I am concerned.[55]

A new local organization made its first public appearance and joined the press, Democratic party spokesmen, and Democratic members of the Knights to foment the white backlash. The "Law and Order League" had been organized by "the best families in the city" to fight boycotts. Its major vehicle was the "Businessmen's Committee of Twenty-Five," under the leadership of militant conservatives. Calling upon its members to be "armed and ready for bloodshed," the league sought a popular base. Its spokesmen organized a group that would patrol the Academy of Music to prevent any further challenges to racial segregation. Shouts of "Coons and Forty-Niners" echoed in the streets around the theater. Swollen to several hundred, augmented by Police Chief Poe and thirty-five white "special deputies," the patrol became a crowd that threatened to attack any black member of the Order who dared show his face. Rather than the unification sought by local black and white militants, virtual race war had become a possibility.[56]

For instance, the October 8 *Dispatch* headlines, "SOCIAL EQUALITY." The "race issue" laced convention debate; *John Swinton's Paper* observed: "One of the things most talked of in Richmond during the sessions has been reference to the social status of the colored delegates." Powderly himself had seemed to sanction an attack on Richmond's racial discrimination. In doing so, he won the enthusiastic support of black militants across the South. At the same time, he provoked a massive attack on the Order in the local and Southern press, reverberating through the membership of the Knights. The *Richmond Whig* warned on October 7:

> If it is the purpose of the demonstration of social equality now being so persistently forced into prominence in our midst to set an example to be followed by the members of the order here, we predict that it will not only fail to accomplish the desired result, but that it will be a serious obstacle in the way of the future extension of the Order among the whites, and cause its abandonment by many of the present members.

The correspondent to the *Montgomery Advertizer* accurately described the spreading repercussions of the "race issue:"

> One result, citizens here say, will follow the admission of Ferrell to the Academy of Music. It will insure the election of George D. Wise, Democratic candidate for Congress in this district. Waddill is the Republican candidate, and Mullen, Master Workman of the Knights of Labor in this district, is the labor candidate. Now they say no white man will vote for him.[57]

Powderly was pressured from all sides. Black activists were united in their support for him. White militants, however, were sharply divided. Some, mostly visitors from the North, led by the radicals from DA 49, advocated a continuing assault on the "color line." Many delegates, including some local militants, granted the moral justice of such actions, but regretted their consequences. Frank Foster, the veteran labor reformer from Massachusetts who advocated the abandonment of Mullen's independent campaign, reported through his *Haverhill Laborer* that "perhaps a little too much of this color line question" had been agitated for the Order's own good. Other white delegates, led by southerners, urged Powderly to repudiate No. 49 and predicted dire consequences if he failed to do so. R. J. Steele, a white delegate from Petersburg, accused No. 49 of "trying to humiliate the white people of Richmond." He warned Powderly:

> I think if this evil is not atoned for and condemned by the General Assembly it will be a drawback in its progress. They should investigate the whole affair and throw this Assembly 49 out of the Order for we had better lose 60 men than 1,000. It has done a great injury to the order and the South, if not rectified at once, and also to our labor candidate for Congress. I will be pleased to hear your public condemnation of the whole affair. For a word from you will perhaps heal up the sore of those that thought a great deal of our Order and was in sympathy with us until this occurred.[58]

Powderly's stance was characteristically ambiguous. Police Chief Poe had warned him that no further episodes such as the Academy of Music controversy would be tolerated. Powderly sent for Ferrell and asked him to refrain from any further provocative actions. He also drafted a lengthy letter to the local press, which was reproduced in newspapers from coast to coast. "It is unfortunate that our coming was at a time when political excitement ran high, and all things serves as an excuse for those who wished to use them," he recognized. The General Master Workman refused to back down from his commitment "to encourage and uplift [the black] race from a bondage worse than that which held them in chains twenty-five years ago—mental slavery," and "to impress upon the minds of white and black that the same result followed action in the field of labor, whether that action was on the part of the Caucasian or the Negro." At the same time, Powderly suggested he did not intend to violate "the sanctity of the fireside circle. . . . Every man has the right to say who shall enter beneath his roof; who shall occupy the same bed, private conveyance, or such other place as he is master of. . . . I have no wish to interfere with this right.

Ultimately, however, Powderly reaffirmed the Knights' commitment to racial equality.

> We have not done a thing since coming to this city that is not countenanced by the laws and Constitution of our country. . . . The equality of American

> citizenship is all that we insist upon, and that equality must not, will not be trampled upon.
>
> To the Convention I say: Let no member surrender an iota of intellectual freedom because of any clamor. Hold fast to that which is true and right. The triumph of noise over reason is but transient. Our principles will be better known, if not today it may be tomorrow; they can bide their time, and will some day have the world for an audience. In the field of labor and American citizenship we recognize no line of race, creed, politics, or color.[59]

Powderly tried to counter the growing public criticism by strengthening his own ties with the local order. He met with Tredegar's management on behalf of the employed Knights, a relatively conservative group of white workers. He visited workplaces organized by the order and several local assembly meetings. He attended services at both black and white Catholic churches, and he was welcomed at meetings of the Catholic Beneficial Society and the John Mitchell Club of the Clan-Na-Gael.[60]

Powderly, however, could not effectively curb the discontent, both within the General Assembly and the local Order. Southern delegates, without Powderly's sanction, successfully promoted a resolution condemning all efforts to "disrupt the social relations which may exist between different races:"

> Whereas, Reports have been circulated and impressions have been created by the press of the country, regarding the position of the Knights of Labor upon the question of social equality; and
>
> Whereas, We believe the welfare of the Order in that section of the country which we represent would be largely enhançed if this General Assembly would take such action as would dispell those wrong impressions, therefore,
>
> Resolved, That the organization of the Knights of Labor recognizes the civil and political equality of all men, and, in the broad field of labor, recognizes no distinction on account of color, but it has no purpose to interfere with or disrupt the social relations which may exist between different races in any portion of our country.[61]

Local white Knights shared in the opposition to any attempt "to build a new social fabric during a two-week visit." A *New York Times* correspondent reported a continuing "storm of indignation and a new hesitancy by whites in their relation to the Order." As a result, none of the critical problems on the agenda—from the Knights' relationship with trade unions to the reunification of the local Reform movement—were addressed and resolved during the delegates' two-week stay in Richmond.[62]

The local black community embraced the Knights with unprecedented enthusiasm. The day of festivities marking the convention's midpoint provided an opportunity for local black workers to demonstrate their allegiance to the Knights. White militants had planned these festivities weeks earlier, with an eye toward rekindling the internal cohesion of the local popular movement. However, the show of popular black support, which followed the turmoil once the delegates convened, was an unintended result. In reflected both a new quality to the relationship between white labor activists and the black popular movement and a deepening tension between these activists and many white workers.[63]

The events of October 11 opened with a parade of Knights officials, General Assembly delegates, and members of local assemblies 84 and 92. Most white Richmond residents boycotted the event, and only the faithful within the Order joined the large number of black marchers. The white participants included Excelsior Assembly No. 3488, Advance Assembly No. 3572, Onward Assembly No. 3471, Marshall Assembly No. 3479, Tuckahoe Assembly No. 4099, Tinners' Assembly No. 5192, Old Dominion Assembly No. 3380, and one women's group, Electric Assembly. Their marchers constituted only a small fraction of Richmond's once impressive white Knights of Labor organization. Local blacks, however, turned out in full force, led by Pioneer Assembly No. 3572, Confidence Assembly No. 3895, Virginia Assembly No. 3564, Sumner Assembly No. 3912, Henrico Assembly No. 3913, Moore Assembly No. 4084, and the huge Mutual Assembly No. 3619 from Manchester. Frank Foster told the readers of his *Haverhill* (Massachusetts) *Laborer* that the turnout was "90 to 1 black." While surely an exaggeration, this observation captured the spirit of the parade. The thousands of black spectators that lined the parade's route led one correspondent to believe that "the entire colored population of Richmond" was in attendance. Black and white local assembly marchers lined up on opposite sides of the street. They followed some forty-odd carriages, bearing local and visiting dignitaries and female delegates, while the male General Assembly delegates marched ahead of the carriages. Powderly, Ferrell, and Mullen were especially cheered. The parade was led by a group of local marshals, black and white, all veteran activists and committed Reformers: J. J. Lynch, John T. Chappell, George E. Conway, Oliver Mountcastle, D. E. DeClay, Charles DeVoto, Dr. Robert E. Jones, Isaiah Pettiford, Lewis Stewart, and coopers' union leader Robert Beecher Taylor. In sum, the parade symbolized the new unity of white activists and the black popular movement, and their growing distance from what once was the white base of the Order. "It was," as the *Whig* stated, "a small army of workingmen, white and black, animated by a common purpose, and marching under a common flag."[64]

The parade concluded at the fairgrounds, where national activists Ralph Beaumont and Charles Lichtman delivered speeches. Track games and other sporting competitions were followed by a banquet where the "races mixed, male and female, but it excited no trouble." Then came a fireworks display and a ball, which was scheduled to close the festivities. Separate dance halls had been rented for whites and blacks, but most of the whites, possibly anticipating a mixed affair, had already left. Instead of promoting the unification of the black and white popular movements, these events commemorated the abiding distance between them. Black militants continued to identify with the Order and to perceive it as the appropriate vehicle for their struggles. When the General Assembly neared its close, black activists organized a banquet to honor the delegates from No. 49. They packed Harris's Hall (above his funeral parlor) and heard speeches by three prominent young black professionals: Dr. John C. Ferguson, *Planet* photographer J. C. Farley, and Republican District Attorney Walter Scott, all of whom praised the maverick New York assembly. Victor Drury, the well-known socialist member of No. 49, struck a popular chord in response: "He said that what forty-eight was to the oppressed millions of Europe, it was hoped forty-nine might be to the struggling masses of Americans in this day, and this play upon words and reference to a red-letter period of the revolutionary spirit nearly forty years ago abroad were received with cheers."[65]

As for the biracial popular movement as a whole, however, the General Assembly had signaled its death-knell. Radical northern delegates had joined with local black activists to challenge the southern racial code. In doing so, they pressed the movement culture, which had germinated in local soil, to break with its most tenaciously held traditions. Few white workers were prepared for such a break, but local conditions would no longer allow postponement. Under such circumstances, many white members fled the Order after its General Assembly concluded.

CHAPTER 11

The Death Throes of the Reform Movement

IN THE spring of 1886, politics had provided both the necessity and the opportunity for the forging of a biracial popular movement in Richmond. Yet, the Reform party's "victory" at the polls generated discord between and within District Assemblies 84 and 92. Over the summer and early fall, black and white working-class activists had drawn closer together in their effort to reunite and revitalize their movements. Their strategy had come to rest on two upcoming events: the Knights of Labor General Assembly, and an independent campaign for Congress.

William Mullen, the controversial District Master Workman of No. 84 and the white architect of biracial cooperation, had assumed the additional role of standard-bearer for the Reform movement. Trouble began with the nominating convention, where his candidacy was weakened by mass defections of both races. Mullen's supporters, white and black alike, hoped that the General Assembly would breathe new life into his campaign and, through it, revive their movement. On the contrary, events surrounding the General Assembly intensified racial conflict to the point where it threatened the order itself. Over the next year, black and white working-class militants desperately battled the trend, but it eventually overwhelmed them.

• • •

The independent congressional campaign was the first casualty of the General Assembly. Veteran black working-class activists Richard Thompson, James Washington, Robert Beecher Taylor, and Ben Scott joined Mullen's campaign with white working-class reformers John Bethel, John Ryall, Dan Alley, Joseph Devine, and John Chappell. Together, they built new bridges between black and white workers—only to find that few of their fellows cared to cross them. With the collapse of Mullen's campaign, racial mistrust destroyed most of these bridges and had a negative impact on what remained of the black and white popular movements.

President Grover Cleveland visited Richmond after the General Assembly adjourned. He mingled with the crowd at the Fairgrounds, where the Knights had earlier held their celebration. Symbolically reclaiming it for the bourgeoisie, he had appeared on the scene specifically to boost George Wise's candidacy and to promote the Democratic party's standing among white workers. Cleveland, a popular figure among whites throughout the country, assisted the local bourgeoisie in its efforts to reassert political hegemony, now challenged by the Knights.[1]

The attack on Mullen continued on both flanks. The hopelessness of his position is suggested by the "Goochland Courthouse" incident. The Clay Ward Democratic committee met the day after Cleveland's visit. Prominent "bolters" G. Waddy Wilde and Henry L. Carter directed the meeting, at which a former knight took the floor and recounted an anecdote, that he claimed showed Mullen's "true colors." He told the white audience that Mullen, while on the campaign trail and in the company of one black and one white associate, sat down at the refreshment stand of "an old colored woman" near the Goochland County courthouse. After she refused to serve the mixed party at the same table, Mullen reportedly arose, left indignantly, and vowed to take his supper elsewhere. The Republicans had their own version of the "Goochland incident," and theirs did not end with a declaration of principle on Mullen's part. John Wise told the largely black audience at another rally, "half an hour afterwards Mullen shook his colored friend and sneaked back to the stand and bought a pie. You see how he went back on the negro there, don't you?" Wise warned, "And if you vote for him, he will fool you."[2]

Democratic orators portrayed Mullen as a secret Republican agent, and George D. Wise stumped white working-class neighborhoods. In a more direct appeal for white plebian support, the Democratic-controlled city council passed election-eve wage increases to selected city employees. For their part, GOP leaders planned the disruption of pro-Mullen meetings in black neighborhoods. On Sunday, October 25, a Jackson Ward rally—organized by veteran black activists Joseph Wilson and Ben Scott, with contributing white activists John M. Ryall and William Mullen—was broken up by a handful of troublemakers. Party leaders published a broadside "To the Republican Voters of Richmond," which urged the rejection of "Mullenism" and claimed that, "with a united party, and the Democrats divided between Geo. D. Wise and Mullen, we are sure to win." They called upon their "Fellow Republicans":

> Spit upon the filth of such miserable rascals. Tell them they lie in their throats and know they are lying for gain, and you, backing our honest, earnest efforts to gain a victory for the Republicans, march in solid phalanx to the polls, deposit your ballots for your candidate, and at the same time that you

> will defeat Democracy you will rebuke the brutes and wretches who are seeking to malign and traduce your trusted servants who have served you long and faithfully—so long and so faithfully that their loyalty is not to be impeached by deserters and hypocrites.[3]

Partisan politicians, acting in public and behind the scenes, saw their efforts rewarded. The original group of "bolters" had been expanded to include experienced and respected white labor activists. They had established a popular-based organization, the "Democratic Knights of Labor," which actively organized white working-class support for George Wise. White support for Mullen, black workers noted, was rapidly slipping into his camp. The Republicans, led by master tactician John S. Wise, experienced comparable success. They now capitalized on the fear that Mullen's candidacy would split the black vote, rather than the white vote, and thereby enable George Wise to gain a plurality. Veteran black militants endorsed Waddill. By late October, the partisan *Richmond Whig* hailed the Republicans' effectiveness: "Two or three weeks ago all the Negroes were said to be for Mullen. Today they are said to be for Waddill." The twin pillars of Mullen's campaign were tottering and the whole edifice threatened to collapse.[4]

On Saturday night, October 30, the Labor Reform Committee of the Third Congressional District—its ranks depleted by the defections of both black and white delegates—held an emergency meeting co-directed by Davey Gaines, District Assembly 84's statistician, and Robert Beecher Taylor, the black leader of the interracial coopers' union. It voted to withdraw support from Mullen and cast it for George Wise. Mullen himself took the floor and pledged to do his utmost "to kill Waddill, [John] Wise, and Co., the deadliest enemies of the Reform party." Shortly afterward he drafted a public letter "To the Workingmen of the Third Congressional District."[5]

Mullen's missive blamed the failure of his campaign on the Republican "ring." Given the latter's midsummer promise to stay out of the canvass, the reformers had expected a head-on fight with the Democrats. But the "ring" leaders violated their pledge, entered a candidate, and altered the whole context of the election. Mullen and his allies, however, had not given up, despite Republican perfidy. Althugh Mullen had hoped "that the colored man would stand with the white man in this contest," black voters deserted the Reform camp en masse. In this, it seemed, Mullen felt the most profound sense of betrayal: "We were willing to lay aside party for the present in order to secure recognition; we held out our hand to the colored man as laboring men, and advised them to act with us politically." And he continued, "While this is a slander on those of our colored brethren who have stood firm, a sufficient number have gone over to make our success doubtful. They have permitted themselves to be whipped into line by the party-lash, and are alone responsible for the defeat of the Labor candidate."[6]

Mullen published a special issue of the *Labor Herald* that featured this public letter along with endorsements of George D. Wise by John Bethel,

Joseph Devine, and John Conner, three of the staunchest reformers among white workers. He added a personal appeal: "The election of Judge Waddill would be one of the severest blows that Labor ever had inflicted upon it. . . . I ask my friends to work as hard to defeat this aspiring dictator as they would have done to secure my election."[7]

Reform clubs across the city met and endorsed Mullen's new position. The Tammany Reform Club, described as the "backbone" of the Reform party, organized a mass meeting in Jefferson Ward, at which veteran white activists Ryall, Conner, and Bethel promoted George Wise. They followed Mullen's lead and pointed the finger of blame at Richmond's GOP politicians and black workers. Of the seventy black activists who had pushed hardest for Mullen at the nominating convention, Bethel claimed only ten could now be counted on. Ryall charged that over four thousand blacks and deserted the Reform party for the Republicans. Now, he and his fellow activists "had taught John S. Wise that he would not be able to say that he had defeated both organized labor and the Democratic Party, and they had taught the colored men a lesson." Mullen, at the podium, told the crowd that "the Labor Party was determined to erect a standard, and if they could not bear to success the one which they had erected of their own they would take the next best one—the one borne by the regular Democratic nominee."[8]

George D. Wise won the election by a margin of more than two-thousand. John S. Wise, manager of the losing campaign, boasted to the *Valley Virginian*: "I feel more pride in the result in the Third Congressional District than in any in the state notwithstanding we were defeated. . . . We acted in the only way we could to preserve the unity of our party." This "only way" included a heavy dose of political venom as well as closed-door double-dealing. The day before the election, an unsigned broadside entitled "A New Mixture" appeared in Richmond. It presented a frontal assault on Mullen (even though he had already dropped out of the campaign) and asked working-class voters: "Men of Richmond, can he sell you like sheep?" The anonymous authors suggested that Mullen had sold out to George Wise. "The only interest the Public will henceforth feel in Mullen will be Curiosity to know what he got."[9]

Recriminations and hostilities echoed within and around the Reform movement itself. An unnamed correspondent wrote *John Swinton's Paper* that Mullen's actions had "not been advantageous to the Order here. A great deal of corresponding has been published concerning the reports of 'trading' that have been associated with Mullen's canvass, from his first dealings with the Republicans till his final surrender to the Democrats." Such rumors were refueled when later in November Mullen fired John S. Wise as his lawyer in the boycott conspiracy case and retained none other than George Wise.[10]

• • •

For the moment at least, the curtain had been lowered on the stage of biracial organization and activity. Black working-class militants, nonetheless, pushed ahead and kept alive the fires of popular struggle among their constituency. They continued to employ DA 92 as the organizational vehicle for their collective effort, whatever the issue.

They recognized that the electoral fiasco had harmed their cause considerably. The day after the votes were tallied, veteran black activist Collin Payne privately cirticized the Republicans' role.

> I am sorry that your opinion was not asked in this district. If it had I think we would of elected the Knights of Labor candidate to Congress and broke up the Democrat party in this district and certainly in Richmond. The Republican party in Richmond are very much divided. The laboring men thinks it was done to defeat them.[11]

In the winter of 1886–1887, these activists agitated for the employment of qualified blacks at skilled jobs on the municipally directed city hall project. A mass petition campaign, organized through No. 92, quickly garnered more than a thousand signatures and was laid before the city council within a month of Mullen's defeat in the congressional campaign. Referred to the Committee on Grounds and Buildings, this petition was tabled and then ignored. The committee explicitly resolved to hire only white workers for skilled jobs, even if these workers were "tramping" whites, in preference to long-time black city residents. It also recommended that the granite contract be awarded to the Westham quarry, whose all-white skilled workforce had long been the core of the local granite cutters' union. This union had recently won a brief strike for higher wages and shorter hours and had rejected William Mullen's plea to admit black skilled granite cutters.[12]

Black activists convened a mass meeting on November 29 at Harris's Hall, where the No. 49 delegation had been honored only a month earlier. With the doors closed to white reporters, the gathering decided upon a new and promising tactic. A committee was selected to draft a letter of protest to various national labor and reform organizations. Frustrated by the city council's unresponsiveness and lacking any direct channels of communication with the white Reform movement, itself in an apparent state of disarray, those in attendance now sought the assistance of national figures who might be sympathetic to their appeal.[13]

These black militants were especially optimistic about Patrick Ford, the controversial editor of the New York–based *Irish World*, a radical pro-Knights and pro-Gaelic weekly with an international readership. Locally, readers of the Irish World included workers of all ethnic and racial groups. Informally, black workers had more contact with the Irish than with any other group. Their neighborhoods frequently bordered each other, sometimes overflowed their respective boundaries, and often shared the same markets and grog shops. Whether in the iron mills or on major constuction projects, black and Irish unskilled laborers worked together and, in hard times, competed for the same jobs, occasionally with explosive results. Bishop Keane, the voice of Catholic Richmond, organized a black congregation in 1879, the first of its kind in the South. By 1885, the new St. Joseph's Church had been built; much of the money for its construction had come from local Irish Catholics. Powderly himself had attended mass at St. Joseph's during the General Assembly session. A few of Richmond's Irish residents found their way into the Republican party after the war. Every venture into "independent" politics on a local level—be it the Workingmen's party of 1877, the Greenbackers, the Readjusters, or the Knights of Labor–based Reform party of 1886—had some base among Irish workers and some candidates drawn from working-class and shop-keeping Irish. Hostile to Grover Cleveland's "pro-British" position on the question of Gaelic independence, some local Irish workers, led by John Ryall and Joseph Devine, had openly defected to the Republicans in 1884. They organized an "Irish National Republican Association" and an "Irish Blaine and Logan Club," which claimed four hundred members.[14]

Though local Irish support for black demands was rarely heard, there was considerable logic in this appeal to Patrick Ford. He had been a staunch public supporter of black popular aspirations since 1874. In the early 1880s, he put the *Irish World* squarely behind the Readjuster movement. The *Irish World* supported Richmond activists campaigning for the inclusion of black men on juries; supported a strike of one thousand Lynchburg tobacco factory workers; praised the April 1879 Richmond celebration of the passage of the Fifteenth Amendment; and gave an enthusiastic account of the September 1883 National Convention of Colored Men in Louisville, hailing their concern with "the Labor Question" and the evidence of "Political independence" they demonstrated.[15]

Black activists, well aware of Ford's support for their activities, had sensed the parallels between their struggle for justice and Ireland's battle against Britain. The fall 1882 National Convention of Colored Men, for example, passed a resolution calling for black popular support for Ireland's independence. Many local black militants responded, donating to Gaelic "Skirmishing" and "Emergency" funds.[16]

Ford had strongly endorsed DA 49's challenge to racial discrimination. The columns of the *Irish World* praised its "manly and significant conduct in maintenance of that grand principle of equal liberty for white and black, . . . an essential plank in a consistent platform of industrial emancipation." Therefore, after November 1886, when black working-class militants, sought the assistance of prominent national labor reformers to influence local white workers, Patrick Ford was a natural choice.[17]

And so, in early December, the committee appointed by the Harris's Hall mass meeting sent Ford an eloquent appeal that was immediately published in the *Irish World*:

> We wish to make known to the justice-loving workmen of the country the bitter opposition and hatred which the colored workingmen of the South are made to feel at the hands of those who hold the reins of government as well

> as many of those whose wealth is the product of colored labor. At a recent meeting of the City Council, a resolution was passed forbidding the employment of colored mechanics on the City Hall work. The colored men have held a meeting to consider what they ought to do in the matter, as they feel that a great wrong has been committed against not them alone but against the just principle of justice and fair play. We would like to know if such conduct has the approval of the workingmen of the country. It was certainly not the spirit manifested by the Knights of Labor at their recent convention in this city.[18]

Ford added some well-chosen words of his own, urging "the organized white workingmen of Richmond" to change their ways:

> It is a duty the organized white workmen of Richmond owe to themselves to publicly repudiate all sympathy with this most unjust prejudice against the colored workingman. . . . Only by making common cause, regardless of color or trade, can the workmen of the country maintain any degree of independence in the face of the forces with which they must contend. Not only justice, therefore, but their selfish interests would demand of the organized workingmen of Richmond that they resist all such unjust discrimination against any class of honest and industrious American citizens.[19]

Ford's support encouraged the black activists. Through James Hayes, they presented the city council with a formal list of questions such as "whether there are any non-resident mechanics employed on the city hall building" and "whether any resolutions have been adopted by this council discriminating against any mechanics of this city." Hayes made an impassioned speech on the subject and demanded that "every [council] man put himself on record on this color question." The *Dispatch* reported: "He wished to know who was and who was not the friend of the colored man." Common council president John S. Bethel intervened to halt the discussion; he used the prerogative of the chair to table the matter.[20]

On January 9, black workers crowded the Gallilee Hall on Broad Street, listened to a number of speeches by militant blacks, and resolved to sustain the struggle for skilled jobs on the city hall project. One month later, a "committee of colored mechanics" called directly on the city engineer and demanded jobs for a number of skilled black stonecutters. He rejected their demand, claiming that he could not hire them because they were not union members. The black committee vainly argued that the union would not allow them to join. The *Dispatch* added: "It seemed understood that the union men would quit work were these outsiders put to work on the building." Undaunted, black activists persisted; in early March, the city council reconsidered its position and agreed, at least in principal, to cease excluding blacks from skilled jobs on the city hall project.[21]

More was involved here than intense lobbying or even winning some specific demands. Black activists directed these popular concerns and energies in such a way as to breathe new life into the black Knights of Labor and the popular movement it represented. District Assembly No. 92 swelled to some thirty black local assemblies, six of them women's. Rather than collapsing, the black movement appeared even stronger in the aftermath of Mullen's disastrous campaign.

• • •

In contrast to the unity of purpose manifested by the black popular movement in the winter of 1886–1887, discord, controversy, and lack of direction plagued veteran white labor activists. The momentum had shifted against them. They were thrown on the defensive by a reawakened local bourgeoisie, aided by national allies from Grover Cleveland to the *New York Times*. In January 1887, for instance, the latter singled out Richmond as the "finest example" of the "New South," "with snap and go, with push and enterprise, with commercial ambition, with industrial purpose, upon development." Special praise was reserved for the local chamber of commerce. The *Times* concluded:

> Here [Richmond] was the very hotbed of "organized labor" all through last year, and Chief Powderly's national convention held here did a lot to make it hotter. Employer and employee were largely on ill terms. There were bitter contests; there was some boycotting; there was idleness; there was crippled industry. All this told severely on the year's trade, as the figures finally collated showed. Had there been no labor turmoil, no strikes, no consequential shutdowning, the annual statement of the city would have redounded to the city's industrial pride.[22]

Barely two months after they welcomed the likes of William Mullen and John Ryall back into the Democratic party, Richmond middle-class leaders launched a full-fledged campaign to finish off labor reform. Veteran reformers were singled out for attack, divisions between craft unionists and the Knights of Labor were fostered, and inducements were held out to disaffected white workers. Mullen, Ryall, Chappell, Bethel, and company barely managed to retain control over DA 84.[23]

In April 1887, the local bourgeoisie issued a symbolic challenge to white working-class activists. With municipal government support, businessmen organized a parade to celebrate the laying of the new city hall's cornerstone. Officers of the Law and Order League directed the planning. White workers were to march by workshop, led by their employers and foremen. Black workers were not invited to participate; nor were the Knights of Labor, who had a central role in the adoption of the construction plans.[24]

DA 84's officers called for a boycott of the parade. Though "representing fully two-thirds of the population," they complained they were "totally and significantly ignored in the arrangements for the laying of the cornerstone."

The "orator of the day" was to be none other than the judge who had decided the Baughman Brothers boycott case against the Knights of Labor, the *Labor Herald*, and the printers' union. The "chief marshal" was the head of the Law and Order League, and his "assistant marshals" were "with but few exceptions selected from members" of that antilabor organization. Among them, "we fail to find the name of one man who was in sympathy with the reform movement, but all are men who were bitterly opposed."

> Having taken such an active part in the building of the new City hall, naturally we should feel a deep interest in the laying of the cornerstone, and do all in our power to make it an occasion worthy of such an important event in the history of our city, but we would be untrue to ourselves, untrue to the principles of our order, untrue to our manhood, should we let these insults pass unnoticed and acquiesce in the present arrangements for laying the cornerstone of the new City Hall. We regret that the course pursued by those making the arrangements had made this action on our part necessary, and trust that those having the authority may yet so change matters that members of our order can participate without sacrificing their manhood.[25]

White workers were forced to choose. If they rejected the traditional relationships of the paternalistic social hierarchy, they had to embrace new relationships of equality with their black counterparts. Few were ready to do so; few could withstand the pressure. Thousands of white workers marched by workshop, led by foremen, managers, shop-keepers, and businessmen. DA 84's appeal failed.[26]

Signs of strain began to appear within the black popular movement. By early spring 1887, three local assemblies had fallen behind in their "defense assessments" and "taxes" due to the national office. DA 92 itself finally appealed on behalf of all "the local assemblies attached to it" for exoneration from all dues and assessments. In mid-March, Harris's Hall, an important meeting place and symbol of black support for No. 49, burned to the ground. Internal conflict spread. The *Planet* attacked John Oliver and the directors of the Moore Street Industrial School for allegedly placing their personal needs ahead of those of the black community. The directors, in turn, sued the *Planet* for libel. The April reorganization of the middle-class Colored Mercantile Society also reflected the disunity growing within black Richmond. Begun before the rise of the Knights, this special interest organization had declined in the midst of the Order's ascendancy. The complaint of the deacons of the First African Baptist Church that congregation donations to their poor fund could no longer support indigent members was still another indication of the diminished commitment to popular uplift felt by the black middle-class. The Knights, and their particular vision of social reform, crumbled in the black community.[27]

Deterioration threatened to turn into a rout. Following the mid-April collapse of the bricklayers' strike for the nine-hour day, the tinners, facing intransigent contractors, drew back from an open confrontation. The coopers lost a brief strike for higher "prices" for flour barrels and nail kegs. The local circuit court convicted William F. Crump of conspiracy in the Baughman Brothers boycott case. Though he was only fined five dollars, the legal precedent in state boycott conflicts was now established; the courts had stripped the labor movement of its most effective tactic for collective action. Black brick moulders lost their fight to maintain the higher wages won in 1886. In disgust and frustration, some turned to "machine-breaking" under cover of night. An attempted strike failed as only a few union members walked off the job. In a clear indication of weakness, when seeking to maintain the Richmond end of a nationwide boycott of several Philadelphia breweries, DA 84 turned to the Liquor Dealers' Protective Association for assistance.[28]

• • •

By mid-summer 1887, militants returned to the idea of political organization in their effort to revive the popular movement. They concentrated on the fall elections to the state legislature. In August and September, they established new "Reform Clubs" throughout Richmond and Manchester as political vehicles independent of both major parties. The initial meeting of the Manchester Reform Club featured speeches by Joseph Devine, Ira Bland, Jacob Lange, and Dr. T. E. Stratton, all veterans of the 1886 Reform campaign. The Alliance Club—with residents of Clay, Jackson, Monroe, and Madison Wards—debated the virtues of John Ryall, John Bethel, and Rowland Hill as potential independent candidates for the state legislature. By mid-September, a Reform executive board was convened by delegates from the Alliance Club, the Tammany Club, and the Rocketts Tammany Club. A number of recognized activists were elected. They met with the Republican party's executive committee to discuss the possibility of joint nominations for the upcoming campaign. But unlike the earlier District Labor Convention that had nominated Mullen, this move was not made by a popularly elected, biracial group of delegates. Rather, whites alone sought to reach the black base of the GOP through the white machine. It was pragmatic rather than popular politics.[29]

This new approach was full of pitfalls. The GOP "ring," continuing its manipulative practices, sought to employ the Reform activists to its own advantage. Initially, the Republican executive committee told the Reformers to nominate their own state legislature ticket. If these candidates pledged to support the Republican nominee for United States senator, the Republican party would endorse them rather than field a competing slate. However, when GOP leaders realized "that the Democratic Party was making no formal overtures to the Reformers," they shifted ground, demanding "that at least one straight out Republican should be placed on the ticket." The Reformers expressed "bitter opposition." An elaborate compromise was finally worked out, in which the Reform clubs would place twelve names in nomination for the four state offices. Then, at a joint meeting of the Reform executive board and the city Republican committee, "first the Republicans will strike off one and then the Reformers one, until there are only four left, who will be the nominees."[30]

These steps toward coalition were not popular among most white workers. A small, self-proclaimed group of "True Reformers" declared themselves "ready and willing to fight for a straight-out Reform ticket, but opposed to being swallowed up by either of the old parties." At the same time, the "Democratic Knights of Labor" conservatives also challenged the political coalition. As one prominent "bolter" told a late September mass meeting, "he would never consent to desert the Democratic party if it were necessary to be a Reformer to do so."[31]

Sticky quesions arose concerning black-white relations. An anonymous Reformer told a *Dispatch* reporter of opposition within the Reform camp to black candidates on the joint ticket. On September 28, delegates from the Reform clubs and colored Reform clubs, which had been organized in every ward, held a stormy meeting. Each of these black clubs had been named after a prominent national Republican—Garfield, Lincoln, and Hayes. The black delegates were adamant in their demand that the ticket include black candidates. But the meeting adjourned with no commitments being made—and no real progress in biracial cooperation.[32]

Despite ths disharmony and confusion, the Reformers aggressively promoted their campaign. The *Labor Herald* carried the September 30 "Address of the Reform Party to the voters of Richmond." It presented the "Reform Council" as an agent of economy in government, a promoter of local economic growth, and a trend-setter in wages, hours, and labor relations. Its platform included state funding of free school books; prohibition of child labor under age fourteen; a law "preventing convicts from being brought into competition with free labor in any way, shape, or form"; a ten-hour day statute for railroad workers; a "graded income tax"; a "mechanics' lien law"; "the abolition of the contract system upon National, State, and Municipal work"; and a measure "prohibiting members of the Legislature from receiving free passes upon railroads" and "from acting as council for railroads or other corporations." It even proposed "such amendments to the present laws as may be necessary to make fewer crimes punishable by confinement in the penitentiary." In a nutshell, the Reform party called for: "the abrogation of all laws that do not bear equally upon capital and labor."[33]

The Reform party depicted the "so-called Democratic party" as the tool of the Law and Order League, and themselves as "not a party of any particular class or color, but . . . of the whole people and for the people." The Democratic party, it claimed, had not fulfilled any of "about a dozen bills" in its 1885 "labor plank." "We challenge our opponents to produce one measure passed which is of any benefit to this city." They, on the other hand, sought to promote the prosperity and vitality of all Richmond, including "the interests of other classes" and the black community. The Reform party's "Address" called on black voters to recognize "that their true interests lie with the Reform party—the party of the people—which guarantees to every man his rights, regardless of color, race, or previous condition."[34]

Some weeks before the election, the Reformers sponsored a mass parade, which culminated in an address by John Ryall, the "silver-tongued orator of the Reform party, the man who has never failed to hold spell-bound the men of the Labor party." From a platform decorated with banners that proclaimed "Vote for Freedom and Liberty" and "Stand by the Reformers, the Party of the People," Ryall urged his racially mixed audience to "hold firm." After a week of discussions in the Reform clubs, four veteran white labor reformers were chosen as nominees for the state legislature. All were white veterans of labor reform politics in Richmond. A short time later the Republican executive committee ratified these choices, as John S. Wise explained that the candidates were committed to voting Republican in all House of Delegates issues. Thus the four labor reformers became the official Republican candidates. The campaign was on in earnest.[35]

The hard core of Knights of Labor activists threw their energy into the campaign. Mullen and the four candidates spoke at several largely black mass meetings in early November. On November 3, Mullen and John S. Wise jointly addressed a sizeable gathering; Mullen and John Mitchell of the *Planet* were the main speakers of a Jackson Ward rally on the following night. "What we want the white man to do in this election is to vote for the coalition ticket," Mitchell told the black audience. "We propose to get the same wages that they do." Lewis Lindsay, the veteran of two decades of struggle, then urged: "Let us shake hands with out brothers, the white workingmen, and vote for Parrish, Bland, Graves, and Ryall." William Fields, a prominent member of DA 92, followed. He declared that "the white laboring men's interests and the negro's interests were mutual in this fight."[36]

These themes were echoed at additional mass meetings right up to the election. Mullen, the candidates, and John S. Bethel enlivened a late night rally at the old Market Hall. The following evening, they joined Lewis Lindsay on the podium of the black Gallilee Hall. Among the activists, at least, there was a new unity and a renewed enthusiasm.[37]

In the preelection issue of the *Labor Herald*, Mullen urged:

> Organization is what will give justice to the laborer. One person can accomplish nothing, but thousands can sweep the field clear of all obstacles. To gain their justice, their liberty, and equal rights, the oppressed must band together and use the ballot box as their weapon. The dawn of the day of the battle had just dawned forth, and by united strength and untiring energy the masses can claim the victory ere the close of the day.

On election eve, he told an open-air meeting at the railroad freight depot "that the conditions of the white workingman would be worse under Democratic rule than the colored man, and that the wealthy whites paid more money in caring for a pointer dog than they gave the workingman for wages."[38]

The Republican-Reform coalition pushed their campaign to a climax on election day. It had faced a powerful opposition rooted in John S. Barbour's railroad empire and George D. Wise's ideological chicanery. It had endured bitter internal conflicts as well as the alienation of the following: some white workers, because the coalition collaborated with the Republican "ring"; other white workers, because it reached out to black workers; and black workers, because it nominated an all-white ticket. The coalition gave the Democratic machine quite a scare. Of the fourteen thousand votes cast, the Democrats won by six hundred, a spread of fifty-two percent to forty-eight percent. Most of the coalition's strength was among black workers. Its weakness appeared to be in Richmond's outlying precincts. Its ticket made a respectable showing in Richmond's white-majority wards, and swept the predominantly black Jackson Ward by a five to one margin.[39]

The strong showing in this electoral venture did little for the resurrection of mass working-class activity among blacks or whites. Despite the parade, open-air orations, and new ward committees among blacks, this campaign had not been an expression of a popular movement. On the contrary, it had rested on a pragmatic alliance between two political central committees, both of which stood at considerable distances from their organizational bases. Hence, the election stood as an end in itself, with no implications for new social relationships or renewed popular activism.

By the end of the year, the popular movements once represented by the Knights of Labor had virtually faded from sight. Once a proud and powerful organization with more than ten thousand local members, the Knights of Labor began 1888 with fewer than fourteen hundred dues-paying members. By mid-year, DA 84 had only 455 members, and District Assembly 92 had only 282. Many local assemblies disbanded, some were consolidated in order to stay alive, and others barely survived. In July 1888, for example, the recording secretary of a once prominent black local assembly informed Powderly: "Our membership has decreased in a short time from 380 down to 20, and they left us with a heavy debt hanging over us." When the women's lecturer for the Knights of Labor stopped in Richmond on an early 1889 national tour to try to revive the Order, she found few members and much bickering among them. "The majority," she lamented, "let go the footing they had secured, and left the few who are capable of realization to suffer without any near prospect of relief."[40]

CHAPTER 12

Race and Class: Legacy and Possibility

Southern society is now virtually divided into two castes. In the first caste are merged indiscriminately gentleman, farmer, overseer, poor white, and each and every one of these, regardless of education, worth, refinement, decency, or morality, belongs to this class simply by reason of a white skin. The second caste is composed promiscuously of all who have a black skin and are related to them, however remotely; and all who are thus marked, however cultured and refined they may be, however able and and however excellent, are confined as by fate to this caste, and are not permitted to throw off its galling chains.[1]

THE KNIGHTS of Labor forged into a single movement the manifold activities undertaken by American workers—skilled and unskilled, black and white, men and women—over the course of the nineteenth century: fraternal and benefit societies, trade unions, "social reform" organizations and movements, self-improvement and self-education campaigns, and independent labor politics. Most important, the Knights were the last and most complete embodiment of labor's struggle against the emergence of a new social order, based on deskilled work, strict hierarchy at the workplace, rigid industrial and social discipline, corporate power in politics, the separation of "life" and "work" between home and workplace, and the development of everyday culture as a collection of purchasable commodities rather than the direct creation of families, workmates, and neighbors. The demise of the Knights signified not only the collapse of this struggle, but also the refragmentation of activities it had tried to pull together. The fragments included pockets of resistance and institutions and activities that were geared to the better integration of workers as subordinate actors within society.

The Knights also represent a particularly critical moment in Afro-American history. Here, too, we find the congealing of earlier activities and experiences: secret societies, reform organizations, trade unions and labor societies, and political struggles. New features are also relevant. The Knights were the first labor organization to welcome blacks on an equal footing with whites. They introduced and assisted a class perspective enfolded within the sense of race pride, and they offered an overall perspective of society, as a whole, in need of reform. Their perspective of society was comparable to the way blacks had perceived society since Emancipation.

The failure of the Knights resulted in a fragmentation of black activities that was similar to that among white workers. The division of rural and urban blacks contributed to the weakness of Virginia's Populism. Race pride shifted from an aggressive to a conservative, defensive ideology in the hands of Booker T. Washington, among others, and it was limited in practice to black consumer support for black businesses. Secret societies, which were transformed into insurance companies and banks, drove a wedge between the social and benefit features of these organizations. The gap between the middle and working classes in the black community grew; ultimately, millions of southern blacks migrated to the urban and industrial North.

• • •

Black Richmond emerged from the Civil War with impressive strength and cohesiveness. Familial and kinship networks provided the foundation for secret societies, which helped generate popular movements. Long-term Richmond residents, many of them former slaves, rose to new positions of social and political leadership. During the brief period of formal Reconstruction, black activists expressed themselves through the local Republican party, often in conflict with the white "ring" of carpetbaggers and professional politicians who headed the GOP. In this way, they played an important role in shaping the new state constitution and, through it, the ground rules for future social and political struggles.

After Virginia's readmission into the Union in 1870, black activists found the Republican apparatus increasingly less viable as a popular vehicle. Even at its best, the use of formal political channels implied popular demobilization, from the denial of the franchise to women to the reliance on elected delegates rather than on direct action. With the creation of Jackson Ward, the black vote was effectively gerrymandered into the first southern ghetto. The white "ring" learned to manipulate and weaken the party, taking black votes for granted. Outright repression and discrimination by employers, by the police, and by the courts further undermined Afro-Americans' political expression.

By the early 1870s, the tightly knit black community, with a predominantly working-class leadership group, adopted the Colored National Labor Union as the primary vehicle for its struggle for "Equal Rights." The CNLU provided a "unitary" structure for black popular organizaiton, addressing simultaneously the social, political, and economic concerns of Richmond Afro-Americans. Despite its promise, however, the CNLU rapidly sank into oblivion; its possibilities were reduced to component parts of the experiences of local black workers.

The depression, ushered in by the national financial collapse of September 1873, took Richmond's black and white workers by surprise. It took a terrible material toll among local working-class families. Especially debilitating was the division created by the color line, for it allowed employers and politicians to play workers against one another, whereas working-class activists of both races had initiated popular movements between 1865 and 1873.

By 1873, the CNLU had faded from view. The opportunistically based factionalism that replaced it poisoned the political atmosphere. The depression threatened to sweep away the institutional foundations of the black community, especially after the collapse of the Freedman's Savings Bank in 1874. Confronted by multiple pressures and disasters, activists—especially the younger generations—began to move in new directions, to develop new ideas. Notions of race pride and self-help evolved; by late 1875, they were underpinning new strategies that revolved around independent black labor and black political organization. Though discrete at the time, these developments signalled the deathknell of the cautious, pro-Republican strategy that had been promoted by an earlier generation of community leaders. They also marked the birth of a revived race pride and mutual dependence, whose vitality would soon become apparent.

The split in the Conservative party and the organization of William Mahone's Readjuster party in 1879 created an environment in which this black awakening could flourish. Between 1880 and 1883, Richmond was swept by a wave of Afro-American militancy unrivaled even by that of a decade earlier. From the workplace to the ballot box, from one corner of the city to another, racial pride and independent organization blossomed with a distinctly working-class flavor. Facing such a challenge, the bourgeoisie turned directly to force in 1883. Outright discrimination, threats, violence, repression, fraud, and finally, the Danville race riot that it provoked, turned aside the black popular thrust.

Conversely, white workers drew closer than ever to the bourgeoisie during the Readjuster years. First of all, the economic recovery that began in 1879 restored much of their faith in the South's employers and political "leaders." But when the economy slowed and then slid backward in 1882–1883, they would blame the Readjusters and their unorthodox economic policies. Moreover, the convergence of Readjusterism and the black popular movement, followed in 1884 by the formal merger of the Readjuster and GOP organizations, seemed to bear out white bourgeois warnings about "independent" politics being merely a tool in Republican hands. Such politics stood discredited among white workers, and Richmond's bourgeoisie appeared to be enjoying their most secure position since the war.[2]

Much to their surprise, however, the next three years witnessed the emergence of the most formidable challenge to their rule in the city's history. By late 1884 and early 1885, black and white popular movements had revived; both were now formally tied to the newly organized Knights of Labor, which was potentially a single powerful movement. The Knights were absorbed into the existing networks of social organization among both black and white workers, and the Order's leaders gave new coherence and articulation to the vision of its members.[3]

The Knights of Labor drew in members through a broadly based boycott of convict-made flour barrels and forged a movement culture in which these recruits could develop new ideas and activities. The Knights stood at the forefront of the struggle against convict labor, which had a negative impact on both black and white workers. They promoted campaigns to build a new city hall out of local materials and with local labor, to build trade unions for all workers, and to win equality before the law for all blacks. By early 1886, such manifold popular efforts had begun to shift power away from the bourgeoisie, who seemed unable to cope with this mounting challenge to their authority.

By late spring 1886, in an apparently logical development, the Knights of Labor extended their activities into independent politics. Their "workingmen's Reform Ticket" won a stunning victory, but it generated problems for which they were unprepared. These problems revolved around racial issues that threatened to destroy the order itself. Activists hoped that the Knights' general assembly, scheduled for Richmond in October, and William Mullen's labor candidacy for Congress would galvanize and focus the movements. Both ventures backfired, however, and left increased, rather than diminished, racial tension in their wake. Each popular movement then caved in, despite the valiant efforts and black and white working-class militants. By the end of 1887, the status quo was no longer imperiled, and the social and racial hierarchies appeared more rigid than ever. In this historical context, Louis Harvie Blair could realistically write of the "two castes" of southern society.[4]

• • •

Over the next fifteen years, black and white activists struggled unsuccessfully to rekindle a popular movement in Richmond. Their efforts came to naught, frustrated by the persistence of the color line, which posed a powerful obstacle to the emergence of shared perspectives among white and black workers. With the collapse of the Knights in the late 1880s, no organizational vehicle that could even potentially mediate between the races existed; therefore, face-to-face experience was rare. In the absence of such personal exchanges, the press, politicians, and employers could easily interject falsehoods, distort attitudes, twist events, and foster prejudices. In fall 1888, for example, a number of local white working-class activists attended a Republican meeting at Petersburg as part of Richmond's predominantly black delegation. The *Dispatch* treated this convention much as it had the October 1886 Knights of Labor General Assembly, when it promoted rumors and discord:

> Some said they were disposed to vote for a protective tariff, but could not stand such close associations with the negroes as they saw at this meeting. They had been led to believe by their leaders in Richmond that the negroes were to be kept in the background, but the negroes predominated, and some of the Richmond visitors declared they could not be used as monkeys to pull chestnuts out of the fire for the negroes.[5]

The collapse of the Knights of Labor effectively eliminated the possibility of biracial action. Thus, in 1888, when a committee of black craftsmen once again appealed to the common council for job opportunities on the city hall project, they discovered that the white members of the stonecutters', blacksmiths', carpenters', and bricklayers' unions would strike rather than work alongside them. Even the possibility of biracial dialogue markedly declined. And there were no channels through which the black and white craftsmen could even discuss their differences or common concerns. By the early 1890s, an all-white Central Trades and Labor Council connecting craftsmen's unions existed in Richmond. Among those absent were coopers—the most integrated trade in the city and the one that saw the most consistent black-white cooperation. Nor were any of the predominantly black trades—teamsters, stevedores, tobacco factory workers, brickmakers, or hod carriers—included. Furthermore, no women, either black or white were represented: thus, the fastest-growing and lowest-paid sector of the workforce had been excluded.[6]

All Richmond workers—black and white, women and men—were affected by the organizational weaknesses rooted in racial separation. When the U.S. Commissioner of Labor studied the conditions of workingwomen in twenty-five cities in 1888, he found their average weekly wages in Richmond—only $3.93 a week!—to be the lowest in the nation. (The national average was $5.24) He concluded: "Among the workingwomen of Richmond nothing is more uncommon than an example of the robust health so frequently met with among the northern working girls."[7]

While Richmond ranked twenty-ninth among all American cities in terms of its workforce in 1890, it fell to forty-first when its wage bill was considered. Richmond workers—women and men, black and white, unskilled and skilled—were paid substantially less for comparable work elsewhere. Skilled iron trades workers—from agricultural implements shops, foundries and machine shops, iron mills, and nail works—earned ten to twenty percent less than the national averages in their respective industries and trades. Building trades fared no better. Plumbers and gasfitters earned about $550 a year in Richmond, more than ten percent below their trade's national average of $627. Richmond carpenters averaged $510 a year, while their counterparts elsewhere averaged $648, almost twenty percent more per year. Plasterers, the only predominantly black building trade in Richmond, did even worse. Their $375 annual earnings were almost thirty percent below the national average of $620. Local coopers earned $300 a year, one-third under the national average of $450. In industry after industry, for occupation after occupation, Richmond employers paid their workers considerably less than the national average.[8]

The prevalence of low wages, combined with the frequency of both seasonal and cyclical layoffs, compounded by the structural unemployment rooted in technological change, made poverty a rather common condition in late nineteenth- and early twentieth-century Richmond. Fully eighty percent of the black workforce was limited to unskilled pursuits in industry, transportation, and service, where they were fortunate to earn even $300 a year. Male tobacco factory workers averaged only $305 a year in 1890. Their female fellow workers, of whom there were more than fourteen hundred, received but $120. White women in textile, wool, and clothing factories earned almost $100 a year more than their black counterparts from the tobacco industry, but even $220 a year fell far short of a living wage. While skilled white workers found themselves earning less than their fellows nationally, black men, black women, white women, and all unskilled workers engaged in a constant struggle for survival.[9]

This struggle took a continuing toll and even affected the very future of Richmond's working class. In 1890, the mortality rate for white infants was more than 90 per 1,000 births, while the rate for blacks was 242 per 1,000. For those who lived, the future remained grim. Less than half of the school-age population attended any school at all in 1890, hardly a hopeful sign in a city with an adult illiteracy rate of more than twenty percent. Nearly 1,000 men and women were imprisoned in the state penitentiary, 230 in the city prison, and another 340 in the city station houses, while 260 called the almshouse "home." Stability, let alone security, continued to escape Richmond's workers.[10]

• • •

Racial separation not only caused the low living standards of Richmond's workers, but also continued to sap the bases of social organization and social protest in the 1890s and early 1900s. The failures of Populism, socialism, trade unionism, and the black struggle against disfranchisement bore testimony to the continuing significance of race.

The Populist movement was of little more than ephemeral significance in Virginia. Working-class activists from Richmond had begun to explore the possibilities of a "farmer-labor alliance" in 1887. Though men from both races were involved initially, nothing permanent evolved. By the time Populists had formally organized statewide in 1890, racial separation was once again the order of the day. The white Virginia Farmers' Alliance and a

Virginia Colored Farmers' Alliance coexisted uneasily. In 1891 and 1892, these alliances waged internal battles over the distribution of power, the issues deserving priority, and the racial basis of representation within the Virginia People's party. The *Richmond Sun*, the voice of the white Farmers' Alliance, could begin an article in 1894 on the rights of blacks by declaring: "This is a white man's country and will always be controlled by whites." For all its potential, Populism, too, had fallen victim to the color line.[11]

Socialism fared no better. In April 1895, twenty-two white workers met at the home of veteran activist John Taylor Chappell and resolved to organize themselves into the "Altrurian Assembly of the Reform Order of the Knights of Labor." Chappell had been secretary of the Knights of Labor Cooperative Building Association and "Reform" alderman from Jefferson Ward in the halcyon days of 1886. He shared the direction of this new organization with young Walter Ramond, an idealistic printer who was new to the local labor movement, and H. A. Muller, a German-born farmer who had served as district chair of the People's party in 1892 and would soon become secretary of the Virginia Socialist Labor party. Chappell, Ramond, and Muller were joined by a core of committed militants from the new generation as well as the ranks of the experienced. They expressed high hopes of reaching workers throughout the Richmond area.

> The policy of Altrurian Assembly K of L would always be to co-operate and move in harmony with all organizations having for their object the amelioration of the physical workers and downtrodden masses, no matter of what calling or trade, it will be our policy in short to assist all in every way we can do so consistently and to fight none unless forced to do so in self-defense.[12]

Harmony and growth eluded the organization. Within a year and a half, it had been dissolved, replaced by "Local Union No. 1 of the Co-operative Commonwealth of Virginia." Though tied to the Virginia Socialist Labor party, the "C.C." served more as a vehicle for the self-education of its members than as the impetus for a popular movement. In 1897 and 1898, discussions and debates centered on "How to Build Here and Now a Co-operative Commonwealth"; "What Effect will Socialism have upon the Tramp element?"; "Would not Socialism destroy man's individuality?"; "Under a Socialistic form of government would there be any overproduction, and, if so, what would be done with the surplus?"; "If God intended a part of the Human Race to be in Slavery (wage and chattel) why did He implant in his breast a thirst for Independence?"; "What is to become of those displaced by machinery whose living depends on physical labor?"; "If the government desired to control the Railroads and Telegraph lines, about what would be the cost to the government and how long would it take to purchase them?"; and so forth. There were also discussions based on shared readings: Bellamy, "Equality"; Baker, "Plea for Communism"; Blatchford, "Merrie England";

Morris, "Useless vs. Useful Toil"; Bellamy, *Parable of the Water Tank* and issues of the *Appeal to Reason*, the *People*, and the *New Charter*, "a socialistic paper published in California." Not once was the issue of race addressed, nor was the problem of local organizing considered. By early 1898, the members explicitly recognized the limited functions of their organization, "and after a short debate it was decided to withdraw and as soon as possible organize into an independent Socialistic educational club."[13]

Trade unionism continued to touch far more working-class lives in Richmond than did Populism or socialism. However, through the 1890s and early 1900s, it remained exceedingly limited and ineffectual. In March 1893, the short-lived *Richmond Labor News* listed fifteen unions and labor organizations in the city. Rather than expanding from its narrow, male, white, craft base, trade union organization barely held its ground over the next decade. *The First Annual Report of the Bureau of Labor and Industrial Statistics of the State of Virginia*, published in 1899, noted only 1,436 trade union members in the entire state of Virginia.[14]

Materially, black workers predictably lagged far behind their white counterparts. Politically and socially, they found their world increasingly restricted. By 1901 they faced a crisis: a constitutional convention that would disenfranchise them. Over the course of the 1890s, black suffrage had been restricted through both legal and extralegal measures, from the poll tax to thinly veiled physical and economic threats. By 1897, only an estimated twenty-two percent of adult black male Virginians voted in the state elections. With the Republican party debilitated, Democratic leaders anticipated little opposition in their drive to constitutionally strip blacks of their right to vote.[15]

Richmond Afro-Americans themselves were isolated and divided in this struggle. White Republican party officials, noting the facility with which Democratic officials manipulated vote tallies in southside "black belt" counties, offered little resistance to disfranchisement proposals. The professional black middle class, desperate to protect its small advantages, suggested that literacy requirements be established. Such a compromise might save their own franchise, but not that of black workers generally. By 1900, 52.5 percent of adult black men in Virginia were still classified as illiterate. Forty-one percent of black voters did turn out in the 1901 election of delegates to the constitutional convention, but this impressive reversal was not enough. The new constitution, adopted in 1902, effectively disfranchised all of black Virginia.[16]

No opposition to the status quo and its bourgeois architects could survive in the Virginia of the 1890s and early 1900s. Fragmentation and division had deepened in the aftermath of the collapse of the Knights. Defeatism and disarray had mounted. And the color line remained where it had been when Richmond was established, where it remains today. No popular movement could flourish in such a climate. In the absence of such a movement, we are left with William Mullen's bitter observation of 1902:

> The growing greed for gain, and the mad rush which men are making with the hope of amassing great fortunes, have so hardened the conscience of men, and so paralyzed their sense of responsibility and justice, that they give no thought as to what suffering their course may bring to others, so long as their ambition for gain is satisfied. . . . And there is little doubt but that a thrill of joy passes through their unholy frame when one who has grown too old to be as valuable as in former years, drops at his post or is ground to fragments in the machinery he works—they see a vacancy for a stronger, younger man—with stronger muscle to work their purpose, from whose healthy veins they can take deeper droughts of blood.[17]

• • •

Racial separation characterized most features of everyday working-class life after 1865. It tended to increase throughout the latter 19th century, in the workplace as well as the community. Inhabiting largely separate worlds, black and white workers had little face-to-face experience with one another, and hence, little opportunity to understand one another.

There were genuine, deep-seated differences between the black and white working-class experiences in Richmond. Material differences—the availability of work, the level of wages, the quality of housing—accompanied major ideological differences: self-images, religious beliefs, familial values, and political allegiances. The differences in the problems they faced, the traditions they drew upon, and the solutions they fashioned led them in different directions. The very rhythms and patterns of their activity diverged. White workers tended to move back and forth from workplace to political activity, depending on which appeared more likely to succeed at the time. Black workers, on the other hand, interwove "economics" and "politics" in a fashion appropriate to their experience of discrimination and oppression. From the ballot box to the shop, conditions for black workers either improved or deteriorated at the same time. They tended to organize and fight—or retreat—in all spheres simultaneously. In the short run, these differences ensured that when white workers zigged, black workers zagged, both for reasons all their own.

With little opportunity to know each other, black and white workers were doomed to misunderstanding. They became vulnerable to the influence of abstract, ideological prejudices and preconceptions. For white workers, a negative image of black workers resulted, inversely reflecting their own self-perceptions. The dependence and bondage experienced by black workers helped describe the independence and freedom white workers claimed as their own and valued highly. No matter how their framework was threatened, materially as well as ideologically, most white workers clung tenaciously to this negative image of their black counterparts. To give it up, we may believe, was to compromise their own integrity and wholeness, to lose hold on their understanding of themselves.

Both black and white workers thirsted for "independence." Yet each pursued its quest alone. Separate camps became hostile camps, each under the direction of politicians, employers, merchants, and demagogues. The thirst for independence brought both black and white workers to drink at bourgeois-controlled wells. As such, it became the greatest chimera of all.

Only a mass-based, biracial popular movement could provide the solution—and bring independence. The Knights of Labor had threatened to become such a movement, coalescing decades of experiences and potentiality. It had only a brief moment in the sun. But its fleeting existence bears witness to the two possibilities long denied by apologists for the southern status quo: (1) that black and white workers could act together and (2) that a working-class reform movement could challenge the status quo. This entire study offers testimony to these possibilities, whose very existence has too long been wished away. Now, we should know—the possibility is there.

Appendixes

Richmond Population, 1870, by Ward

Ward	*Total*	*Native*	*Foreign-born*	*White*	*Black*
Richmond	51,038	47,260	3,778	27,928 (55%)	23,110 (45%)
Clay	6,101	5,654	447	3,469 (57%)	2,632 (43%)
Jefferson	13,565	12,476	1,089	7,406 (55%)	6,159 (45%)
Madison	11,802	10,760	1,042	6,741 (57%)	5,061 (43%)
Marshall	5,276	4,976	300	2,857 (54%)	2,419 (46%)
Monroe	14,294	13,394	900	7,455 (52%)	6,839 (48%)

Source: A Compendium of the Ninth Census (Washington: GPO, 1872), 472–473.

Male, Female, and Child Labor in Tobacco Manufacturing, 1870

Firm	*Men*	*Women*	*Children*
Alex Cameron	150	100	100
J. H. Greanor	120	8	50
Jemes H. Grant	50	0	20
P. H. Mayo	150	35	10
T. W. Pemberton	40	20	25
L. Lottier	70	6	25
E. J. Pilkinton	91	10	16
Yarborough & Sons (stems)	61	10	37
John Enders	40	6	25
Unintelligible	500	6	20
Unintelligible	30	4	30
Unintelligible	40	10	10
Unintelligible	150	10	0
Unintelligible	80	5	0
Unintelligible	60	0	15
R. J. Christian	60	19	0
Royster	50	25	25
Baldwin Chase	50	10	0
D. C. Mayo	110	30	40
T. J. Hargrove	28	8	15
American Tobacco Co.	20	0	10
John Allen (smoking)	5	6	0
Ragland & Jones (stems)	40	6	12
Winne & Talbot (stems)	45	6	26
J. G. Dill	105	40	62
L. H. Frayser	50	15	25
John K. Childrey	125	25	35
A. M. Lyons	50	20	30
Turpin & Bros. (stems)	75	20	30
J. B. Pace	130	35	55
TOTAL (3,982)	2,677 (67%)	512 (13%)	793 (67%)

Source: 1870 Manuscript Census of Manufactures. Figures do not add up due to the inclusion of some factories too small to list individually.

Tobacco Manufacturing In Richmond, 1880

Firm	*Capital*	*Men*	*Women*	*Children*
P. H. Mayo	$ 80,000	200	100	50
Banner	50,000	200	100	100
Callingworth & Ellison	40,000	150	75	75
Jas. Leigh Jones	65,000	50	20	20
J. B. Pace	250,000	200	100	100
Shockhoe Stream	100,000	200	50	50
Turpin & Bros.	30,000	100	70	30
Jackson Turpin	10,000	20	20	10
W. T. Yarborough	30,000	150	75	100
Alex Cameron	400,000	150	100	50
Geo. Campbell	50,000	90	25	50
O. P. Gregory	15,000	120	80	45
J. G. Dill	30,000	100	85	0
Larus & Bros.	30,000	162	28	30
R. J. Christian	10,000	30	20	15
J. K. Childrey	35,000	62	7	21
T. C. Williams	110,500	222	94	55
R. A. Patterson	64,500	133	24	43
L. H. Frayser	20,000	50	60	15
W. C. Thomas	10,000	42	10	23
Hardgrove & Co.	20,000	50	60	15
T. T. Mayo	5,000	35	25	15
Prescott & Osgood	7,000	30	10	22
A. M. Lyon	30,000	59	46	35
T. W. Pemberton	5,000	24	7	19
Whitlock & Northern	1,000	3	2	0
J. W. Phillips	1,500	3	5	0
G. K. Wren	1,500	3	4	2
R. J. Christian	5,000	4	6	2
Chas. Early	8,000	5	14	1
Allen & Ginter	25,000	40	200	60
Pilkinton & Co.	4,000	10	20	15
Sullivan, Word, & Co.	5,500	50	25	50
Oliver & Robinson	100,000	75	75	50
H. Blackmeer	25,000	5	40	7
TOTALS	$1,683,000	2,843 (50%)	1,644 (29%)	1,169 (21%)

Source: 1880 Manuscript Census of Manufactures. Figures do not add up due to the inclusion of some firms too small to list individually.

Tobacco Stemming and Reprizing, 1880

Firm	*Capital*	*Men*	*Women*	*Children*
Christian & Gunn	$ 29,000	20	15	5
Alex. Kear	12,000	7	20	20
Geo. Thompson	15,000	50	100	50
F. H. Deane	5,000	4	21	0
T. C. Williams	29,000	11	2	14
Harwood	5,584	8	2	0
E. M. Moore	5,000	3	0	0
J. Peyton Wise	16,000	15	1	0
B. C. Gray	6,000	8	12	0
J. M. Armistead	25,000	28	7	0
W. H. Connell	10,000	6	0	9
S. A. Ellison	50,000	15	5	0
W. E. Dibrell	5,000	4	0	0
W. H. Perkins	2,500	14	6	0
J. N. Boyd	13,000	10	30	10
A. B. Eddins	15,000	6	10	4
Alex Cameron	10,000	50	30	20
Unintelligible	10,000	7	18	0
Woodbridge	10,000	11	14	0
W. M. Bridges	16,000	4	5	1
A. J. Ford	20,000	10	40	3
Boykin	25,000	9	9	2
Scott & Clarke	30,000	12	54	24
Geo. Campbell	10,000	20	30	25
Hinton	1,000	5	3	5
Barksdale	40,000	30	30	20
Unintelligible	20,000	15	6	4
TOTAL	$435,084	382 (36%)	470 (44%)	216 (20%)

Source: 1880 Manuscript Census of Manufactures.

Tobacco Industry Wages, 1870–1880
O. P. Gregory & Co., Richmond, Virginia

Classes of employes	*Unit of payment*	*Dates* 1880	1879	1878	1877	1876	1875	1874	1873	1872	1871	1870
Plug tobacco												
Sorter	Day	$1.00	$1.00	$1.00	$1.00	$1.00	$1.00	$1.00	$1.00	$1.00	$1.00	$1.00
Stripper	Day	1.00	1.00	1.00	1.00	1.00	1.00	1.00	1.00	1.00	1.00	1.00
Caser	Day	1.16⅔	1.16⅔	1.16⅔	1.16⅔	1.16⅔	1.16⅔	1.16⅔	1.16⅔	1.16⅔	1.16⅔	1.16⅔
Plug-maker	Day	1.25	1.25	1.25	1.25	1.25	1.25	1.25	1.25	1.25	1.25	1.25
Wrapper	Day	1.25	1.25	1.25	1.25	1.25	1.25	1.25	1.25	1.25	1.25	1.25
Pressman	Day	1.25	1.25	1.25	1.25	1.25	1.25	1.25	1.25	1.25	1.25	1.25
Packer	Day	1.00	1.00	1.00	1.00	1.00	1.00	1.00	1.00	1.00	1.00	1.00
Laborer	Day	1.00	1.00	1.00	1.00	1.00	1.00	1.00	1.00	1.00	1.00	1.00
Roller	Day	.83	.83	.83	.83	.83	.83	.83	.83	.83	.83	.83
Stemmer	Day	.50	.50	.50	.50	.50	.50	.50	.50	.50	.50	.50

Tobacco Industry Wages, 1870–1880 *(continued)*
Robert W. Oliver, Richmond, Virginia

Classes of employes	*Unit of payment*	*Dates* 1880	1879	1878	1877	1876	1875	1874	1873	1872	1871
Cigars											
Twister	Per lb.	$0.01¾	$0.01¾	$0.01¾	$0.01¾	$0.01¾	$0.01¾	$0.01¾	$0.01¾	$0.01¾	$0.01¾
Job-Hand	Week	5.00	5.00	6.00	6.00	6.00	6.00	6.00	6.00	6.00	6.00
Maker	Per 1,000	7.00	7.00	7.00	7.00	7.00	7.00	7.00	7.00	7.00	7.00
Girl	Week	3.00	3.00	3.00	3.00	3.00	3.00	3.00	3.00	3.00	3.00
Boy	Week	2.50	2.50	2.50	2.50	2.50	2.50	2.50	2.50	2.50	2.50
Cigarette-maker	Per 1,000	.50	.50	.50	.50	.50	.50	.50	.50	.50	.50

REMARKS.—The following statement regarding the prices of tobacco, cigars, etc., is given in this schedule:

Year	*Prices* Plug tobacco	Smoking tobacco	Cigarettes	Cigars	*Cost of Labor* Plug tobacco	Smoking tobacco	Cigarettes	Cigars
	Per pound	*Per pound*	*Per 1,000*	*Per 1,000*	*Per pound*	*Per pound*	*Per 1,000*	*Per 1,000*
1870	$0.59	$0.64	$5.00	$26.00	$0.15	$0.16	$1.10	$11.10
1875	.47	.54	5.00	26.00	.11	.11	1.20	11.00
1880	.38	.45	5.00	26.00	.08	.10	1.20	11.00

The difference between prices of plug and smoking tobacco in different years is largely due to the difference in tax. In the above percentage the United States tax is ignored, it being calculated upon gross cost excluding the tax.

Source: Report on the Statistics of Wages in Manufacturing Industries, 1880, Tenth Census , XX (Washington: GPO, 1886), 49.

Manufacturing in Richmond, 1880

Industry	*Capital*	*Men*	*Women*	*Children*
Agricultural implements	$ 219,000	246	—	2
Blacksmithing	1,925	15	—	—
Boots and shoes	30,900	224	13	3
Boxes, cigar	6,100	15	9	5
Boxes, fancy and paper	18,000	52	87	102
Boxes, wooden	97,600	121	—	12
Bread & bakery	59,000	74	14	1
Brick and tile	21,500	64	—	19
Carpentry	41,000	158	—	2
Carriages & wagons	63,000	101	—	2
Clothing, men's	155,367	163	405	2
Coffee and spices	46,000	36	1	1
Confectionary	69,700	63	7	0
Cooperage	33,700	238	—	9
Drugs & chemicals	142,500	247	0	3
Dyeing & cleaning	5,150	12	7	1
Fertilizers	298,000	172	3	0
Flour & grist mills	1,226,500	191	—	—
Foundry & machine shops	523,500	1,044	—	61
Furniture	108,650	124	10	13
Hairwork	7,500	5	36	0
Iron and steel	702,000	1,004	—	50
Lock & gun-smithing	4,400	11	—	—
Looking-glass & frames	8,950	28	—	9
Marble & stone work	20,400	56	—	—
Oil lubricating	12,000	7	—	1
Painting & paperhanging	14,200	36	—	—
Patent medicines	37,000	32	1	0
Photographing	21,000	36	1	2
Plumbing & gas-fitting	22,000	28	—	7
Printing & publishing	177,300	241	4	24
Saddlery & harness	38,100	74	—	9
Sash, doors, & blinds	73,500	100	—	0
Shipbuilding	3,500	23	—	0
Soap & candles	26,000	17	1	0
Tinware, copperware	88,050	143	—	3
Tobacco: chewing, snuff & smoking	1,333,100	2,838	1,704	1,179
Tobacco: cigarettes & cigars	140,430	261	19	78
Tobacco stemming	435,184	369	470	202
Watch & clocks	15,700	16	—	3
Wheelwrighting	27,450	77	—	1
All other industries	509,000	456	80	145
TOTALS	$6,884,386	9,218	2,872	1,957

Source: *Report on the Manufactures of the United States, Tenth Census*, 1880, pt. 2 (Washington: GPO, 1883), 430. Totals do not add due to errors in original.

The Development of Manufacturing in Richmond During the 1880s, Industry by Industry

Industry	*Capital per Firm* 1880	1885	1890	*Workers per Firm* 1880	1885	1890	*Capital per Worker* 1880	1885	1890
Agricultural implements	$ 43,900	$ 51,000	$ 51,000	49	49	36	$ 885	$1,049	$1,397
Blacksmith	240	900	735	2	6	2	128	148	420
Carriages & wagons	7,000	10,000	15,280	11	11	11	612	935	1,451
Cooperage	2,247	2,507	2,697	16	16	13	136	157	212
Carpenters	1,206	1,673	9,007	5	9	9	256	188	1,126
Bakery	2,950	4,781	7,992	4	7	7	663	736	1,151
Brick & Tile	5,375	9,941	22,200	21	29	24	259	340	938
Confections	5,362	6,227	4,795	6	10	3	917	623	2,038
Fertilizers	59,600	107,143	36,913	35	27	27	1,702	3,947	1,367
Flour & grist mills	245,300	179,300	213,737	38	43	40	6,421	4,154	5,343
Foundry & machine shops	40,269	—	157,564	85	—	85	474	—	1,848
Plumbing	4,400	—	11,285	7	—	8	629	—	1,449
Saddlery & harnesses	3,175	4,867	6,724	7	9	5	459	573	1,327
Chewing, snuff, & smoking	34,182	48,365	106,538	147	134	145	233	360	734
Cigars & cigarettes	5,400	4,089	37,752	14	23	44	392	179	841
Tobacco: stemming & reprizing	16,118	26,500	50,574	39	44	66	418	690	764
Marble & stone	2,914	3,845	13,158	8	8	23	364	470	564
Painting	1,578	—	1,913	4	—	5	394	—	356

Sources: *Report on the Manufactures of the United States, Tenth Census, 1880,* pt. 2 (Washington: GPO, 1883), 430; J. D. Imboden, "Virginia," in *Report on the Internal Commerce of the United States* (Washington: GPO, 1886), 80; *Report on the Manufacturing Industries of the United States at the Eleventh Census, 1890, pt. 2, "Statistics of Cities"* (Washington: GPO, 1895), xiv, xxxi, xxxviii, 5.

Male, Female, and Child Labor in Tobacco Manufacturing, 1870–1890

Industry	*Men*	*Women*	*Children*
Tobacco manufacturing, 1870 (gross totals for chewing, snuff, smoking, cigars, and cigarettes)	2,677	512	793
Chewing, smoking, & snuff, 1880	2,838	1,704	1,179
Chewing, smoking, & snuff, 1890	2,060	1,045	223
Stemming & reprizing, 1880	369	470	202
Stemming & reprizing, 1890	386	365	43
Cigars & Cigarettes, 1880	261	19	78
Cigars & cigarettes, 1890	531	1,323	94

Sources: 1870, 1880, 1890 Manuscript Census of Manufactures.

Cooperage in Richmond, 1880

			Wages		
Firm	*Capital*	*Workers*	*Skilled*	*Unskilled*	*Months off*
J. Whitworth	$ 2,000	45	2.40	1.00	6
A. Gaskins	200	6	1.50	—	—
W. H. Manning	150	4	1.25	1.00	—
B. Branch	100	1	—	—	2
A. Whitworth	500	20	1.25	1.00	8
M. Murphy	3,000	15–20	1.00	.75	—
H. Metzger	8,000	15–20	1.25	.75	—
Scott & Clarke	850	2	2.00	—	8
Shea & McCarthy	350	8	1.00	.75	9
M. E. Gary	3,000	35	1.00	.30	8
Va. Penitentiary	8,000	110	.25	.25	—
S. G. Fairbanks	7,000	77	1.25	1.00	6
W. L. Krug	250	2	1.25	.75	—
Henry Nolte	300	1	1.00	—	—
W. Redd	1,000	5	.75	.30	8
TOTAL	$34,700	346–356			

Source: 1880 Manuscript Census of Manufactures.

Iron Manufacture in Richmond, 1880

Firm	*Capital*	*Men*	*Boys*	*Wages*	*Months off*	*Product*
Tredegar	$500,000	760	40	$1.00–2.50	—	$1,917,000
J. R. Johnson	60,000	58	0	1.00–3.50	—	210,000
Vulcan Iron Works	30,000	60	80	1.00–2.25	—	240,000
Old Dominion Nail	375,000	534	20	1.00–5.75	4	409,000
Richmond Stove	211,500	40	0	.75–2.00	2	75,000
Richmond Iron	45,000	70	0	1.00–2.50	—	36,000
A. J. Miller	12,000	15	0	1.00–2.15	—	12,000
Walsh & McGlaughlin	3,000	12	0	1.00–1.75	—	7,000
Ettinger & Edmund	12,000	60	0	1.00–2.00	—	61,000
Wm. E. Tanner	70,000	172	28	1.00–2.00	—	180,000
Talbott & Sons	100,000	175	0	1.00–1.75	—	200,000
W. A. Waldron	1,000	9	0	1.00–1.75	—	8,500
J. W. Cardwell	27,000	40	0	1.10–1.80	4	30,000
H. M. Smith	10,000	12	3	1.25–2.25	6	10,000
C. T. Palmer	3,500	12	0	1.00–2.00	2	14,800
Asa Snyder	30,000	25	4	1.00–2.00	—	17,600
W. Moore	2,000	7	0	1.75–2.50	1	25,000
J. E. Lintz	1,000	1	1	.40	—	3,000
Variety Iron Works	400	5	2	.75–2.50	—	2,200
H. L. Pelouze	5,000	6	4	1.00–2.00	—	10,000
M. E. Gary	5,000	10	1	.75–2.50	2	16,000
D. M. O'Brian	1,400	3	0	1.00–4.00	—	5,200
W. L. Cox	3,000	4	0	1.00–2.50	—	12,000
McIntyre	1,500	3	2	.50–1.50	—	6,000
Ed. Vial	1,500	6	0	1.00–2.00	6	6,000
W. B. Cook	4,000	17	0	1.00–2.00	—	30,000
J. W. Cardwell & Co. agricultural implements	82,530	75	0	1.10–1.80	4	77,143
C. T. Palmer Plows	30,000	73	0	1.00–2.25	2	63,000
P. H. Starke	30,000	40	0	1.00–2.25	—	70,000
Watt & Call	27,000	52	0	1.00–2.75	—	60,845
H. H. Smith Plows	50,000	75	0	1.00–2.75	6	50,000

Source: 1880 Manuscript Census of Manufactures.

Manufacturing in Richmond, 1880–1890

Characteristic	*1880*	*1890*
Number of establishments	598	966
Total capital	$6,884,386	$16,785,242
Capital per establishment	$11,512	$17,376
Gross value of product	$20,790,106	$27,792,672
Net value of product	$8,648,594	$13,778,458
Average amount of capital to produce a product of $100 value	$33.11	$60.39
Employees	14,047	18,512
males	9,218	13,838
females	2,872	4,127
children	1,957	547
Workers per establishment	23	17
Average capital per worker	$491	$994

Source: *Report on the Manufacturing Industries of the U.S. at the Eleventh Census, 1890, pt. 2, "Statistics of Cities"* (Washington: GPO, 1895), xiv, xxxi, xxxviii, 5.

The Industrial Working Class (black and white), 1880: Structural Composition

Industry	*Workers*	*% of Workforce*
Tobacco: snuff, chewing, smoking, cigars, cigarettes, stemming, and reprizing	7,120	51%
Metal trades: tinware, copperware, sheet-iron, foundry & machine, iron & steel, agricultural implements, blacksmithing	2,568	18%
Building trades: brick & tile, carpentry, furniture, marble & stone, plumbing & gas-fitting, sash, doors, blinds, ship-building, painting	640	5%
Clothing: boots and shoes, men's clothing, women's goods	810	6%
Packaging: cigar boxes, fancy & paper boxes, wooden boxes, paper bags, cooperage	650	5%
Chemicals: drugs & chemicals, dyeing & cleaning, fertilizer, oil, patent medicine, soap & candles	632	4%
Food products: bread & bakery, confectionary, coffee & spices, flour	394	3%

Source: *Report on the Manufactures of the United States, Tenth Census, 1880*, pt. 2, (Washington: GPO, 1883), 430.

The Industrial Working Class (black and white), 1885: Structural Composition

Industry	*Workers*	*% of Workforce*
Tobacco: cigars, cigarettes, snuff, chewing, smoking, stemming, and reprizing	7,311	42%
Building trades: carpentry, granite, marble & stone, sash, doors, blinds, plumbers, bricklayers, masons, painters, plasterers	1,456	8%
Metal trades: agricultural implements, blacksmiths, wheelwrights, iron & steel, nails, type foundries	2,647	15%
Factories: bags, boxes, cotton, paper mills, underwear, furniture	1,601	9%
Clothing: the hand trades—tailors, boot & shoe, repairs	1,485	8%
Food: bakers, confectioners, flour, coffee, butchers, ale & beer	539	3%
Chemicals: fertilizers, drugs, soap & candles, sulphuric acid	415	2%
Printing: job, newspaper, engraving	295	2%
Transportation: saddles, harnesses, carriages, and wagons	241	1%
Barrels & hogsheads	224	1%
Bricks	497	3%
TOTAL	17,522	

Source: J. D. Imboden, "Virginia," in *Report on the Internal Commerce of the United States* (Washington: GPO, 1886), 80. Totals do not add up due to inclusion of all of workforce, not just industries enumerated.

Notes

Chapter One

1. David Brody, "The Old Labor History and the New: In Search of an American Working Class," *Labor History* 20 (1979): 111–126; David Montgomery, "To Study the People: The American Working Class," *Labor History* 21 (1980): 485–512.

2. Herbert Gutman, *The Black Family in Slavery and Freedom* (New York: Pantheon, 1976); George Rawick, *The American Slave* (Westport: Greenwood, 1972); Ira Berlin, *Slaves Without Masters* (New York: Pantheon, 1974); Tony Martin, *Race First* (Westport: Greenwood, 1976); Allen Spear, *Black Chicago* (Chicago: University of Chicago Press, 1969); August Meier and Elliott Rudwick, *Black Detroit and the Rise of the UAW* (New York: Oxford University Press, 1979).

3. Joel Kovel, *White Racism: A Psychohistory* (New York: Vintage, 1971); Roger Ransom and Richard Sutch, *One Kind of Freedom* (Cambridge, Eng.: Cambridge University Press, 1977); J. Morgan Kousser, *The Shaping of Southern Politics* (New Haven: Yale University Press, 1974).

4. C. Vann Woodward, *Origins of the New South, 1877–1913* (Baton Rouge: Louisiana State University Press, 1951); James Tice Moore, *Two Paths to the New South* (Lexington: University of Kentucky Press, 1974); Peter Kolchin, *First Freedom* (Westport: Greenwood, 1972); Thomas Holt, *Black Over White* (Urbana: University of Illinois Press, 1977).

5. Robert S. Starobin, *Industrial Slavery in the Old South* (New York: Oxford University Press, 1970); Leon Fink. *Workingmen's Democracy* (Urbana: University of Illinois Press, 1983); John T. O'Brien, "From Bondage to Citizenship: The Richmond Black Community, 1865–1867" (Ph.D. diss., University of Rochester, 1974); Herbert Gutman, "The Negro and the United Mine Workers," *Work, Culture, and Society in Industrializing America* (New York: Knopf, 1976); Steve Brier, "The Persistence of the Knights of Labor in the Southern West Virginia Coal fields," unpublished paper.

6. *Preliminary Report on the Eighth Census, 1860*, United States Census, Eighth, Schedule 5, *Products of Industry during the year ending June 1, 1860, Virginia, Eastern Division, Henrico County* (Washington: GPO, 1862), 221; David R. Goldfield, *Urban Growth in the Age of Sectionalism, Virginia, 1847–1861* (Baton Rouge: Louisiana State University Press, 1977); Starobin, *Industrial Slavery*.

7. Goldfield, *Urban Growth*, 29–96; Henry G. Ellis, "The Influence of Industrial

and Educational Leaders on the Secession of Virginia," *South Atlantic Quarterly*, 9/4 (October 1910); Virginius Dabney, *Richmond: The Story of a City* (Garden City: Doubleday, 1976), 129–39.

8. Jack Maddex, Jr., *The Virginia Conservatives, 1867–1879* (Chapel Hill: University of North Carolina Press, 1970); Charles B. Dew, *Ironmaker to the Confederacy: Joseph R. Anderson and the Tredegar Iron Works* (New Haven: Yale University Press, 1966).

9. Herbert Gutman and Ira Berlin, "Slaves, Free Workers, and the Social Order of the Urban South," Davis Center Seminar, 1976; Starobin, *Industrial Slavery*; Claudia Goldin, *Urban Slavery in the American South, 1820–1860* (Chicago: University of Chicago Press, 1976); James H. Brewer, *The Confederate Negro: Virginia's Craftsmen and Military Laborers* (Durham: Duke University Press, 1969); Dew, *Ironmaker to the Confederacy*.

10. *Proceedings and Debates of the Virginia State Convention, 1829–1830* (Richmond: Ritchie and Cook, 1830), 25–31; *Richmond Enquirer*, 27 August 1857.

11. Goldfield, *Urban Growth*, 61–62, 91–92; Kathleen Bruce, *Virginia Iron Manufacture in the Slave Era* (New York: Century, 1930); William Still, *The Underground Railroad* (New York: Arno Press, 1968 [1872]).

12. Starobin, *Industrial Slavery*; Richard C. Wade, *Slavery in the Cities* (New York: Oxford University Press, 1964); Goldin, *Urban Slavery*.

13. Starobin, *Industrial Slavery*, 16–17; Joseph C. Robert, *The Story of Tobacco in America* (New York: Knopf, 1949), 70; Wade, *Slavery in the Cities*, 33; Schedule 5, *Products of Industry During the Year ending June 1, 1860* (Manuscript Census of Manufactures) *Virginia Eastern Division, Henrico County*.

14. Wade, *Slavery in the Cities*, 43; Robert, *Tobacco in America*, 83–86; Nannie Mae Tilley, *The Bright Tobacco Industry, 1860–1929* (Chapel Hill: University of North Carolina Press, 1948), 491.

15. Tilley, *The Bright Tobacco Industry*, 491; Robert, *Tobacco in America*, 85.

16. Robert, *Tobacco in America*, 86.

17. Tilley, *The Bright Tobacco Industry*, 498.

18. Berlin, *Slaves Without Masters*, 219–39; Gutman and Berlin, "Slaves, Free Workers, Social Order"; Herbert Gutman, "The World Two Cliometricians Made," *Journal of Negro History* 60/1 (January 1975): 101; Luther P. Jackson, *Free Negro Labor and Property-Holding in Virginia, 1830–1860* (New York: Appleton-Century, 1942), 151.

19. Frederick Law Olmstead, *Journey in the Seaboard Slave States* (New York: Mason Brothers, 1856), 103, 127; Wade, *Slavery in the Cities*, 35.

20. Wade, *Slavery in the Cities*, 71; O'Brien, "From Bondage to Citizenship," 23–28.

21. Lawrence Levine, *Black Culture and Black Consciousness* (New York: Oxford University Press, 1977), 6–7; Catherine C. Hopley, *Life in the South from the Commencement of the War*, vol. 1 (New York: Da Capo, 1974 [1863]), 152–53.

22. O'Brien, "From Bondage to Citizenship," 28; Robert Ryland, *The First Century of the First Baptist Church of Richmond, Virginia, 1780–1880* (Richmond: Carlton McCarthy, 1880), 257–58; Still, *The Underground Railroad*, 377.

23. Dew, *Ironmaker to the Confederacy*; Charles B. Dew, "Disciplining Slave Ironworkers in the Antebellum South: Coercion, Conciliation, and Accommodation," *American Historical Review* 79/2 (April 1974): 393–418; Sidney Bradford, "The Negro Ironworker in Antebellum Virginia," *Journal of Southern History* XXV/2 (May 1959): 194–206; Bruce, *Virginia Iron Manufacture*.

24. Dew, *Ironmaker to the Confederacy*, 250–55, 262.

25. Goldin, *Urban Slavery*, 36; Clement Eaton, "Slave Hiring in the Upper South: A Step Towards Freedom," *Mississippi Valley Historical Review* 46/4 (March 1960): 663–78.

26. Hopley, *Life in the South*, 170–71 (emphasis added).

27. O'Brien, "From Bondage to Citizenship," 22.

28. Gutman, "Two Cliometricians," 264.

29. O'Brien, "From Bondage to Citizenship," 46–49; First African Baptist Church, Richmond, Minutes, Book I: 1841–1859 (Virginia State Library),; Herbert Gutman, *The Black Family in Slavery and Freedom, 1750–1925* (New York: Pantheon, 1975).

30. O'Brien, "From Bondage to Citizenship," 67–68; Luther P. Jackson, "Religious Development of the Negro in Virginia, 1760–1860," *Journal of Negro History* 16/2 (April 1931): 168–239; Robert Ryland, *The Baptists of Virginia, 1699–1929* (Richmond: Virginia Baptist Board of Missions and Education, 1955); *The First Century of the First Baptist Church of Richmond, Virginia, 1780–1880* (Richmond: Carlton McCarthy, 1880); Carter G. Woodson, *The History of the Negro Church* (Washington: Associated Publishers, 1921), 108–9; W. Harrison Daniel, "Virginia Baptists and the Negro in the Antebellum Era," *Journal of Negro History* 56/1 (January 1971): 1–16.

31. O'Brien, "From Bondage to Citizenship," 52; Luther P. Jackson, "Manumission in Certain Virginia Cities," *Journal of Negro History* 15/3 (July 1930): 278–314; Jackson, "Early Strivings of the Negro in Virginia," *Journal of Negro History* 25 (January 1940): 24–34; John W. Cromwell, "The Aftermath of Nat Turner's Rebellion," *Journal of Negro History* 5/2 (1920): 208–34.

32. Henry L. Swint, ed., *Dear Ones at Home* (Nashville: Vanderbilt University Press, 1966), 155.

Chapter Two

1. *New York Tribune*, 17 June 1865.

2. Freedmen's Bureau Papers, Virginia, Assistant Commissioner reports, box 48, National Archives, courtesy John O'Brien; Jane P. Guild, *Black Laws of Virginia* (New York: Negro Universities Press, 1969 [1936]); John P. McConnell, *Negroes and Their Treatment in Virginia from 1865 to 1867* (New York: Negro Universities Press, 1969 [1910]).

3. Henry L. Swint, ed., *Dear Ones at Home* (Nashville: Vanderbilt University Press, 1966), 121; Population of the United States in 1860, United States Census, Eighth, (Washington: GPO, 1864), xiii; Andrew Washburn to Rev. George Whipple, 22 May 1866, American Missionary Association Manuscripts, Amistad Research Center, Dillard University, New Orleans; Peter Randolph, *From Slave Cabin to the Pulpit* (Boston: Earle, 1893), 59. (Randolph became the first black pastor of the Ebenezer Baptist Church in June 1865.).

4. Leon F. Litwack, *Been in the Storm So Long* (New York: Knopf, 1979), 310–22; Charles L. Perdue, Jr., Thomas E. Barden, and Robert K. Phillips, *Weevils in the Wheat* (Charlottesville: University of Virginia Press, 1976), 165–170.

5. *New York Tribune*, 17 June 1865.

6. Randolph, *From Slave Cabin to the Pulpit*, 91; Colonel Brown's "Circular No. 11," 19 March 1866, American Missionary Association Manuscripts. On Drew, see: Manuscript Census of Population for Richmond, 1860, 1870, 1880; Records of the Freedman's Savings Bank, Richmond Branch, 1867–1874; Records of the First African Baptist Church; Herbert G. Gutman, *The Black Family in Slavery and Freedom* (New York: Pantheon, 1976); George B. Rawick, *The American Slave* (Westport: Greenwood, 1972).

7. Manuscript Census of Population for Richmond, 1860, 1870, 1880; Records of the Freedman's Savings Bank, Richmond Branch, 1867–1874; Records of the First African Baptist Church, 1840–1890.

8. Manuscript Census of Population for Richmond, 1870.

9. Records of the Freedman's Savings Bank, Richmond Branch; Manuscript Census of Population for Richmond, 1870, 1880.

10. Gutman, *The Black Family*.
11. Records of the Freedman's Savings Bank; Manuscript Census of Population, 1860, 1870, 1880.
12. Records of the Freedman's Savings Bank; Manuscript Census of Population, 1860, 1870, 1880.
13. Records of the Freedman's Savings Bank; Manuscript Census of Population, 1860, 1870, 1880.
14. Records of the Freedman's Savings Bank.
15. Ibid.
16. Records of the Freedman's Savings Bank.
17. Ibid.
18. Records of the Freedman's Savings Bank.
19. Ibid.
20. Records of the Freedman's Savings Bank.
21. Ibid.
22. Records of the Freedman's Savings Bank.
23. Ibid.
24. Records of the Freedman's Savings Bank.
25. Ibid.; Gutman, *The Black Family*, passim.
26. J. T. Trowbridge, *The South: A Tour of its Battlefields and Ruined Cities* (Hartford: L. Stebbins, 1866), 151.
27. E. A. Randolph, *The Life of Rev. John Jasper* (Richmond: R. T. Hill, 1884); Carter G. Woodson, *The History of the Negro Church* (Washington: Associated Publishers, 1921); Randolph, *From Slave Cabin to the Pulpit*, 89; Rev. W. D. Harris to Rev. George Whipple, 1866, 1868, American Missionary Association Manuscripts; D. B. Williams, *A Sketch of the Life and Times of Captain R. A. Paul* (Richmond: Johns & Goolsby, 1884); John T. O'Brien, "From Bondage to Citizenship: The Richmond Black Community, 1865–1867," (Ph.D. diss., University of Rochester, 1974).
28. Records of the First African Baptist Church.
29. Ibid.
30. Lawrence W. Levine, *Black Culture and Black Consciousness* (New York: Oxford University Press, 1977), 32–33, 137–38.
31. O'Brien, "From Bondage to Citizenship," 255; W. D. Harris to Rev. Whipple, 17 Feb. 1866, American Missionary Association Manuscripts.
32. *New York Tribune*, 17 June 1865; John Dennett, *The South As It Is, 1865–1866*, ed. Henry Christman, (New York: Viking, 1965 [1866]), 25.
33. *Richmond Republic*, 22 January 1866; O'Brien, "From Bondage to Citizenship," 329–31.
34. Records of the Freedman's Savings Bank; U.S. Congress, *Report of the Joint Committee on Reconstruction* (Washington: GPO, 1866), 128; Margaret R. Neary, "Some Aspects of Negro Social Life in Richmond, Virginia, 1865–1880," *Maryland Historian* 1/2 (1970).
35. Records of the Freedman's Savings Bank.
36. Ibid.; Records of the First African Baptist Church; Manuscript Census of Population for Richmond, 1860, 1870, 1880.
37. Records of the Freedman's Savings Bank; Records of the First African Baptist Church; Manuscript Census of Population for Richmond, 1860, 1870, 1880.
38. Records of the Freedman's Savings Bank; Records of the First African Baptist Church; Manuscript Census of Population for Richmond, 1860, 1870, 1880.
39. Records of the Freedman's Savings Bank, Records of the First African Baptist Church, Manuscript Census of Population for Richmond, 1860, 1870, 1880.
40. Records of the Freedman's Savings Bank, Records of the First African Baptist Church; Manuscript Census of Population for Richmond, 1860, 1870, 1880.

41. Petition, 12 October 1865, courtesy of John T. O'Brien.

42. Records of the Freedman's Savings Bank; Manuscript Census of Population for Richmond, 1860, 1870, 1880; *Richmond Dispatch*, passim, 1866–73.

43. Records of the Freedman's Savings Bank, Manuscript Census of Population for Richmond, 1860, 1870, 1880; *Richmond Dispatch*, passim, 1866–73; *Workingman's Advocate*, 26 July 1873.

44. Records of the Freedman's Savings Bank; Manuscript Census of Population for Richmond, 1860, 1870, 1880.

45. Myrta Lockett Avary, *Dixie After the War* (Boston: Houghton-Mifflin, 1937 [1906]), 264.

46. Records of the Freedman's Savings Bank; Manuscript Census of Population for Richmond, 1860, 1870, 1880.

47. Records of the Freedman's Savings Bank; Manuscript Census of Population for Richmond, 1860, 1870, 1880.

48. Records of the Freedman's Savings Bank; Manuscript Census of Population for Richmond, 1860, 1870, 1880.

49. Records of the Freedman's Savings Bank; Manuscript Census of Population for Richmond, 1860, 1870, 1880.

Chapter Three

1. Thomas Holt, *Black Over White* (Urbana: University of Illinois Press, 1977); Peter Kolchin, *First Freedom: The Responses of Alabama's Blacks to Emancipation and Reconstruction* (Westport: Greenwood, 1972); Edward Magdol, *A Right to the Land* (Westport: Greenwood, 1977).

2. Ira Berlin and Herbert Gutman, "Slaves, Free Workers, and the Social Order of the Urban South," Davis Center Seminar, 1976; Howard Rabinowitz, "The Search for Social Control: Race Relations in the Urban South, 1865–1890" (Ph.D. diss., University of Chicago, 1973).

3. General E. O. C. Ord, Richmond, to General Stanton, 19 April 1865; *The War of the Rebellion: A Compilation of the Official Records of the Union and Confederate Armies*, 1st Ser., vol. 46, pt. 3 (Washington: GPO, 1894), 835. Also, General Halleck to Stanton, *The War of the Rebellion*, 11 May 1865, 1131–32.

4. *New York Tribune*, 12, 17 June 1865.

5. *New York Tribune*, 12, 17 June 1865; Deposition of Albert R. Brooks, Freedman's Bureau Records, courtesy of John O'Brien.

6. General Orlando Brown to Rev. George Whipple, 14 June 1865, American Missionary Association Manuscripts; Deposition of John Oliver, Freedman's Bureau Records, courtesy of John O'Brien.

7. *New York Tribune*, 17 June 1865; Deposition of Stephen D. Jones, Freedmen's Bureau Records.

8. *New York Tribune*, 12 17 June 1865.

9. General Terry, "General Orders No. 77," *The War of the Rebellion*, 1293; *The Liberator*, 23 June 1865.

10. *Proceedings of the Convention of the Colored People of Virginia* (Alexandria: August, 1865), 12; *Richmond Republic*, 11 October 1865; *The Liberator*, 8 Sept. 1865.

11. *The Liberator*, 20 October 1865; Rev. W. D. Harris to Rev. George Whipple, 1 February 1867, American Missionary Association Manuscripts.

12. Sloan to Rev. Strieby, 30 April 1865, American Missionary Association Manuscripts; Joseph T. Wilson, *Emancipation: Its Course and Progress* (New York: Negro Universities Press, 1969 [1882]), 141–42; *A Compendium of the Ninth Census, 1870* (Washington: GPO, 1872), 472–73; Howard N. Rabinowitz, "Half a Loaf:

The Shift from White to Black Teachers in the Negro Schools of the Urban South, 1865–1890," *Journal of Southern History*, 40 (November 1974): 569; Charles L. Perdue, Jr., Thomas E. Barden, and Robert K. Phillips, *Weevils in the Wheat* (Charlottesville: University of Virginia Press, 1976), 196–97.

13. Rev. W. D. Harris to Rev. George Whipple, 17 February 1866, American Missionary Association Manuscripts; *Richmond Times*, 2 October 1865.

14. Records of the Freedman's Savings Bank, Richmond Branch, 1867–1874.

15. Ibid; Walter L. Fleming, *The Freedman's Savings Bank* (Westport: Negro Universities Press, 1970 [1927]), 99, 160.

16. *New York Times*, 4 April 1866; *Richmond Citizen*, 4 April 1866.

17. *New York Times*, 4 April 1866; *Richmond Citizen*, 4 April 1866; *Richmond Dispatch*, 9 April 1866; *Richmond Republic*, 9 April 1866.

18. *Richmond Dispatch*, 9 April 1866; *Richmond New Nation*, 5 April 1866.

19. Rev. W. D. Harris to Rev. W. J. Bell, 5 July 1866, American Missionary Association Manuscripts; *Richmond Dispatch*, 6 July 1866.

20. Harris to Bell, 5 July 1866, American Missionary Association Manuscripts; *Richmond Dispatch*, 22 May, 28 December 1866.

21. Harris to Bell, 5 July 1866, American Missionary Association Manuscripts; John T. O'Brien, "From Bondage to Citizenship," (Ph.D. diss., University of Rochester, 1974), 320–22; *Richmond Dispatch*, 22 June, 30 July, 1 August, 13 December 1866.

22. *Richmond Dispatch* 8, 9, 13 March 1867.

23. Ibid., 4 April 1867.

24. Ibid., 18 April 1867; Luther Porter Jackson, *Negro Office Holders in Virginia, 1865–1895* (Norfolk: Guide Quality Press, 1945).

25. *Richmond Dispatch*, 19 April 1867; *New York Times*, 19 April 1867.

26. *Richmond Dispatch*, 12 April 1867.

27. Ibid. 24 April, 1 May 1867.

28. *Richmond Dispatch*, 30 April 1867.

29. Ibid.

30. Records of the First African Baptist Church, Richmond, February 1853; Manuscript Census of Population for Richmond, 1860, 1870, 1880; Records of the Freedman's Savings Bank, Richmond Branch; Jackson, *Negro Office Holders*, 57.

31. *Richmond Dispatch*, 10, 13, 15 May 1867; *New York Times*, 13 May 1867; *Report of the Secretary of War*, Executive Documents, House of Representatives, 40th Cong., 2d sess., 1867–1868, 1 (GPO, 1868), 286.

32. *Richmond Dispatch*, 16 May 1867.

33. Ibid., 13, 14, 15 June and 5 July 1867.

34. *Richmond Dispatch*, 1 August 1867; *New York Times*, 1 August 1867.

35. *Richmond Dispatch*, 1, 2 August 1867; *New York Times*, 2 August 1867.

36. *New York Times*, 6 August 1867.

37. *Richmond Dispatch*, 30 September and 9 October 1867; *New York Times*, 15, 18 October 1867.

38. *New York Times*, 18 October 1867; *Richmond Dispatch*, 15, 20, 21 October 1867.

39. *New York Times*, 15, 29 October 1867; *Richmond Dispatch*, 20, 23, 25, 26 October and 2 November 1867.

40. *Richmond Dispatch*, 25 February 1868.

41. *The Debates and Proceedings of the Constitutional Convention of the State of Virginia, Assembled at the City of Richmond* (Richmond: Office of the New Nation, 1868), 63; "Freedmen's Bureau Report," *Report of the Secretary of War*, Executive Documents, House of Representatives, 40th Cong., 3d sess., 1868–1869 (Washington: GPO, 1869), 1036.

42. *Debates and Proceedings*, 35–36, 60–64, 487, and 521.

43. *Debates and Proceedings*, 150–51, 447.
44. *Richmond Dispatch*, 2, 4, 14, 23 January, 15 February, 3, 25 April 1868; John S. Wise, *The Lion's Skin* (New York: Doubleday & Page, 1905), 214.
45. *Richmond Dispatch*, 8 April 1868.
46. Ibid., 4, 14, 24 January 1868.
47. *Richmond Dispatch*, 7 April 1868.
48. *Richmond Dispatch*, 8 April 1868.
49. Records of the First African Baptist Church 1840–1890; Records of the Freedman's Savings Bank; 1870 Manuscript Census of Population of Richmond.
50. *Richmond Dispatch*, 6 May 1868.
51. *Richmond Dispatch*, 9 May, 6 July, 16 August 1868; *New York Times*, 30 August 1868.
52. Richmond City Council Minutes, September 1867–December 1868.
53. *Richmond Dispatch*, 29 January, 10–12 March 1969.
54. *Richmond Dispatch*, 28 May, 5, 9, 23, 25 June 1869.
55. Ibid., 12 July 1869.
56. *Richmond Dispatch*, 19 August, 25 October, 22 November 1869; William A. Christian, *Richmond: Her Past and Present* (Richmond: L. H. Jenkins, 1912), 302.
57. *Proceedings of the Colored National Labor Convention, Washington, D.C., December 6–10, 1869* (Washington: New Era, 1870), 23; *New York Times*, 11 Ocober 1869.
58. *Richmond Dispatch*, 3 January 1870.
59. Ibid., 27, 29 January 1870.
60. *Richmond Dispatch*, 28 February, 14 March 1870.
61. *Richmond Dispatch*, 16–18 March 1870; Richmond City Council Minutes, March 16 and 18, 1870.
62. *Richmond Dispatch*, 18 March 1870.
63. Ibid., 19 March 1870.

Chapter Four

1. Philip S. Foner and Ronald Lewis, eds., *The Black Worker During the Era of the National Labor Union* (Philadelphia: Temple University Press, 1978).
2. *New National Era*, 21 April 1870.
3. Ibid.; Manuscript Census of Population for Richmond, 1860, 1870, 1880; Records of the Freedman's Savings Bank, Richmond Branch, 1867–1974; Records of the First African Baptist Church, 1840–1890.
4. Manuscript Census of Population, 1860, 1870, 1880; Records of the Freedman's Savings Bank; Records of the First African Baptist Church.
5. Manuscript Census of Population, 1860, 1870, 1880; Records of the Freedman's Savings Bank; Records of the First African Baptist Church.
6. Manuscript Census of Population, 1860, 1870, 1880; Records of the Freedman's Savings Bank; Records of the First African Baptist Church.
7. Manuscript Census of Population, 1860, 1870, 1880; Records of the Freedman's Savings Bank; Records of the First African Baptist Church.
8. Manuscript Census of Population, 1860, 1870, 1880; Records of the Freedman's Savings Bank; Records of the First African Baptist Church.
9. *New National Era*, 21 April 1870.
10. Ibid.
11. *New National Era*, 21 April 1870.
12. Ibid.
13. *Richmond Dispatch*, 21 April 1870.
14. Ibid.; *New National Era*, 28 April 1870.
15. *Richmond Dispatch*, 21 April 1870; *New National Era*, 28 April 1870.

16. *Richmond Dispatch*, 22, 23 April; 23–25, 28, 31 May; 21 July; 1, 3 August; 23 September; 4, 5 November 1870.

17. *New York Times*, 13 June 1870.

18. *Coopers' Union Monthly Journal*, July 1870.

19. *Richmond Dispatch*, June, July, August 1870, passim.

20. *New National Era*, 12, 17 January, 1871.

21. Ibid.; Records of the Freedman's Savings Bank, Richmond Branch.

22. *Richmond Dispatch*, 21 April 1871.

23. Richmond City Council Minutes, 20, 21 April, 1871.

24. *Richmond Dispatch*, 25 September 1871; *Whig*, 17 January 1871.

25. *New National Era*, 3 November 1871.

26. Richmond City Council Minutes, October–November, 1871.

27. *New National Era*, 23 November, 7 December, 1871.

28. *Richmond Dispatch*, 12, 13 March 1872.

29. Ibid., 15 March 1872.

30. *Richmond Dispatch*, 18, 19, 23, 30 April, 25 May 1872.

31. Ibid., 1, 25 July, 8 August, 6 September 1872; *New York Times*, 9 December 1872.

Chapter Five

1. Philip S. Foner and Ronald L. Lewis, eds., *The Black Worker during the Era of the National Labor Union* (Philadelphia: Temple University Press, 1978).

2. *Richmond State*, 20–24 September 1873; *Richmond Dispatch*, 8 October 1873; *Workingman's Advocate*, 27 September 1873.

3. *Richmond Dispatch*, 29 September, 14–15 October, 5 November 1873; *Workingman's Advocate*, 27 September, 15 November 1873; *Iron Molders' International Journal*, (October 1873).

4. Walter L. Fleming, *The Freedman's Savings Bank* (Westport, Conn.: Negro Universities Press, 1970 [1927]), 99, 142, 160–61; *Richmond Dispatch*, 2 July 1874; Carl R. Osthaus, *Freedmen, Philanthropy, and Fraud* (Urbana: University of Illinois Press, 1970), 138–200; Records of the Freedman's Savings Bank, Richmond branch.

5. *Annual Report of the City Almshouse* (Richmond: Evening News Steam Press, 1873, 1874, 1875).

6. David Montgomery, *Beyond Equality* (New York: Random House, 1967), 176–196; *Workingman's Advocate*, 19 July 1873; Nathan Fine, *Labor and Farmer Parties in the United States, 1828–1928* (New York: Rand, 1928), 26–32; John B. Andrews, "Nationalisation," in John R. Commons et al., *History of Labor in the United States, II* (New York: McMillan, 1918), 135–45.

7. Records of The Freedman's Savings Bank, Richmond branch, 1867–1874; Records of the First African Baptist Church, 1840–1890; Manuscript Census of Population for Richmond, 1870 and 1880.

8. *Richmond Dispatch*, 1 December 1873; I. M. St. John, *Notes on the Coal Trade of the Chesapeake and Ohio Railroad, in its Bearing upon the Commercial Interests of Richmond, Virginia* (Richmond: Chesapeake and Ohio Railroad, 1878).

9. *Richmond Dispatch*, 28 July 1874.

10. "Warehouse Laborers" to Governor Kemper, September 9, 1874, *James Lawson Kamper Executive Papers*, Virginia State Library; Records of the Freedman's Savings Bank; Manuscript Census of Population for Richmond, 1870 and 1880; Records of the First African Baptist Church.

11. *New National Era*, 28 May, 25 June, 6 August, and 1 October 1874; *Richmond Dispatch*, 15 October 1873; 15 Sepember 1874.

12. *Workingman's Advocate*, 25 April 1874; William Still, *The Underground Railroad*, (New York: Arno, 1968 [1872]); Records of the Freedman's Savings Bank; Records of the First African Baptist Church; Manuscript Census of Population for Richmond, 1870 and 1880.

13. *Richmond Dispatch*, 9 March 1874; Annual Report of the Board of Directors of the Virginia Penitentiary, 1872, 1873, 1875, 1879; T.V. Powderly, *Thirty Years of Labor* (Columbus, Ohio: Excelsior, 1889), 113; *Workingman's Advocate*, 25 April 1874; Records of the Freedman's Savings Bank.

14. Manuscript Census of Population for Richmond, 1870; Records of the Freedman's Savings Bank.

15. *Workingman's Advocate*, 25 April 1874.

16. Ibid., 20 March 1875.

17. *Richmond Dispatch*, 31 March 1875; *New York Times*, 22 August 1875.

18. Powderly, *Thirty Years of Labor*, 121.

19. *New York Times*, 22 August 1875.

20. *New York Times*, 21 August 1875; *Richmond Dispatch*, 20 August 1875; *Address of the Republican State Committee to the People of Virginia* (Richmond: B. W. Gillis, 1871).

21. *New York Times*, 21 August 1875; *Richmond Dispatch*, 20 August 1875.

22. *New York Times*, 21 August 1875; *Richmond Dispatch*, 21 and 23 August 1875; *Workingman's Advocate*, 25 April 1874 and 24 April 1875.

23. *New York Times*, 21 August 1875. Wilson would later refine his views and write two brilliant expositions on "race pride": *Emancipation: Its Course and Progress* (1882) and *The Black Phalanx* (1890).

24. Luther Porter Jackson, *Negro Office Holders in Virginia, 1865–1895* (Norfolk: Guide Quality Press, 1945), 14–15, 73–74.

25. *Richmond Dispatch*, 20 August 1875; *New York Times*, 22 August 1875.

26. *Richmond Dispatch*, 15 September 1875; Records of the Freedman's Savings Bank; Records of the First African Baptist Church; Manuscript Census of Population for Richmond, 1870 and 1880.

27. *Richmond Dispatch*, November 1876–March 1877, passim; *Richmond State*, 4 December 1876, 17 January 1877.

28. Richmond City Council Minutes, July 1876–May 1877; *Richmond State*, 17 April 1877.

29. *Richmond State*, 23 April 1877.

30. Ibid., 24 July, and 12 September 1877.

31. Ibid., 29 September 1877; *Richmond Dispatch*, 26 September 1877; *Annual Report of the Board of Directors of the Virginia Penitentiary*, 1876 and 1878.

32. *Richmond State*, 1 October 1877.

33. *Richmond Dispatch*, 5, 7 November 1877; *Richmond State*, May 1878.

34. James Tice Moore, *Two Paths to the New South* (Lexington: University of Kentucky Press, 1974), 23–44; C. C. Pearson, *The Readjuster Movement in Virginia* (New Haven: Yale University Press, 1917), 51–53.

35. Pearson, *Readjuster Movement*, 61–63; *Richmond Dispatch*, 5 October 1877; *Richmond State*, 10 January, 1 March 1878.

36. *Richmond Dispatch*, 5 October 1877.

37. Richmond City Council Minutes, 4 November 1878; Howard N. Rabinowitz, "Half a Loaf: The Shift from White to Black Teachers in the Negro Schools of the Urban South," *Journal of Southern History*, 40 (November 1974): 592.

38. Pearson, *Readjuster Movement*; Moore, *Two Paths*.

39. *Richmond State*, 25 September, 24 October 1878.

40. *New York Times*, 7 October 1878.

41. *Richmond State*, 19 and 24 October, 6 November 1878.

Chapter Six

1. The best overall analysis of the Readjuster movement has been provided by James Tice Moore, in his *Two Paths to the New South* (Lexington: University of Kentucky Press, 1974).

2. Herbert Northrup, *The Negro in the Tobacco Industry* (Philadelphia: University of Pennsylvania, 1970), 3; Nannie Mae Tilley, *The Bright Tobacco Industry, 1860–1929* (Chapel Hill: University of North Carolina Press, 1948), 515, 572; Charles S. Johnson, "The Conflict of Caste and Class in an American Industry," *American Journal of Sociology*, 42/1, (July 1936): 64; *Richmond Dispatch*, 1 January 1882; *Richmond Industrial South*, 10 September, 27 October 1881; *Report on the Manufacturing Industries in the United States at the Eleventh Census, 1890*, part. 3, *"Selected Industries"* (Washington: G.P.O. 1895), 808–815; Manuscript Census of Manufactures, Richmond, 1880.

3. James T. Moore, "Black Militancy in Readjuster Virginia," *Journal of Southern History*, 41 (May 1975).

4. *Richmond State*, 19 February, 10 March 1879.

5. Manuscript Census of Population for Richmond, 1870; Records of the Freedman's Savings Bank, Richmond branch, 1867–1874; *Richmond Dispatch*, 21 April 1874, 11 January 1875, 1 January 1885.

6. Manuscript Census of Population, 1870; Records of the Freedman's Savings Bank; Records of the First African Baptist Church, Richmond, 1840–1890.

7. *Irish World*, 3 May 1879; *Richmond State*, 21 April 1879; *New York Times*, 19 March 1879.

8. *Richmond State*, 17 May 1879; Records of the First African Baptist Church; Records of the Freedman's Savings Bank; Manuscript Census of Population for Richmond, 1870 and 1880.

9. *New York Times*, 20, 21 May 1879; *Irish World*, 31 May 1879.

10. *Richmond State*, 21 May 1879.

11. Ibid., 29 May, 2 June 1879; *New York Times*, 3 June 1879; "Official List of Colored Persons Convicted of Felony or Petit Larceny in the Hustings Court of the City of Richmond and Thereby Disenfranchised, from 1870 to October 1892," (N.p., n.d.); House of Representatives, "Papers and Testimony in the Contested Election Case of John E. Massey vs. John S. Wise, from the state of Virginia at Large," 48th Cong., 1st Sess., Mis Documents, 27, 1883–1884, 1, 748.

12. *Richmond State*, 9 June 1879.

13. Moore, "Black Militancy" 170.

14. R. E. Withers, *The Autobiography of an Octogenarian*, 249, quoted in James Hugo Johnston, "The Participation of Negroes in the Government of Virginia from 1877 to 1888," *Journal of Negro History*, 14 (July 1929): 255–56.

15. Elizabeth H. Hancock, ed., *Autobiography of John E. Massey* (New York: Neale, 1909); C. C. Pearson, *The Readjuster Movement in Virginia* (New Haven: Yale University Press, 1917), 128; Nelson M. Blake, *William Mahone of Virginia* (Richmond: Garrett and Massie, 1935), 180; William C. Pendleton, *Political History of Appalachian Virginia* (Dayton, Va.: Shenandoah Press, 1927), 345; Moore, "Black Militancy," 171.

16. *Richmond State*, 1 October 1879, described the Manchester Readjuster organization as "red hot Greenbackers in the last canvass"; D. B. Williams, *A Sketch of the Life and Times of Capt. R. A. Paul* (Richmond: Johns and Goolsby, 1885), 12–16; Richmond *Virginia Star*, 27 September 1879.

17. Moore, "Black Militancy," 171; *Richmond State*, 20 October 1879; Stanley P. Hirshson, *Farewell to the Bloody Shirt* (Bloomington: University of Indiana Press, 1962), 95.

18. Moore, "Black Militancy," 171; *Richmond State*, 23 October 1879.

19. Moore, "Black Militancy," 171; *Richmond State*, 10 November 1879.

20. Moore, "Black Militancy," 171; *New York Times*, 30 November 1879.

21. Moore, "Black Militancy," 172; George Freeman Bragg, letter of August 26, 1926, in *Journal of Negro History*, 11/4 (October 1926): 675.

22. *Richmond State*, 18 November, 2, 3, 4 December 1879; *New York Times*, 3 December 1879; T. Thomas Fortune, *Black and White: Land, Labor, and Politics in the South* (New York: Arno, 1968 [1884]), 45.

23. Moore, "Black Militancy," 172; *New York Times*, 21 March 1880; C. C. Pearson, "William Henry Ruffner: Reconstruction Statesman of Virginia," *South Atlantic Quarterly*, 20 no.1 (January 1921), and no. 2 (April 1921); Richmond *Southern Intelligencer*, 29 March 1880; Blake, *William Mahone*, 189.

24. Moore, "Black Militancy," 173.

25. *Richmond State*, 21, 29 January 1880.

26. Williams, *Capt. R. A. Paul*, 5–16; Manuscript Census of Population for Richmond, 1880; Records of the Freedman's Savings Bank.

27. Manuscript Census of Population for Richmond, 1870 and 1880; Records of the Freedman's Savings Bank.

28. For their family relationships, see Chapter Four; Manuscript Census of Population for Richmond, 1870 and 1880; Records of the Freedman's Savings Bank; Records of the First African Baptist Church.

29. *Richmond State*, 7 February 1880; Richmond *Southern Intelligencer*, 9 February 1880.

30. *Richmond State*, 10 February, 28 March, 1 April 1880.

31. *New York Times*, 27 April 1880.

32. *New York Times*, 7 October 1878, 27 April 1880; Elsie M. Lewis, "The Political Mind of the Negro, 1865–1900," *Journal of Southern History*, 20, (1955): 201; Carter G. Woodson, *History of the Negro Church* (Washington: Associated Publishers, 1921), 248–249; *Report on the Population of the United States at the Eleventh Census 1890* (Washington: GPO, 1895), lvi; (Black illiteracy in Richmond fell from 66 percent in 1870 to 45 percent in 1890.) *A Compendium of the Ninth Census, 1870* (Washington: GPO, 1872), 472–73.

33. Zane L. Miller, "Urban Blacks in the South, 1865–1920," in Leo F. Schnore, ed., *The New Urban History* (Princeton: Princeton University Press, 1975), 198; George W. Williams, *History of the Negro Race in America, II: 1800–1880* (New York: G. P. Putnam, 1883), 397.

34. *Richmond Planet*, 21 February 1885; New York *Globe*, 1883–1884, passim.

35. Williams, *Capt. R. A. Paul*, 52; E. A. Randolph, *The Life of Rev. John Jasper* (Richmond: R. T. Hill, 1884); *Washington Bee*, 12 May 1883; *New York Globe*, 5 May, 6 October 1883; *Richmond Planet*, 21 February 1885.

36. *New York Globe*, 23 June, 7 July, 18 August 1883 and 15 March 1884.

37. *New York Freeman*, 10 January 1885.

38. Williams, *History of the Negro Race*, 63.

39. Williams, *Capt. R. A. Paul*, 63; *Washington Bee*, 24 March 1883.

40. Records of the First African Baptist Church, April 1880.

41. Ibid.; Records of the Freedman's Savings Bank; Manuscript Census of Population for Richmond, 1870 and 1880.

42. Records of the First African Baptist Church, May and June 1880.

43. Ibid.

44. Ibid.; Woodson, (*The History of the Negro Church* (Washington: Associated Publishers, 1921),) 248–52; Records of the First African Baptist Church, *Statement to Ecclesiastical Council of Black Churches*, April 1881.

45. *Richmond Dispatch*, 1 September 1882; *New York Globe*, 23 June, 20 October 1883; *Report of the Senate Committee upon the Relations Between Labor and Capital* (Washington: GPO., 1884), 343.

46. *New York Globe*, 23 June, 20 October 1883.
47. *Virginia Star*, 11 May 1878.
48. *Richmond State*, 6, 9, 15 April 1880.
49. Williams, *Capt. R. A. Paul*, 18–19; Pearson, *The Readjuster Movement*, 136–37; *Richmond State*, 24 April 1880; *New York Times*, 27 April 1880.
50. *Richmond State*, 28 May 1880.
51. *New York Times*, 28 April 1880; *Southern Intelligencer*, 19 April 1880.
52. *Richmond State*, 7, 8, 30 July 1880.
53. *Richmond State*, 30 July, 9 August 1880; *New York Times*, 4 October 1880.
54. Moore, "Black Militancy," 175; *Richmond State*, 19 August, 15 September 1880.
55. *Richmond State*, 3 November 1880.
56. Moore, "Black Militancy," 176–77.
57. J. T. Stovall to Mahone, November 19, 1880, Mahone Papers, courtesy of James T. Moore.
58. *New York Times*, 14 January 1881; *Richmond State*, 15 March 1881; Moore, "Black Militancy," 177.
59. *Richmond State*, 30 May 1881.
60. F. E. Wolfe, *Admission to American Trade Unions* (Baltimore: Johns Hopkins, 1912), 19; *Proceedings of the Sixth Annual Convention of the Amalgamated Association of Iron and Steel Workers* (Pittsburgh, n.p., 1881), 747, 781; *National Labor Tribune*, 18 February, 25 March 1881.
61. *Richmond State*, n.d.; "Report on the Alleged Outrages in Virginia," *Senate Reports*, 48th Cong., 1st sess., no. 579, May 1884, 418–422.
62. *Richmond State*, 2, 3, 4 June 1881; *New York Times*, 2, 3 June 1881; Moore, "Black Militancy," 178.
63. *Richmond State*, 21 June 1881; Frederick Douglass himself made a similar suggestion in a public letter to Virginia blacks published in the Washington *National Republican*, reprinted in the *New York Times*, 16 July 1881.
64. Bragg letter, *Journal of Negro History*, 677.
65. "To the Republicans of Virginia," Virginia Historical Society, Broadside Files; *New York Times*, 25 July 1881; *Richmond State*, 29 June 1881; Moore, "Black Militancy," 178–79.
66. Moore, "Black Militancy," 180; Bragg letter, *Journal of Negro History*, 239–44; W. A. Butterworth to George K. Gilmer, September 29, 1881, Gilmer Papers, Virginia State Library; Teamon to Lewis, March 1, 1881, Mahone Papers, courtesy of James T. Moore.
67. Moore, "Black Militancy," 179–81; Williams, *Capt. R. A. Paul*, 25–28; *New York Globe*, 2 January 1883; Howard N. Rabinowitz, "Half a Loaf: The Shift from White to Black Teachers in the Negro Schools of the Urban South, 1865–1890," *Journal of Southern History*, 40 no. 4 (November 1974): 565–94.
68. *New York Globe*, 7 April 1883.
69. Williams, *Capt. R. A. Paul*, 28, 48.
70. W. A. Butterworth to George K. Gilmer (September 29, 1881), William Mahone to Gilmer (February 11, 1881), J. W. Southward to Gilmer (July 24, 1884) Gilmer Papers; Bragg letter, *Journal of Negro History*, 243.
71. Steward to Mahone, September 21, 1883, quoted in Rabinowitz, "The Search for Social Control," (Ph.D. diss., University of Chicago, 1973), 737.
72. *Washington Bee*, 10 March 1883.
73. "To the Republicans of Virginia," broadside, Virginia Historical Society; *Richmond State*, 27 October 1880; 29 June 1881; *New York Times*, 25 July 1881; *Richmond Dispatch*, 10 January 1882; E.H. Hancock, ed., *Autobiography of John E. Massey* (New York: Neale, 1909).
74. *Richmond Dispatch*, 22 January 1882.

75. Manuscript Census of Population for Richmond, 1880; Records of the Freedman's Savings Bank; *New York Globe*, 27 October 1883.

76. *Proceedings of the Seventh Annual Convention of the Amalgamated Association of Iron and Steel Workers*, (Pittsburgh: n.p., 1882), 953.

77. *National Labor Tribune*, 14 October 1882; *Richmond Dispatch*, 10, 17 October 1882.

78. Moore, "Black Militancy," 182.

79. *Richmond Dispatch*, 25 July 1883; *New York Times*, 26 July 1883; Allen S. Moger, "The Origin of the Democratic Machine in Virginia," *Journal of Southern History*, 8, no. 2 (May 1942): 187–89.

80. John S. Goode, *Recollections of a Lifetime* (New York: Neale, 1906), 226–27; "Report on the Alleged Outrages in Virginia," Senate Reports, 48th Cong., 1st sess., no. 579, May 1884, 418–22; Moore, *Two Paths to the New South*, 115–17; Frank G. Ruffin, *The Negro as a Political and Social Factor* (Richmond: Randolph and English, 1888), 24.

81. "Report on the Alleged Outrages in Virginia," Senate Reports, 418–22; Moore, *Two Paths to the New South*, 116.

82. *New York Globe*, 17 November 1883.

83. Williams, *Capt. R. A. Paul*, 61.

Chapter Seven

1. Ira Berlin and Herbert Gutman, "Slaves, Free Workers, and the Social Order of the Urban South," unpublished paper, Davis Center Seminar, Princeton University, 1976, 31, 47, 53.

2. Allen W. Moger, "The Origin of the Democratic Machine in Virginia," *Journal of Southern History*, 8/2 (1942); James Tice Moore, *Two Paths to the New South* (Lexington: University of Kentucky Press, 1974); J. Morgan Kousser, *The Shaping of Southern Politics* (New Haven: Yale University Press, 1974); George Freeman Brugg, Jr., to *Journal of Negro History*, 5/2 (April 1920): 243; *Report on the Alleged Outrages in Virginia*, Senate Reports, Forty-eighth Cong., First sess., May 1884, 449; John S. Wise Scrapbook, Wise Family Papers, Virginia Historical Society.

3. See Chapters Two and Three of this book.

4. *Industrial South*, 10 September 1881; Nannie Mae Tilley, *The Bright Tobacco Industry, 1860–1929* (Chapel Hill: University of North Carolina Press, 1948), 494; Meyer Jacobsen, *The Tobacco Industry in the U.S.* (New York: Columbia University Press, 1907), 92–93.

5. Testimony of E. Lewis Evans, Secretary-Treasurer of the Tobacco Workers' International Union, in *Report of the Industrial Commission on the Relations and Conditions of Capital and Labor* 7 (Washington: GPO, 1901), 399–405; *Report of the Commissioner of Corporations on the Tobacco Industry: Part I: Position of the Tobacco Combination in the Industry* (Washington: GPO, 1909), 51, 94, 253–354, 375; Joseph C. Robert, *The Story of Tobacco in America* (New York: Knopf, 1949), 135; Charles E. Landon, "Tobacco Manufacturing in the South" in *The Coming of Industry to the South* ed. William J. Carson, ed., (Philadelphia: Annals of the American Academy of Political and Social Science, 1931), 43–53; T. Arnold Hill, "Negroes in Southern Industry," Carson, *Coming of Industry*, 170–81; *Industrial South*, 21 October 1882.

6. Franklin E. Coyne, *The Development of the Cooperage Industry in the United States, 1620–1940* (Chicago: Lumber Buyers' Publishing Company, 1940), 14–22.

7. Ibid., 23–24.

8. *Richmond Planet*, 21 February 1885; *New York Globe*, 17 May, 19 July 1884.

9. *New York Globe*, 22 June 1883.

10. Ibid., 1884, passim.

11. *New York Freeman*, 17 January 1885.
12. *New York Globe*, 25 October 1884; *New York Freeman*, 20 December 1884.
13. D. B. Williams, *A Sketch of the Life and Times of Capt. R. A. Paul* (Richmond: Johns and Goolsby, 1885), 67; *New York Globe*, 15 March, 1884; *New York Freeman*, 10 January 1885.
14. *Richmond Planet*, 21 February 1885.
15. Terence V. Powderly, *The Path I Trod* (New York: Columbia University Press, 1940); David Montgomery, "Labor and the Republic in Industrial America, 1860–1920," *Le Mouvement Social*, no. 111 (April–June, 1980); Paul Buhle, "The Knights of Labor in Rhode Island," *Radical History Review*, 17 (Spring 1978); Richard Oestreicher, "Solidarity and Fragmentation: Working People and Class Consciousness in Detroit, 1877–1895" (Ph.D. diss., Michigan State University, 1979); Jonathan Garlock, ed., *All Branches of Honorable Toil, All Conditions of Men* (Urbana: University of Illinois Press, forthcoming).
16. Herbert G. Gutman, "Protestantism and the American Labor Movement: The Christian Spirit in the Gilded Age," in *Work, Culture, and Society in Industrializing America* (New York: Random House, 1976).
17. *Journal of United Labor*, 10 May 1884; Hermann Schuricht, *History of the German Element in Virginia, II* (Baltimore: Kroh, 1900), 72–73; *Richmond State*, 15 June 1878; *Richmond Dispatch*, 5 January 1869, 29 December 1873, 4 February 1874, 9 January 1883; Manuscript Census of Population for Richmond, 1860 and 1870; Richmond Gesangverein records, 1879 membership list, Virginia Historical Society, Richmond; *Richmond Dispatch*, 15 January 1874; *Richmond State*, 12 October 1877; *Journal of United Labor*, 10 May 1884.
18. *Record of the Proceedings of the Eighth Regular Session of the General Assembly of the Knights of Labor*, Philadelphia, September 1884; *Journal of United Labor*, 25 November 1884; *Richmond Dispatch*, 25 July 1884; Richmond City Council Minutes, 18 December 1883; *Richmond Dispatch*, 1, 6 January, 24 April, 25 July, 11 October, 1, 4 November 1884.
19. *Richmond Dispatch*, 11, 25, 31 October, 1, 4 November 1884.
20. Ibid., 25 October, 8, 9, 19 November 1884.
21. Manuscript Census of Population, 1860; John J. Laferty, *Sketches and Portraits of the Virginia Conference, Methodist Episcopal Church, South* (Richmond: Christian Advocate Office, 1891), 215–16; *Richmond Dispatch*, 8 July 1879; *Proceedings* of the Annual Sessions of the International Typographical Union, 1878–1885.
22. Mullen to Powderly, 10 October 1884, Powderly to Mullen, 22 October 1884. Mullen to Powderly, 30 October 1884, Powderly Papers.
23. *Journal of United Labor*, 25 November 1884; Mullen to Powderly, 30 October 1884; Jon Garlock, "Knights of Labor Data Bank", unpublished manuscript; Richmond 25 September 1884, 1, 2 January, 8 February 1885; *Irish World*, 4 October 1884; *Record of the Proceedings of the Ninth Annual Session of the General Assembly*, Hamilton, Ontario, 1885, p. 202.
24. *Cigarmakers' Official Journal*, October and December 1884, May 1885, September 1889; *Journal of United Labor*, 25 November 1884; Harry W. Laidler, *Boycotts and the Labor Struggle* (New York: Russell & Russell, 1968 [1913]), 72–73; *Report of Proceedings of the Thirty-third Annual Session of the International Typographical Union*, June 1885, pp. 35, 117, 128; *Iron Molders' International Journal*, October, November, December 1884 and January 1885; *Granite Cutters' National Journal*, August, November 1883; September, October, November 1884; Frederick S. Deibler, *The Amalgamated Wood Workers' International Union* (Madison: University of Wisconsin Press, 1912), 13; R.A. Christie, *Empire in Wood*, 61ff.; *The Carpenter*, September 1883, December 1885; *Proceedings of the Twenty-first Annual Convention of the Bricklayers' and Masons' International Union*, 1887, 39.

25. Charles M. Miller to Powderly, 20 December 1884, Powderly Papers; Melton A. McLaurin, "The Racial Policies of the Knights of Labor and the Organization of Southern Black Workers," *Labor History*, 17, no. 4, (Fall 1976): 568–85.

26. Powderly's scrapbook and diary, Powderly Papers; *Richmond Dispatch*, 27 January 1885.

27. *Richmond Dispatch*, 9, 27 January 1885.

28. Ibid., 27 January 1885; Powderly's diary, Powderly Papers.

29. *Richmond Dispatch*, 27 January 1885.

30. Ibid.; Scranton *Truth* clippings in Powderly's scrapbook, Powderly Papers.

31. *Richmond Dispatch*, 27 January 1885.

32. Ibid.

33. Untitled clipping, 4 February 1885, Powderly Papers.

34. *Richmond Dispatch*, 27 January 1885; *Journal of United Labor*, 25 January, 10 February 1885; *Record of the Proceedings of the Ninth Annual General Assembly*, 1885, 202, 205.

35. *John Swinton's Paper*, 15 February 1885.

36. Angle to Powderly, 27 February 1885; Powderly to Angle, 20 March 1885, Powderly Papers.

37. *Richmond Dispatch*, 8, 12 February 1885; *Irish World*, 3 October 1885.

38. *John Swinton's Paper*, 1 March, 12 April 1885; *Journal of United Labor*, February–May 1885.

39. *Granite Cutters' National Journal*, March 1885; *John Swinton's Paper*, 12, 19 April 1885; *Cigarmakers' Office Journal*, May 1885; *Cigarmakers' Official Journal*, 12 September 1889; *Iron Molders' International Journal*, March, April, May 1885; Mullen to Powderly, 7 March 1885, Powderly Papers.

40. *Irish World*, 11 April, 30 May, 13 September, 3 October 1885.

41. Mullen to Powderly, 7 April 1885, Powderly Papers; *Journal of United Labor*, 10 April 1885; *John Swinton's Paper*, 19 April 1885.

42. *Proceedings of the Ninth Annual General Assembly*, 1885, p. 205.

43. Ibid.; Mullen to Powderly, 7 March 1885, Powderly Papers.

44. *Proceedings of the Ninth General Assembly, 1885*, 205; Mullen to Powderly. 7 March, 7 April 1885, Powderly Papers; *Journal of United Labor*, 10 April, 10 May 1885.

45. *John Swinton's Paper*, 12 April 1885; *Journal of United Labor*, 10 June 1885.

46. *John Swinton's Paper*, 12 April, 14 June 1885; *Journal of United Labor*, 14 June 1885.

Chapter Eight

1. For the concept of a "movement culture," see Lawrence Goodwyn, *The Populist Moment* (New York: Oxford, 1976), 33; Jonathan Garlock, "Knights of Labor Data Bank," University of Pittsburgh, unpublished computer printout; Jonathan Garlock, ed., *All Branches of Honorable Toil, All Conditions of Men* (forthcoming, University of Illinois Press); Knights of Labor Centennial Symposium, unpublished papers (Chicago: Newberry Library, 1979).

2. 1880 Manuscript Census of Manufactures; Knight Neftel, "Report on Flour-Milling Processes," in *Report of the Productions of Agriculture, Tenth Census, 1880*, pt. 3 (Washington: GPO, 1883); *The Statistics of Wealth and Industry of the United States, Ninth Census*, pt. 3 (Washington: GPO, 1872), 739; *Report on the Manufactures of the United States, Tenth Census, 1880*, pt. 2 (Washington: GPO, 1883), 430; *Report on the Manufacturing Industries of the United States at the Eleventh Census, 1890*, pt. 2, (Washington: GPO, 1895), 718–19; Franklin E. Coyne, *The Development of the Cooperage Industry in the United States, 1620–1940* (Chicago: Lumber

Buyers Publishing Company, 1940), 24; *Second Annual Report of the Commissioner of Labor, 1886; Convict Labor* (Washington: GPO, 1887), 114–15, 192–93, 208, 302–3; *Report on the Manufacturing Industries of the United States at the Eleventh Census, 1890*, pt. 2 "Statistics of Cities" (Washington: GPO, 1893), 718–19.

3. *Richmond Labor Herald*, 17 October 1885; Clipping in Powderly's scrapbook, Powderly Papers.

4. *Granite Cutters' National Journal*, June 1885; *Richmond Labor Herald*, 17 October 1885; Harry W. Laidler, *Boycotts and the Labor Struggle* (New York: Russell and Russell, 1968 [1913]), 160–62; Leo Wolman, *The Boycott in American Trade Unions* (Baltimore: Johns Hopkins University Press, 1916), 29.

5. *Granite Cutters' National Journal*, July, August, September, October 1885; *Richmond Dispatch*, 18 April, 11 October 1885; W. H. Mullen to T. V. Powderly, 24 August 1885, Powderly Papers.

6. *New York Globe*, 27 September 1884; *New York Freeman*, 10 October 1885; Vincent P. DeSantis, "Negro Dissatisfaction with Republican Policy in the South, 1882–1884," *Journal of Negro History*, 37, 1, (February 1971): 41–65.

7. *New York Freeman*, 28 March 1885.

8. *Richmond Dispatch*, 22 September 1885.

9. Unpublished papers and discussion at the Knights of Labor Centennial Symposium (Chicago: Newberry Library, May 1979).

10. *Journal of United Labor*, 25 September 1885; Mullen's cohorts were James A. Healy, Perry Jones, and John M. Lewis.

11. No actual copies of the *Labor Herald* exist in U.S. libraries or repositories; however, more than twenty clippings can be found in Powderly's scrapbook.

12. *Richmond Dispatch*, 10 June, 6 October 1885; *Irish World*, 12 September 1885.

13. Clare A. Horner, "The Knights of Labor and Producers' Co-operation," unpublished paper, Knights of Labor Centennial Symposium; *Journal of United Labor*, 25 March 1885.

14. *John Swinton's Paper*, 28 June 1885.

15. *Chicago Knights of Labor*, October 1885.

16. Knights of Labor Building Association, minutes, courtesy of Warren Chappell, grandson of John T. Chappell. (All the quotations in this chapter pertaining to the Building Association have been taken from this ledger book, unless otherwise noted.)

17. *Report on the Population of the United States at the Eleventh Census, 1890*, pt. 1 (Washington: GPO, 1895), 949–52.

18. Constitution and By-laws, Richmond Knights of Labor Building Association, adopted 19 February 1886.

19. Ibid.

20. Preamble, Constitution and By-Laws, Richmond Knights of Labor Building Association.

21. Dion Boucicault, *The Long Strike*, (New York: Samuel French, 1866).

22. Ibid.; *Richmond Dispatch*, 15 November 1885.

23. Terrence V. Powderly, *The Path I Trod*, (New York: Columbia University Press, 1940), 54.

24. Knights of Labor, *Illustrated "Adelphon Kruptos": The Secret Work of the Knights of Labor* (Chicago: Ezra A. Cook, 1886), 29.

25. Ibid., 29–32; Powderly, "Appendix II: Secret Circular: Explanation of the Signs and Symbols of the Order" in *The Path I Trod*.

26. *Adelphon Kruptos*; Powderly, *The Path I Trod*.

27. *Adelphon Kruptos*; Powderly, *The Path I Trod*.

28. Kenneth Kann, "The Knights of Labor and Southern Black Workers," *Labor History*, 17, no. 3, 1976; Melton McLaurin, "The Racial Policies of the Knights of

Labor and the Organization of Southern Black Workers," *Labor History*, 17, no. 4, 1976.

29. Mullen to Powderly, 26 October 1885, Powderly Papers; Jonathan Garlock, "Knights of Labor Courts," unpublished paper, 1979.

30. *Journal of United Labor*, July, September 1885.

31. *John Swinton's Paper*, 25 October 1885; *Record of the Proceedings of the Ninth Annual General Assembly of the Knights of Labor*, Hamilton, Ontario, October 1885.

32. *John Swinton's Paper*, 25 October 1885; *Proceedings of the Ninth Annual General Assembly*, 1885; Mullen's speech was also reprinted in the *Journal of United Labor*, 25 October 1885.

33. *Journal of United Labor*, 25 October 1885.

34. Ibid.

35. *Journal of United Labor*, 25 October 1885.

36. C. E. Jefferson to J. B. Johnson, 10 November 1885, Johnson to Powderly, 5 December 1885, Powderly Papers; *Journal of United Labor*, January 1886.

37. Rudd to Powderly, 7 December, 1885, Powderly Papers; *Journal of United Labor*, December 1885, January 1886; *John Swinton's Paper*, 8 November 1885.

38. Rudd to Powderly, 7 December 1885.

39. *Richmond Dispatch*, 3 November 1885; Ellyson to Powderly, 9 November 1885, Powderly Papers; *Journal of United Labor*, 25 December 1885; *Richmond Dispatch*, 3, 17 November 1885.

40. *Richmond Dispatch*, 31 December 1885.

41. *Richmond Dispatch*, 22 December 1885; Richmond City Council Minutes, December 1885; Richmond letters to the *Granite Cutters' National Journal*, August, September, October 1885.

42. *John Swinton's Paper*, 10, 24 January 1886; *Journal of United Labor*, February, March 1886; R. W. Kruse (Petersburg) to Powderly, 19 January, 7 February 1886, R. J. Steele (Petersburg) to Powderly, 17 February 1886, Powderly Papers.

Chapter Nine

1. *Journal of United Labor*, 25 January, 24 August 1886; *John Swinton's Paper*, 21 March 1886; Manuscript Census of Population for Richmond, 1870 and 1880; Records of the Freedman's Savings Bank 1867–1874; Records of the First African Baptist Church, 1840–1890; *Richmond Dispatch*, March 8, 1869.

2. Manuscript Census of Population for Richmond, 1870 and 1880; Records of the Freedman's Savings Bank; Records of the First African Baptist Church.

3. *Richmond Dispatch*, 15 September 1875, 16 April 1884; Thompson to Powderly, 17 July 1886, Powderly Papers.

4. *New York Freeman*, 20 March 1886.

5. *John Swinton's Paper*, 12 April 1885.

6. Childress to Powderly, 1 March 1886, R. D. Hall to Powderly, 4 March 1886, Powderly Papers.

7. *Third Annual Report of the Commissioner of Labor, 1887: Strikes and Lockouts* (Washington: GPO, 1888), 588–95.

8. *Richmond Dispatch*, 2, 7–9, 15, 17 April 1886; *John Swinton's Paper*, 2 May, 11 July, 1, 8 August, 12 September 1886.

9. *Journal of United Labor*, May, June 1886; *Richmond Dispatch*, 12 April 1886.

10. *Richmond Dispatch*, 14 July 1874; J. D. Imboden, "Virginia," in *Report on the Internal Commerce of the United States* (Washington: GPO, 1886), 179–80.

11. Annual Report of the Board of Directors of the Virginia State Penitentiary, 1872 and 1873.

12. 1880 Manuscript Census of Manufactures; Edna Bonacich, "A Theory of Ethnic Antagonism: The Split Labor Market," *American Sociological Review*, 37, (October 1972): 547–59.

13. The 1880 Manuscript Census of Manufactures; *Report on the Mineral Industries of the U.S. at The Eleventh Census, 1890* (Washington: GPO, 1892), 613–17.

14. *Granite Cutters' National Journal*, August and December 1885.

15. Ibid., March 1886.

16. Annual Report of the Board of Directors of the Virginia State Penitentiary, 1879; *Granite Cutters' National Journal, 1881–1886*, passim, especially May 1885 and June 1886; Dyer to Powderly, 15 June 1885, Powderly Papers; Richmond City Council Minutes, 1884–1886, passim; *Richmond Dispatch*, 22 December 1885; Manuscript Census of Manufactures, 1880; *Report on the Manufacturing Industries of the U.S. at the Eleventh Census, 1890*, pt. 1 "Totals for States and Industries" (Washington: GPO, 1895), 23–27 and pt. 2, 486–89.

17. Johnson to Powderly, 5 December 1885, Powderly Papers.

18. *Third Annual Report of the Commissioner of Labor, 1887: Strikes and Lockouts* (Washington: GPO, 1888), 588–95; *Richmond Dispatch*, 15 April 1886; *Granite Cutters' National Journal*, April 1886; *John Swinton's Paper*, 2 May 1886.

19. Third Annual Report of the Commissioner of Labor, 588–95; *Granite Cutters' National Journal*, April–September 1886; *Richmond Dispatch*, 15, 17 April 1886; *John Swinton's Paper*, 2 May, 11 July, 1, 8 August, 12 September 1886.

20. Leon Fink, "The Uses of Political Power: Towards a Theory of the Labor Movement in the Era of the Knights of Labor" (unpublished paper, Knights of Labor Centennial Symposium, Chicago, May 1979), 1316. For other examles of local movements, see the range of papers delivered at the conference.

21. Ibid.; *Richmond Dispatch*, 23 March 1886; *John Swinton's Paper*, 28 March 1886; *Labor Herald*, 22 March 1886, courtesy Joseph Carvalho.

22. *Richmond Dispatch*, 6 May 1886; *Labor Herald*, 8 May 1886, courtesy of Joseph Carvalho; letter from John T. Chappell to *Richmond Dispatch*, 14 May 1886; "Mechanic," *Richmond State*, 11 May 1886.

23. *Richmond Dispatch*, 18 May 1886.

24. Ibid.; Manuscript Census of Population for Richmond, 1860, 1870, and 1880.

25. Manuscript Census of Population for Richmond, 1860, 1870, 1880.; *Report on the Population of the United States at the Eleventh Census, 1890*, pt. 1 (Washington: GPO, 1895), 483, 557.

26. *Richmond Dispatch*, 18 May 1886.

27. Ibid.

28. Ibid.

29. Ibid.

30. Luther P. Jackson, *Negro Office Holders in Virginia, 1865–1895* (Norfolk: Guide Quality Press, 1945), 57; Manuscript Census of Population for Richmond, 1880; Richmond City Directory, 1880–1886.

31. Jackson, *Negro Office Holders*; Richmond City Directory, 1880–86. Manuscript Census of Population for Richmond, 1860, 1870, 1880.

32. *Richmond Dispatch*, 25 May 1886.

33. *Labor Herald*, 8, 22 May 1886, courtesy of Joseph Carvalho.

34. Ibid., 13 March, 22 May 1886; *Richmond Dispatch*, 28 May 1886.

35. *Richmond Dispatch*, 28 May 1886; *Labor Herald*, 29 May 1886, courtesy Joseph Carvalho; R. T. Hubard to William Mahone, 1 June 1886, courtesy Leon Fink.

36. *Granite Cutters' National Journal*, June 1886.

Chapter Ten

1. C. C. Clarke to William Mahone, 29 May 1886, courtesy of Leon Fink; *Richmond Planet*, 12 June 1886.

2. See Chapter Nine.

3. Manuscript Census of Manufactures, 1860, 1870, 1880; Manuscript Census of Population for Richmond, 1860: Slave Schedules; J. D. Imboden, "Virginia," *Report on the Internal Commerce of the United States* (Washington: GPO, 1886), 80; *John Swinton's Paper*, 20, 30 June 1886.

4. *Richmond Mercantile and Manufacturing Journal*, November 1883.

5. *Richmond Dispatch*, 8 June 1886; *Third Annual Report of the Commissioner of Labor: Strikes and Lockouts* (Washington: GPO, 1888), 588–95.

6. *Richmond Dispatch*, 9, 18, 22, 23 June, 1 July 1886.

7. Ibid., 8, 9 June, 7 July 1886.

8. Ibid., 9 June, 7 July 1886.

9. Ibid., 29, 30 May 1886.

10. Ibid., 1, 6 June 1886; *John Swinton's Paper*, 12 June 1886.

11. *Richmond Dispatch*, 1, 5, 8 June 1886; John S. Wise Papers, in Wise Family Papers, Virginia Historical Society, Richmond.

12. *Richmond Dispatch*, 16, 18, 22, 24 June 1886.

13. Ibid., 2 July 1886; John S. Wise to William Mahone, 25 June 1886, courtesy of Leon Fink.

14. *Richmond Dispatch*, 18 June 1886; Wise to Mahone, 25 June 1886.

15. *Richmond Dispatch*, 24 June 1886.

16. Ibid., 24, 25, 26, 30 June 1886.

17. Ibid., 30 June 1886.

18. Ibid., *John Swinton's Paper*, 11 July 1886.

19. *Richmond Dispatch*, 4 July 1886; Wise to Mahone, 25 June and 2 July 1886; B. Taylor McCue to Mahone, 17 July 1886, courtesy of Leon Fink.

20. *John Swinton's Paper*, 6 June 1886; *Cleveland Plain Dealer*, 3 June 1886; *Chicago Tribune*, 12 June 1886; *Labor Herald*, 12 June 1886, clippings in Powderly Papers.

21. *Richmond Dispatch*, 25 June, 14, 20, 23, 25 July 1886; *Third Annual Report of the Commissioner of Labor*, 588–95; *Labor Herald*, 5, 17 June 1866; Testimony of E. A. Baughman and deposition of J. H. Schonberger, courtesy of Joseph Carvalho; Thomas S. Atkins, "The Criminality of Boycotting: Charge to the Grand Jury of the Hustings Court of Richmond, Va.," *Virginia Law Journal* 10 (December 1886): 707–8; McCue to Mahone, 17 July 1886, courtesy of Leon Fink.

22. *Richmond Dispatch*, 25, 27, 28, 31 July, 3, 10, 12, 19, 27 August, 2 September 1886; Richmond City Council Minutes, July 1886.

23. *Richmond Dispatch*, 27, 28 July 1886; Clipping, n.p., n.d., Wise Papers.

24. Lee A. Nelson, District Assembly No. 120, Petersburg, to Powderly, 21 June 1886, Richard Thompson to Powderly, 17 July 1886, R. W. Kruse, Local Assembly No. 4313, Petersburg, to Powderly, 3 August 1886, J. M. Bingham, Local Assembly No. 3606, Raleigh, North Carolina, to Powderly, 16 August 1886, Powderly Papers; *John Swinton's Paper*, 11 July, 8 August 1886; *Granite Cutters' National Journal* (October 1886).

25. Minutes of the Knights of Labor Building Association, July 12 to August 31, 1886, courtesy of Warren Chappell.

26. Wise to Mahone, 25 June 1886.

27. *Richmond Dispatch*, 22 August 1886; *John Swinton's Paper*, 29 August 1886.

28. *John Swinton's Paper*, 5 September 1886; *Richmond Dispatch*, 2, 3 September 1886; *Richmond Whig*, 3 September 1886.

29. Cornelius Harris to Mahone, 18 June 1886, Daniel Alley to Mahone, 6 September 1886, Richard F. Walker to Mahone, 8 September 1886, all courtesy of Leon Fink.

30. *Richmond Dispatch*, 6, 7, 11 September 1886; *John Swinton's Paper*, 5 September 1886.

31. *Richmond Dispatch*, 11 September 1886.

32. Ibid.; *John Swinton's Paper*, 19 September 1886; *Chicago Knights of Labor*, 18 September 1886; Wade B. DeClay to Mahone, 12 September 1886, courtesy of Leon Fink.

33. *Richmond Dispatch*, 13 September 1886.

34. Ibid., 16 September 1886.

35. Wise to Mahone, 23, 24, 27 September 1886; *Richmond Dispatch*, 12 August, 25 September 1886; Minutes of International Typographical Union No. 90, 6 August, 1886.

36. Wise to Mahone, 23, 24, 27 September 1886; *Richmond Dispatch*, 25 September 1886.

37. *John Swinton's Paper*, 3 October 1886; *Richmond Dispatch*, 22 August, 19 September, 2 October 1886.

38. *Jonn Swinton's Paper*, 3 October 1886; *Richmond Dispatch*, 19 September, 2 October 1886.

39. John Swinton's Paper, 3 October 1886; *Richmond Dispatch*, 2 October 1886.

40. Wise to *Valley Virginian*, clipping, n.d., Wise Papers; *Richmond Dispatch*, 3 October 1886; Waddill, Wise, and Southward, "To the Republican Voters of Richmond," campaign broadside, n.d., Virginia Historical Society.

41. "To the Republican Voters of Richmond," campaign broadside; Petersburg *Index-Appeal*, quoted in Richmond *Whig*, 10 October 1886.

42. Frederick Turner to Powderly, 14, 31 August 1886; *Richmond Dispatch*, 10, 11, 22, 27 August, 28 September 1886.

43. Clipping, n.d., Powderly Papers.

44. Joseph R. Buchanan, *The Story of a Labor Agitator* (New York: Outlook, 1903), 314; Bishop Keane quoted in Henry J. Browne, *The Catholic Church and the Knights of Labor* (Washington: Catholic University Press, 1949), 364.

45. *Record of the Proceedings of the Ninth General Assembly of the Knights of Labor of America*, October 1886, pp. 4–7, 243–55; *Richmond State*, 10 October 1886.

46. *John Swinton's Paper*, 3 October 1886.

47. *Washington Bee*, 21 August 1886; *Richmond Dispatch*, 30 September 1886; *New York Freeman*, 20 March, 1 May 1886.

48. *Richmond Dispatch*, 30 September 1886.

49. *New York Sun*, n.d., cited in *Richmond Dispatch*, 28 September 1886.

50. *Richmond Dispatch*, 5 October 1886; *New York Tribune*, 6, 9 October 1886.

51. *John Swinton's Paper*, 10 October 1886.

52. *Proceedings of the Ninth General Assembly*, pp. 4–12; Chicago *Knights of Labor*, 16 October 1886; Terrence V. Powderly, *Thirty Years of Labor* (Columbus: Excelsior, 1889), 652.

53. *Proceedings of the Ninth General Assembly*, 4–12.

54. *Richmond Dispatch*, 6 October 1886.

55. *Richmond State*, 9 October 1886; *Richmond Dispatch*, 5–8 October 1886; *Richmond Whig*, 10 October 1886.

56. *Richmond Dispatch*, 6–8 October 1886.

57. *John Swinton's Paper*, 10 October 1886; *Whig*, 7 October 1886; *Montgomery Advertizer*, 6 October 1886.

58. *Haverhill Laborer*, 16 October 1886, courtesy of Leon Fink; R. J. Steele, Petersburg, to Powderly, 6 October 1886.

59. *Richmond Dispatch*, 12 October 1886; Terrence V. Powderly, "Knights of Labor and the Color Line," *Public Opinion*, 2, 27, 16 October 1886.

60. Robert E. Masters, Tredegar Foundry Manager, to Powderly, 4 October 1886; Joseph R. Anderson to Powderly, 11 October 1886; John W. Higgins, Catholic Beneficial Society, to Powderly, 5 October 1886; James T. Ashby, Local Assembly No. 7764, Petersburg, to Powderly, 5 October 1886; W.W. Foster, Local Assembly No. 3380, to Powderly, 8 October 1886; Patrick Diamond, John Mitchell, Club of the Clan-Na-Gael, to Powderly, 9 October 1886; Hall and Nichols, Manchester, to Powderly, 4 October 1886; all from Powderly Papers; *Baltimore Sun* 3 October 1886; Browne, *Catholic Church and Knights of Labor*, 203–6, 363–64.

61. *Report of the Proceedings of the General Assembly*, p. 254.

62. *Richmond Dispatch*, 8 October 1886; *New York Times*, 7 October 1886; Buchanan, *The Labor Agitator*, 314.

63. *Richmond Dispatch*, 9, 10, 12 October 1886; *New York Tribune*, 6, 9 October 1886.

64. *Richmond Dispatch*, 9, 10, 12 October 1886; *Haverhill Laborer*, 23 October 1886, courtesy of Leon Fink; *Richmond Whig*, 12 October 1886.

65. *Richmond Dispatch*, 12, 17 October 1886.

Chapter Eleven

1. *Richmond Dispatch*, 22 October 1886.

2. Ibid., 23, 24, 29 October 1886; John S. Wise to *Richmond Dispatch*, 26 April 1886.

3. Richmond Common Council Journal, 6 November 1886; *Whig*, 27, 30 October 1886.

4. *Whig*, 30 October 1886.

5. Ibid., 31 October 1886; *John Swinton's Paper*, 7 November 1886.

6. *Richmond Dispatch*, 31 October 1886.

7. Ibid., 3 November 1886.

8. Ibid.

9. Ibid.; John S. Wise to *Valley Virginian*, n.d., clipping, Wise Family Papers; "A New Mixture," broadside, Virginia Historical Society.

10. *John Swinton's Paper*, 14 November 1886; *Richmond Dispatch*, 23 November 1886.

11. Collin T. Payne to Mahone, 3 November 1886, courtesy of Leon Fink; *Richmond Dispatch*, 16 April 1890.

12. *Richmond Dispatch*, 21, 28 November 1886; *John Swinton's Paper*, 21 November 1886.

13. *Richmond Dispatch*, 30 November 1886.

14. Manuscript Census of Population for Richmond, 1860, 1870, 1880; Richmond City Directory, 1880–1890; Ira Berlin and Herbert Gutman, "Slaves, Free Workers, and the Social Order of the Urban South," (Davis Center Seminar, May 1976), 9–11, 26–29, 32–34; Howard N. Rabinowitz, "The Search for Social Control: Race Relations in the Urban South, 1865–1890," (Ph.D. diss., University of Chicago, 1976), 95, 100, 115–17, 420, 511–12, 701, 783, 820–21; *Irish World*, passim, 1871–1886, especially 18 January 1879 and 3 March 1885 (St. Joseph's Church), 26 June, 4 October 1884 (Irish Blaine and Logan Club and Irish National Republican Association); John Jeter Crutchfield Scrapbook, Virginia Historical Society; *New*

York Freeman, 10 January 1885; The Rev. F. Joseph Magri, "Historical Sketch of the Catholic Church in the City and Diocese of Richmond," (unpublished manuscript, Virginia Historical Society); James H. Bailey, *History of St. Peter's Church, 1834–1959* (Richmond: Lewis, 1959); James J. Green, "American Catholics and the Irish Land League, 1879–1882," *Catholic Historical Review*, 35, no. 1, (April 1949): 19–42; Mary Wingfield Scott, *Old Richmond Neighborhoods* (Richmond: Whittet and Shepperson, 1950), 18–20, 24, 29, 51–52, 215, 245–55.

15. *Irish World*, 3 August 1872, 3, 13 February 1875, 12 September 1874, 15 November, 20 December 1879, 10 April 1880, 14 April, 10 October 1883.

16. Ibid., 26 January 1878, 13 October 1883, 4 October 1884.

17. Ibid., 16, 23 October 1886.

18. Ibid., 12 December 1886, letter dated December 8.

19. Ibid.

20. *Richmond Dispatch*, 24 December 1886; 1, 4 January 1887; *John Swinton's Paper*, 12 December 1886.

21. *Richmond Dispatch*, 10 January, 18 February, 8 March 1887; *Richmond* City Council Minutes, 21 Feburary, 3 March 1887.

22. *New York Times*, 14 January 1887.

23. *Richmond Dispatch*, 8 January, 9 March 1887; *Cigar Makers' Official Journal*, (March 1887); *Granite Cutters' National Journal* (February 1887); Waddill to Mahone, 10 November 1886, courtesy of Leon Fink.

24. *Richmond Dispatch*, 3 April 1887.

25. Ibid., 3, 5 April 1887.

26. *Richmond Dispatch*, 6 April 1887; *Ceremonies Incident to the Laying of the Cornerstone of the New City Hall, April 5, 1887* (Richmond: Everett Waddy Co., 1887).

27. *Proceedings of the General Assembly of the Knights of Labor, Eleventh Regular Session*, (1888), pp. 1305, 1313, 1380, 1401, 1415; *Richmond Dispatch*, 13, 16, 19 March, 20 April 1887; Records of the First African Baptist Church, meeting of September 1887.

28. *Richmond Dispatch*, 3, 14, 24, 26, 28 May 1887; Richard C. Trent, secretary of the Coopers' Protective Union, to John Stewart, Lynchburg, 4 May 1887, sent to Powderly, Powderly Papers.

29. *Richmond Dispatch*, 18 August, 17, 18, 25 September 1887.

30. Ibid., John S. Wise Scrapbook, Wise Family Papers, Virginia Historical Society.

31. Wise Scrapbook, Wise Family Papers.

32. *Richmond Dispatch*, 29 September 1887.

33. *Labor Herald*, 3 October 1887.

34. Ibid.

35. *Richmond Dispatch*, 5 October 1887.

36. Ibid., 4, 5 November 1887.

37. Ibid.

38. *Journal of United Labor*, 5 November 1887; *Richmond Dispatch*, 8 November 1887.

39. *Richmond Dispatch*, November 9, 1887; John S. Wise Scrapbook, Wise Family Papers.

40. Mullen to Powderly, 2 December 1887, Powderly to Mullen, 2 January 1888, John T. Mitchell to Powderly, 2 January 1888, Powderly to Mitchell, 6 January 1888, William Fields to Powderly, 8 March 1888, Powderly to Fields, 14 March 1888, Mullen to Powderly, 28 May 1888, W. Woolridge, Local Assembly 3675, to Powderly, 7 July 1888, C. E. Hill, Local Assembly 3519, to Powderly, 23 March, 1888, all from Powderly Papers; *Proceedings of the General Assembly*, Twelfth Regular Session, 1888, pp. 13–27; *Journal of United Labor*, 2, 16 June, 5 July 1888.

CHAPTER TWELVE

1. Lewis Harvie Blair, *A Southern Prophecy: The Prosperity of the South Dependent upon the Elevation of the Negro* (Boston: Little Brown, 1964 reprint [1889]), 77.

2. Peter J. Rachleff, "Black, White, and Gray: Race and Working-class Activism in Richmond, Virginia, 1865–1890," (Ph.D. diss., University of Pittsburgh, 1981), Chapter 8: "White Workingmen and Women in the Readjuster Period, 1879–1883."

3. Ibid., Chapter 9: "The Resurgence of Popular Activity and the Emergence of the Knights of Labor."

4. Blair, *A Southern Prophecy*, 77.

5. *Richmond Dispatch*, 23 October 1888.

6. Ibid., 31 January 1888, 15 January 1889; *Central Trade and Labor Directory of Richmond*, Virginia (Richmond, n.p., 1895).

7. *Fourth Annual Report of the Commissioner of Labor, 1888: Working Women in Large Cities* (Washington: GPO, 1889), 24, 68.

8. *Report on Manufacturing Industries of the United States at the Eleventh Census: 1890, Part II. Statistics of Cities* (Washington: GPO, 1895), xxxi, 23–27, 486–89.

9. Ibid.

10. *Report on the Population of the U.S. at the Eleventh Census, 1890, Part I* (Washington: GPO, 1895), 742, and *Part II* (Washington: GPO, 1897), 184; 222–45; *Report on Vital and Social Statistics in the United States at the Eleventh Census, 1890, Part I—Analysis and Rate Tables* (Washington: GPO, 1896), 652–53; *Report on Crime, Pauperism, and Benevolence in the United States at the Eleventh Census, 1890: Part II* (Washington: GPO, 1896), 17, 105, 109, 111, 693, 732, 765.

11. William D. Sheldon, *Populism in the Old Dominion* (Princeton: Princeton University Press, 1935); William E. Spriggs, "The Virginia Colored Farmers' Alliance: A Case Study of Race and Class Identity," *Journal of Negro History*, 64 (1979); *Richmond Sun*, 20 December 1894.

12. Charter of Local Assembly 15002 of the "Independent Order of the Knights of Labor," Virginia Historical Society, Richmond; Minutes of "Altrurian Assembly," 5 April 1895, in John T. Chappell ledgerbook, courtesy of Warren Chappell.

13. Minutes of Local Union No. 1, Co-operative Commonwealth of Virginia, John T. Chappell, secretary, in Chappell ledgerbook, 1897–1898.

14. *Richmond Labor News*, 11 March 1893; *Central Trade and Labor Directory of Richmond, Virginia* (Richmond: Central Trade and Labor Union, 1895); *First Annual Report of the Bureau of Labor and Industrial Statistics of the State of Virginia, 1898–1899* (Richmond: Clyde W. Saunders, 1899), 361.

15. Zane L. Miller, "Urban Blacks in the South, 1865–1920," in *The New Urban History*, ed. Leo F. Schnore, (Princeton: Princeton University Press, 1974); Raymond B. Pinchbeck, *The Virginia Negro Artisan and Tradesman* (Richmond: William Byrd Press, 1926); W.H. Brown, *The Education and Economic Development of the Negro in Virginia* (Charlottesville: University of Virginia, 1923); Charles L. Knight, *Negro Housing in Certain Virginia Cities* (Richmond: William Byrd Press, 1927); J. Morgan Kousser, *The Shaping of Southern Politics: Suffrage Restriction and the Establishment of the One-party South, 1880–1910* (New Haven: Yale University Press, 1974), 63, 171–74; John Mercer Langston, *From the Virginia Plantation to the National Capital* (New York: Kraus, 1969 [1894]).

16. Kousser, *Shaping of Southern Politics*, 177–78; James H. Brewer, "Editorials from the Damned," *Journal of Southern History*, 28/2 (May 1962): 225–33; Willard B. Gatewood, "Virginia's Negro Regiment in the Spanish-American War," *Virginia Magazine of History and Biography*, 80/2 (April 1972): 193–217; Giles B. Jackson and D. Webster Davis, *The Industrial History of the Negro Race* (Freeport, New York: Books for Libraries, 1971 [1908]); August Meier and Elliot Rudwick, "Negro

Boycotts of Segregated Streetcars in Virginia, 1904–1907," *Virginia Magazine of History and Biography*, 81/4 (October 1973): 457–78; Andrew Buni, *The Negro in Virginia Politics, 1902–1965* (Charlottesville: University of Virginia Press, 1967).

17. W. H. Mullen, *Virginia State Federation of Labor Directory* (Richmond: State Federation of Labor, 1902), 15–17.

A Note on the Primary Sources

The basic research for this study rests on a foundation of primary sources. In sketching the structures and relationships of black Richmond, I drew upon the unpublished manuscript population and industry censuses for 1860, 1870, 1880, and the extraordinarily rich records of the Richmond branch of the Freedman's Savings Bank. The multi-volume published federal census compilations were also useful.

Local newspapers—the *New Nation*, the *Richmond Dispatch*, the *Whig*, the *Richmond State*—provided the beginning point for my analysis of Afro-American activities. I supplemented these sources with a few extant issues of local black newspapers: the *Planet*, the *Industrial Herald*, and the *Virginia Star*. Black and labor periodicals produced for a national audience were helpful: the *New National Era*, the *New York Globe*, the *New York Freeman*, the *Workingman's Advocate*, the *National Labor Tribune*, the *Journal of United Labor, John Swinton's Paper*, the *Cooper's Monthly Journal*, the *Granite Cutters' National Journal*, and the *Irish World*. Proceedings of state constitutional conventions, of national labor and trade union conventions, and of the Knights of Labor were also useful. Additional information was located in the records of the First African Baptist Church, local city council minutes, congressional committee hearing transcripts and reports, and federal and state labor department studies.

Contemporary Afro-American publications were vital to my understanding of evolving perspectives: Joseph T. Wilson's *The Black Phalanx and Emancipation*, Daniel Williams's *The Life and Times of Captain R. A. Paul*, E. A. Randolph's *The Life of Rev. John Jasper*, Peter Randolph's *From Slave Cabin to the Pulpit*, and George Washington Williams's *History of the Negro Race in America*.

Terence V. Powderly's papers, over 100 rolls of microfilm, yielded a number of letters from Richmond black activists during the era of the Knights of Labor. Two sets of unpublished materials in private possession were helpful: the minutes of International Typographical Union No. 90 and John Taylor Chappell's ledgerbooks, which contain the minutes of the Knights of Labor Co-operative Building Association and local socialist meetings in the 1890s. The Tredegar Iron Works manuscript collection also includes valuable data on Afro-American workers. Some information was also gleaned from the private papers and manuscripts of various politicians: John S. Wise, Frank G. Ruffin, Robert M. T. Hunter, James Lawson Kemper, George K. Gilmer, Lewis E. Harvie, Gilbert C. Walker, and William Mahone. These materials were located at the Virginia Historical Society and the Virginia State Library, both in Richmond.

Index